HAVING IT ALL?

AMBITION CAREER FAMILY RELATIONSHIPS EMPOWERMENT MOTHERHOOD

HAVING IT ALL?

RESPONSIBILITY BALANCE | BLACK WOMEN AND SUCCESS |

VERONICA CHAMBERS

HARLEM MOON | BROADWAY BOOKS | NEW YORK

This book is for the women who took me under their wing:
especially Edna Chatmon, Jacque Alexander, Jill Adams,
Benilde Little and Cassandra Butcher.

AND FOR THE CLAIR HUXTABLES EVERYWHERE

"She had nothing to fall back on; not maleness, not whiteness, not ladyhood, not anything. And out of the profound desolation of her reality she may well have invented herself."

—TONI MORRISON

Contents

FAMILY RESPONSIBILITY RELATIONSHIPS SUCCESS MOTHERHOOD BALANCE

Foreword by Karen Grigsby Bates   *xiii*

Introduction: That Girl   *1*

CHAPTER 1: Aunt Jemima's Granddaughters:
From the Kitchen to the Boardroom   *12*

CHAPTER 2: What We Mean When We Say Home   *27*

CHAPTER 3: To Whom Much Is Given, Much Is
Expected: Successful Women, Family and Responsibility   *45*

CHAPTER 4: The Mommy Track: How It's Different
for Sisters   *61*

CHAPTER 5: At Home in Her World: Empowerment
and Entitlement   *82*

CHAPTER 6: Taking Sides Against Ourselves:
The Push and Pull of Race and Gender   *102*

CHAPTER 7: The Onlys: Success and Isolation   *116*

CHAPTER 8: Black Swans: Women of Privilege
across the Generations   *134*

CHAPTER 9: Invisible Women: Professional Women
and the Media   *149*

CHAPTER 10: Guess Who's Coming to Dinner Now?
Black Women and Relationships   *166*

CHAPTER 11: The Price of the Ticket: New Challenges
and Old Demons   *190*

CHAPTER 12: Black Cinderellas: Finally, Sisters Are
Going to the Ball   *201*

Notes   *216*

Bibliography   *220*

Acknowledgments   *223*

Foreword

SEVERAL YEARS AGO, Anna Perez, the former press secretary to First lady Barbara Bush, came up to me at a party with a request. "I hear you're writing an etiquette book," she began briskly. "I would like for you to do me a favor: Please include some advice on what you should do when you're shopping in Beverly Hills and a white woman comes up, thrusts a dress in your face and says, 'Does this come in a size 6?' " It was not, Perez says, the first time she'd been mistaken for the help. ("I wonder what gave them that impression?" she laughed dryly: "The briefcase and purse slung over my shoulder?")

Perez, of course, is not the only black woman who was assumed to be there to serve rather than to *be* served. Literally, any black celebrity in a rarefied environment has an anecdote about being mistaken for someone other than the paying customer she turned out to be.

Welcome to the land of diminished expectations. Where black women, to paraphrase an Army ad, are encouraged to Be All That You

Can Be—As Long As It Doesn't Conflict with Our Perception of What We Think You Are.

If you are American and of a certain age, even if you've never met any black women, you have seen us. On television, in old movies and sitcom reruns we show up as kindly mammies and sassy maids and opinionated fishwives whose blistering harangue could peel paint from a living room wall. For a very long while, the little media box we were forced into was uncomfortably tight, leaving some of us to stoutly declare, as did Hattie McDaniel when scolded for playing Mammy to Vivian Leigh's Scarlett, "I'd rather play a maid than be one."

A half century later, America is finally catching up. Clair Huxtable broke the mold in the 1980s and allowed little girls to dream that they could be more than mammies, maids or long-suffering matriarchs (playwright George C. Wolfe's impishly described the latter as the "Last Mama on the Couch"). Clair Huxtable, Esq., broke the mold, but there was still a secret much of America didn't get: she wasn't a figment of a television writer's imagination, and she wasn't the Only One.

Veronica Chambers has shed light on an often-neglected segment of the African-American population: middle- and upper-class black women who are accomplished, who have managed—by plan, design or just plain old good luck—to create lives that encompass professional success, emotional fulfillment, prosperity and commitment to the black community.

Women like the women in this book are not hallucinations. They are the natural progression of a post–civil rights inheritance, where race is less of a constraint than it was in the 1960s, but it is still very much both lodestone and touchstone. Chambers has gained entrée into these rarefied social and business circles and allowed her subjects to express themselves with candor, humor and some astringency, to tell us how they manage—and sometimes don't—to try to Have It All.

As Chambers' subjects will show, it can be rough sledding. Some of her subjects are self-made women, round-the-way sisters, whose success has distanced them from their friends and relatives: folks assume that because these women have done well that they will have little in common with the friends of their youth. Or their hard-won prosperity, glimmering like a tantalizing oasis in a sea of want, puts them in the uncomfortable position of being Lady Bountifuls to somewhat resentful friends and relatives who, as one wryly pointed out, "don't even say thank you."

And some of her subjects are women whose families have lived well for generations, who have no guilt about possessing standards of living well above most of black (and for that matter, white) America's, and who feel their social utility comes in broadening the perception of what black is and what it can be. Showing up, guilt-free, in the pages of *Vogue, Town & Country* and *W* is a small step for black womankind, a way, says one, to encourage little black girls who may happen to scan the pages of these glossies to understand that this option is no longer the exclusive purview of white women.

Chambers talks to a lot of First and Only women, sisters whose education and determination have taken them into the thin air of the corporate stratosphere, or into jobs in fields that never considered black women as potential players, let alone power players.

As you'll see in *Having It All?*, the road isn't always an easy one. The pressure of juggling career, family obligations and personal interests can be unrelenting. There's always the danger of being told "real black women don't give up good jobs to become stay at home mothers/take jobs in elite white institutions/show up in the society pages/employ daily, full-time household help/move comfortably around in white society by choice."

Ah, but they do. And the value of this book is that people of all kinds will see—some for the first time—what many of us have known for generations: Black women are so much more than the narrow vision originally offered us by mainstream media. We work. We marry. We have babies. We may stay at home with them or we may return to work and have someone else care for them in our absence. We travel and balance budgets (corporate and domestic) and do volunteer work in our own community and beyond. And we have made a world for the next generation of young black women that is broader than the box we inherited, but not as large as the world they will leave for the generation behind *them*.

From what Chambers' interviewees are telling us, the key to having it All is deciding what "all" is for any one woman. And, perhaps, deciding to have it all sequentially, rather than concurrently. And planning in which sequence those things will happen. In other words, they are shaping their own lives in ways they hope will work for *them*. They're coloring outside the lines, changing the beat of the drummer to which they're marching, cooking by not slavishly sticking to the recipe, but throwing in a little this, a touch of that, until the dish they've made is totally their own. They are making their mothers and grand mothers and the ancestors on whose shoulders they are standing proud.

Go on, girls!

—KAREN GRIGSBY BATES
Los Angeles
September 2002

Introduction: That Girl

FAMILY   RESPONSIBILITY   RELATIONSHIPS   SUCCESS   MOTHERHOOD   BALANCE

THANK GOD FOR Clair Huxtable. If it wasn't for her character on *The Cosby Show,* I might never have had a glimpse of what it was like to be a smart, beautiful black woman—who made her own money, lived in a gorgeous house and was adored by a handsome, charming man. Not to mention, Clair Huxtable could be fabulous without ever being trifling.

When I ask professional black women to talk about a character from television or film that reflects their lives most accurately, they inevitably mention Clair Huxtable even though she hasn't been on TV in years (though the show can be viewed on Nick at Night). Sure, *The Cosby Show* had a "let's be real" quality to it. Their house was obscenely big, as improbable in the '80s New York real estate market as the gargantuan apartments occupied by America's favorite slackers, *Friends.* As a lawyer married to a successful doctor who managed to raise five kids without so much as a nanny, Clair Huxtable gave Wonder Woman a bad name. Yet she wasn't a mythic character. The number of black women entering law school and graduate school has increased more than 120 percent in the last 20 years. Clair Huxtable was, as a character, both inspirational and aspirational.

How many of us have been inspired to shape our lives by what we saw on TV? My friend John, who lives in Los Angeles, loves to visit me in New York. He laughs at the stories about my love life, listens attentively as I talk about my career plans—apprentice at a Claymation studio! move to Paris! join the circus! He loves my apartment, a tiny bachelorette pad with a view of the city skyline. "You're Marlo Thomas," he says, chuckling to himself. "You're *That Girl*." And inevitably, this makes me beam. I love that he compares me to a character that still exemplifies to me what it means to be a young career woman in the big city. I love that he doesn't qualify it by saying, "You're a black Marlo Thomas." To him, I'm *That Girl*. Period.

Everywhere you turn, there are images of sisters who have made it. From National Security Advisor Condoleezza Rice to Brown University president Ruth Simmons to Elektra Records president Sylvia Rhone— the list goes on and on. For a long time, the media portrayed these women as glorious exceptions to the welfare mother rule. But over the past years, several prominent studies have shown that women like these are only public examples of the sea change in the lives of everyday black women.

The news is this—in a single generation, black women's lives have improved vastly on key fronts: professionally, academically and financially. A 2000 report by the Frederick D. Patterson Research Institute found that the number of African-American women earning bachelor's degrees has increased 73 percent in the past ten years alone. (This is compared to just 47 percent for African-American men.) In the past decade, the number of black families earning $100,000 or more almost doubled from 220,400 to 415,500 in 1998. Black women's increased earning power was the rocket fuel for that stratospheric rise. In management positions, white women still outearn black women. But in fields such as sales and administrative support roles, a 1998 survey found that black women are beginning to earn slightly more.

It would be easy to say that this is the natural order of things, that each generation will do a little better than their parents and grandparents. But how do you explain the fact that black men are falling so far behind? And even the civil rights gains don't explain the force we've become in the American workplace. Between 1976 and 2006, the number of black women in the workplace will have increased by 35 percent. This is in comparison with white women, up by 10 percent in the same 30 years, and with white men, down by 17 percent.

There's a deeper story here than statistics can explain, a question that I've heard from every successful black woman that I've interviewed—which is namely, how did we get here? We know we are strong. Yet our strength has often been used against us, most notoriously in the 1965 Moynihan report that blamed single female family heads for the poverty in the black community. In song, poetry and prose, Nina Simone, Maya Angelou and a host of others have praised our inventiveness, our ability to make a way out of no way. But how did that creativity and indomitable spirit manifest itself into corporate reality—into stock portfolios, law partnerships and corner offices?

The success I'm referring to, however, goes deeper than money. Somewhere along the line, black women have become more comfortable in our own skin. We started looking in the mirror and liking what we saw. Above and beyond the black is beautiful rhetoric, we began to fall in love with our nappy hair, our full lips, our ample behinds. Whereas some of us may have thought that the white man's ice was colder, the phenomenal success of icons like Oprah has taught us that we could make it being exactly who we are. We are also the largest generation to know white women, not as strangers or employers, but as childhood friends, college roommates, lifelong pals. That closeness has demystified a lot of what we once imagined was unattainable for us. "I went to private school my whole life and was the only black girl in my class from first grade through twelfth grade," says the designer Sheila Bridges. "My friends were going to Europe when we were 12 years old. All of that made me feel like there's no reason that I can't have that, too."

Her friendships with some white women have taught writer Yvonne Durant that while "I envy their 'cushions'—husbands, parents with money, trust funds—I have learned that when it comes to affairs of the heart, they hurt just like we do. They get burned, too. Palimony wasn't a word created due to the multitude of black men leaving their women high and dry."

As black middle-class women, my friends and I often speak about living in a space between two worlds. Dining at Asia de Cuba on Madison Avenue on a Saturday night, brunching at Sylvia's in Harlem on Sunday morning. Our CD players feature heavy rotations of Lauryn Hill, Fiona Apple and Zap Mama. Though sometimes we go out dressed to kill in outfits that would make Lil' Kim blush, we also enjoy more classic styles. "Very Audrey," we'll compliment each other at a girls' lunch, referring to our all-time style icon, Audrey Hepburn. "Quite Kelly," we'll say, referring of course, to Grace Kelly. In order to fully express who we are as 21st-century black women, we draw from a wide range of influences from Gloria Steinem to Angela Davis, from Marlo Thomas to Paule Marshall. When we play, we want both the black doll and the white doll.

Yet who we are as black professional women remains largely a mystery to mainstream America. Everyone knows Oprah, everyone loves Oprah, but popular wisdom dictates that most black women are suffering, struggling and striving. Because there are precious few images of us in popular culture, it seems like the media—and therefore the world—don't know how well many black women are doing. "We are invisible," my friend Tracie tells me over brunch in Manhattan's financial district. Tracie is 5'10" with a short, cropped haircut that brings to mind the model Alek Wek. The first time we went out to lunch, Tracie's chocolate-colored skin had the sun-kissed glow of someone who'd just returned from a Mediterranean vacation. (She had recently attended a friend's wedding on the island of Capri.) It was October when we had lunch and Tracie met me at my office wearing a black leather pantsuit, complete with Gucci bag and shoes. Like so many women I know, Tracie blends the dichotomy between race and class with seeming effortlessness. She's a homegirl, but she could also give even the baddest Bond girl a run for her money. Yet most white people—and many black people—don't know that women like Tracie and my other friends exist. Or rather, they insist that we are the exception, as exotic and rare as Josephine Baker doing the cakewalk in a banana skirt.

I don't remember the first time I heard the phrase, "You're not like other black girls," though I suspect that those words—and the double-edged compliment they represented—were first uttered to me in college. Since then it's a phrase I've heard with disturbing regularity. I'm supposedly not like other black girls because: I've studied Russian, am bookish, have been snowboarding, traveled to Shanghai, Morocco, fill-in-the-blank. Whether the words are spoken or implied, there's a constant assumption that I've had experiences that can be dismissed as not part of a black woman's lifestyle. The more I researched this book, the more I discovered how untrue this was. Yes, there are vast numbers of black women living in poverty and beaten down by all that implies. Most black women don't go for ski vacations at Whistler or spend their Friday nights drinking splits of champagne at the Bubble Lounge— neither do most white women. But it's never been more untrue that my experiences as a successful black woman are unique. I am like other black women. Lots of them.

Despite the fact that *The Cosby Show* broke down racial barriers by making a black middle-class brood America's favorite family, for the women that I spoke to, invisibility and isolation, not race and class, were the double burdens that haunted their daily life. "Unless you're at a black professional event," said one woman, "then you're just sprinkles. Sprinkles of black folks at the charity auctions or ski resorts or country clubs." This, she explains, is why department store clerks, taxi drivers and uppity maitre d's don't know how to treat a black middle-class person. My friend, the writer Yvonne Durant, tells a story about getting into a taxi one blustery evening in her full-length mink coat. The cab picked her up in front of Yvonne's Upper East Side address, but it was still his assumption that she couldn't possibly live there. He asked her if she was coming from work. "What kind of work would I be doing in this fine mink?" she asked herself, but decided not to voice the question, afraid she would be insulted even further by his answer.

Yet there's a certain freedom inherent in being what a former television producer calls "the Onlys." Sometimes, being the unknown quantity can work to your advantage. "Working on Wall Street, forget about people seeing you," one financial advisor told me. "You're a black female, you're an anomaly. Don't even cry about it. That's the way it is. But because you are an anomaly, nobody knows what to expect. You have to work with it and say, I don't do this or that. I don't want to drink beer with you. Or I don't eat that food or I don't want to go there. It's not my lifestyle or it is. Then they say, 'Okay.' They don't know anything about you. You make your own rules."

The experiences of the women I discuss in this book, for the most part, reflect women who are first- or second-generation college educated and relatively new to the lifestyle that their success affords them. From the days of Reconstruction, however, there have been black women who have lived lives of absolute privilege; women who are used to summer homes in the exclusive enclaves of the black elite in Martha's Vineyard and Sag Harbor, women whose coming of age was marked by couture clothes and coming out balls. While their process of discovery regarding race, class and gender is very different from my own, I think the challenges and choices are not dissimilar. Rather, I think the experience of black women born into wealth is made richer and, perhaps, more complicated by the growing number of successful black women joining their ranks.

While most of the women in this book are college-educated professionals, I use the term successful here in the broadest terms. There are secretaries and schoolteachers and full-time moms quoted here. What I was looking for were women whose salaries gave them enough disposable income to live a middle-class lifestyle. I wanted to talk to women whose working and living situations afforded them the luxury to ponder the deeper questions about what they wanted from life. I truly believe that we are at a historic point in our journey as black women. We are no longer, as Zora Neale Hurston once famously said, "the mules of the world." More than our grandmothers, or even our mothers, ours is a generation with the time, energy and desire to look at the choices that are set before us. Our mothers may have snubbed the women's movement as being too white, but we are the daughters of both the civil rights movement and the women's rights movement and this gives us an unprecedented amount of freedom as well as a unique perspective.

One of the questions we're wrestling with as black women is what does "having it all" mean to *us*? We're certain that it means something different than it has meant to white women—if only because we've listened to their debate for so long. For Victoria Campbell Carter, a 32-year-old divorced mother of two, it means letting herself off the hook. "Life is so fragile and so valuable," she says. "My life is a 24-hour shot at doing my best to make the world a better place for having had me— and my children—in it. If I make mistakes, if I don't quite hit the mark, I pray each evening for a do-over: waking up the next day."

When Helen Gurley Brown wrote a book called *Having It All* in 1982, it was full of the same kind of sassy, sexy rhetoric that had propelled her hit magazine, *Cosmopolitan*, for close to 30 years. But as women swelled the work place in the go-go-go '80s, "having it all" became more than a catch phrase, it became a goal, an increasingly lofty and seemingly unachievable barometer of our worth as modern women. As black women begin to close the financial gap with white women, the phrase resonates for us, too. Well, some of us. "I get exhausted just hearing the phrase," moans Leslie, a 36-year-old magazine editor. "Do we really *want* it all? I'm trying to learn to want what I have —which keeps me plenty busy—and let God take care of the rest. That said, I do believe that any woman, regardless of race, who wants it 'all' badly enough can probably create that in her life. To her, I say, 'You go, girl.'" The God reference in Leslie's words is worth noting. Forty-nine of the fifty women I interviewed noted that cultivating a spiritual life— be it Buddhism or Baptist—is a core part of their definition of "having it all."

"How do you do it all? You make choices," says Janet Hill, mother of professional basketball player Grant Hill and vice president of a Washington, D.C., consulting firm. "The whole business of being an adult is making choices. If you miss the soccer game today, then you'll go next week. Better yet, if you can walk out of the office at 3:00 and go to the game, just decide that you won't go next Thursday. No guilt about work and no guilt about your children, as long as you know they're safe."

Among her circle of friends, Margaret Porter Troupe, founder of San Diego's Porter Troupe art gallery, is the original "You go, girl." At 53, if Margaret doesn't have it all, she doesn't know what the term means. She's blessed with good looks and good health, and if it wasn't for the strands of silver in her jet-black dreadlocks, she could easily pass for a 35-year-old yoga instructor. She and her husband, award-winning poet and biographer Quincy Troupe, have residences in New York City and La Jolla, California. Her 19-year-old son is a happy college sophomore. While she doesn't attend a specific church, Margaret echoed her peers when she spoke of the importance of faith in her life. Since its opening in 1991, her gallery has gained an international reputation among artists, critics, collectors and museum personnel. Margaret has managed to avoid being pigeonholed as an African-American art dealer and has become a prominent part of San Diego's art scene. "This is a *tremendous* achievement of which I'm *enormously* proud," Margaret says fiercely. "It's also a testament to my mother's faith that I could do whatever I set my mind to." Porter Troupe's life is also a testament to the sweeping gains of her generation. "My mother married at 14, gave birth to 15 children and worked on the farm during and in between pregnancies," she recalls. "She cooked, sewed our clothes, washed, ironed, cleaned house, sun up to sun down 365 days a year. I don't re-member her ever having a vacation until she was in her '60s."

In comparison to the ways our mothers toiled, much of what I heard while reporting this book could be easily dismissed as "high-class problems." Talk about guilt. Try bemoaning the fact you were treated poorly by a snobby salesperson at Bergdorf's to your grandmother, the daughter of a slave. And really should the world weep for the sister who drives a Lexus and is the only black soccer mom on her block? Is it shallow for a black woman doctoral candidate to worry about meeting a black man who will match her earning potential? As my own life went through transformations that were mirrored in my work, I worried about revealing too much of myself and I worried about whining. Were I and the women profiled little more than Scarlett O'Haras made legitimate by the legacy of historical oppression?

I don't think so. The questions we are asking matter because they form the lines with which we draw our lives. Moreover, the matter of our success goes right to the heart of not only our lives as individuals, but the changing fabric of the black community.

While I was writing the final draft of this book, the having it all debate exploded again around the release of a book by Sylvia Ann Hewlett called *Creating a Life: Professional Women and the Quest for Children.* Hewlett lobbed her stats like hand grenades at America's working women: 33 percent of high-achieving women, in general, are childless at 40; 42 percent of the women in corporate America are childless; 49 percent of "ultra achievers" (those earning more than $100K a year) are childless. But it gets worse. According to the author, the fertility gods frown on women who decided to feed their "baby hunger" after the age of 35: the process is heartbreakingly painful, mind-bogglingly expensive and, alas, often futile. The book was hotly debated in newspapers and magazines nationwide, with the assumption that the opinions of middle-class white women spoke for us all. If they had specifically looked at the experience of professional black women, they would have seen a very different perspective.

Like other American women, many of the 30-something and even 40-something women interviewed in this book are childless. Unlike the panicked portraits of professional women depicted in the media, the women I spoke to routinely expressed no sense of regret, no Lichtenstein-like cartoon horror of "Damn, I forgot to have a baby." For one, these women were all—in their own eyes and in the eyes of the people who surrounded them—successful. As children of the civil rights generation, achievement is still seen as being more than individual. There is still very much a feeling, in the community, that when a young black person succeeds, all ships rise. Furthermore, as African Americans, we still live in a world of extended family and created family—from the neighbor's kid who was in your house so often that you began to introduce him as "your cousin" to the tight bond of friendships between the non-blood relatives that we honor with the title of "sister." All of the women I interviewed for this book spoke, with warmth and joy, about the children—nieces, nephews, godchildren, neighbors—in their lives.

Finally, while I wouldn't attempt to deny that some of the women I spoke to were sometimes lonely and hoped to have families of their own, no one ever once used the term "biological clock." In fact, on more than one occasion when I used the term, I was stared at as if I'd just grown two heads and begun spouting pig Latin. The successful black women that I interviewed spoke, instead, about all the options that were open to them: more than one woman spoke to me about adoption and the lack of long waiting lists for black children who need a home. Again and again, in the conversations about marriage, motherhood and the personal elements of "having it all," I was struck by the patience in the voices of even the most high-powered, ambitious women. For most successful black women, life has been a long series of negotiations between real and imagined obstacles, between low expectations, stereotypes and limited resources. While many of the women I interviewed are considered miracle workers in their fields, at the very core they all confessed a deep humility that ultimately there were things they couldn't control and wouldn't even try. I suspect that, subliminally, the mainstream debate about biological clocks and "baby hunger" falls under that rubric for many professional black women. You can't control it. Why even try?

I'm sure that many of the women I interviewed would agree with the words of Leslie, the 36-year-old editor, who is single and childless. "I'm trying to learn to want what I have...and let God take care of the rest."

I didn't know when I started this project that I would be writing a history book, but to a certain extent that's what this is. A purely contemporary survey of successful black women had the danger of being just a bunch of talking heads. It was only when I started listening to the women in this book, when I sat down to talk to them for the second and third time, that I heard their mothers' voices and their grandmothers' voices, too. Our language is steeped in history. "To whom much is given, much is expected," is one phrase that kept cropping up, and I ended up writing an entire chapter about what this means to us as black women. One woman told me that she never goes to work expecting it to be easy, which means she's a little more prepared for the battles she has to wage every day in her corporate environment. "You can't wear the crown, if you don't carry the cross," she said. I began to understand that in order to fully appreciate the crowns we now don as successful women, I needed to trace the lineage of those who bore the cross for us. As James Baldwin once famously remarked, "Our crowns have been bought and paid for, all we have to do is wear them."

I can hardly do justice to the scholarly work that I draw on for this book, work by women like Paula Giddings, bell hooks and Patricia Collins. I will say that there is a bibliography attached with enough summer reading to last a bookish sister a lifetime. I hope you will seek those texts out. What I set out to do is write something between the great scholarly canon about black women's lives and the fluffy sister-girl-friend-honey-chile-please advice books that crowd bookshelves. (Mine included!) I wanted this to be a smart, sister-girlfriend book, and I hope it is.

The women in this book are the peers of Clair Huxtable and they are her daughters. They are Pam Grier in *Foxy Brown* and Marlo Thomas in *That Girl*. In one generation, they have experienced the greatest increase in educational and financial success that black America has ever known. And they are the role models of the next generation. Astronaut Mae Jemison, who became the first black woman to go into space and currently directs the Jemison Institute at Dartmouth, has said, "Images are important because going back to the 1960s, when

I was convinced I was going to go into space, I had to be very stubborn. When I would say I want to be an astronaut, [people] said that women couldn't go up. There were no African Americans. People laughed at me. Literally outright, straight-up laughed. And so there was a certain stubbornness that I had to have just to keep on. It would have been wonderful just to have seen an image. But I didn't have to sit and hold and touch and feel. Sometimes it was enough just to see somebody in a book."[1]

It's my hope that for some girl, somewhere, this is that book.

CHAPTER 1

Aunt Jemima's Granddaughters:
From the Kitchen to the Boardroom

CONGRESSWOMAN MAXINE WATERS collects Aunt Jemima memorabilia. She is lauded as one of the most influential women in California politics and in the Democratic Party. But when she needs a symbol of power, Maxine Waters looks toward the world's most famous pancake pitchwoman. "She's very special," Waters has said. "She symbolizes the strength of our people and the strength of black women. Aunt Jemima is the black woman who cooked and cleaned, struggled, brought up her own family and a white family. And if I'm ashamed of Aunt Jemima—her head rag, her hips, her color—then I'm ashamed of my people."[2]

It has been more than a century since Aunt Jemima made her debut as the spokesperson for the first instant pancake mix. To this day, she remains one of the most well-known brand symbols in the world. The arc of her evolution—physical, emotional, psychological—is remarkably true in its telling of black women's experience. Like Aunt Jemima, our grandmothers, mothers and ourselves have gone from being unpaid slave labor, to disregarded mammies, to invisible domestics, to savvy businesswomen. In "Women of Color Executives: Their Voices, Their Journeys," a 2001 study by the Catalyst Foundation, one senior-level African-American woman says, "Well, I am overweight. I have brown skin and my hair is short. Now, by the stereotypes, I ought to be a mammy taking care of some white kid. But I am so wild about me and that comes out very quickly."[3]

Aunt Jemima was created by two white businessmen; inspired by a minstrel show in 1889. The show featured black men wearing aprons and red bandanas performing a jazzy cakewalk to the tune of a popular folk song, "Aunt Jemima." A star was born. From the beginning, Aunt Jemima was something out of *Uncle Tom's Cabin.* She was the very embodiment of the loving mammy—dark-skinned, heavy-set, capable— an asexual workhorse. She was also a direct counterpart to the exalted Southern belle who was white, delicate, desired but sexually pure. Aunt Jemima has always been a controversial figure among blacks. But we were only her community of genesis, not her audience. In the unsettling post-Reconstruction era, she was a reassuring image to whites that the country had not gone to hell in a handbasket. Not everything had changed: black women were still going to cook and clean, Aunt Jemima would still make pancakes.

Whose Aunt Is She Anyway?

IN THE LATE 1800S, even Aunt Jemima's name was a wound to black women. Throughout slavery and Reconstruction, whites routinely denied older blacks the honorific of "Mr." and "Mrs.," choosing instead to refer to them as "aunt" and "uncle." (Note, for example, Aunt Jemima's male counterpart in advertising, Uncle Ben.) James Webb Young, a savvy "adman" as they were called then, created an entire fictional history for Jemima. A typical ad of the time featured a heavy-set, very dark woman chatting away while an attentive, scholarly white man took notes. We learn that Jemima was born and raised on the plantation of an imaginary Colonel Higbee. "After the Civil War, after her master's death," the ad copy read, "Aunt Jemima was finally persuaded to sell her famous pancake recipe to the representative of a northern milling company."

In her book, *Slave in a Box: The Strange Career of Aunt Jemima*, M. M. Manring tells us that Young, "exploited the loves, hates and aspirations of the target market: white housewives eager to please their husbands and experiencing servant problems. [She was] a symbol of racial order and white leisure."

Over the years, dozens of women were hired to play Aunt Jemima at expos, state fairs, in-store events and, later, in television commercials. Her creation marked a revolutionary moment in American advertising. The Aunt Jemima brand was the first product to use a person as a symbol of its brand. Venus and Serena Williams may rack up millions from Avon, sneaker companies and other big businesses eager to be associated with their name, but Aunt Jemima was the first celebrity endorser. Even in the late 1800s, agreeing to don a red bandana and apron and go on the road as Jemima meant that you were essentially signing up to be part of a minstrel show, confirming every mammy stereotype that existed. But as Hattie McDaniel so famously stated about her career of playing servants in films, "I'd rather make $700 a week playing a maid in a movie, than be one for $7."

Nancy Green took on the role of Aunt Jemima at the 1893 World's Fair; she reputedly made a million pancakes that week. In addition to passing out pamphlets with her "life story," she also sang songs and told stories about the old South. The idea of dressing up as a maid, making pancakes and singing songs may make modern black women cringe, but Nancy Green's job—and her popularity—were groundbreaking. The pancake company treated its Aunt Jemima spokespersons as celebrities. They were photographed for the covers of the pancake boxes (supermodels!). They traveled, all expenses paid, with a company escort. The job of being Aunt Jemima, while requiring the women to speak in an uneducated dialect, was a tremendous opportunity for self-improvement. The spokeswomen got to see more of America than they had ever dreamed. Rosie Lee Moore, who played Aunt Jemima during the civil rights battles of the '50s and '60s, is reported to have "dazzled her sisters with tales of her adventures," admonishing them that they should follow her lead. "Y'all have to get out and meet people. Like me," she said.[4]

Over the years, Aunt Jemima experienced a number of makeovers. In the years after the civil rights movement, the headscarf became a headband. In the 1990s, she lost the head wrapping altogether and got a relaxer. Her current image is of a well-coiffed, professional-looking black woman. She even wears a demure set of pearls. She could be a teacher or an executive secretary. Although today the Quaker Oats Company won't comment on her meaning, perhaps well aware of how controversial she still is, some hypothesize that the new Aunt Jemima is a food professional—perhaps a restaurant owner. Her history may still be shrouded in painful stereotype and subjugation, but today's Aunt Jemima, like today's black woman, has got a new deal.

Aunt Jemima Goes Shopping

IN HER POEM, "What Happened to Aunt Jemima?," Sylvia Dunnavant imagines an encounter with a liberated pitchwoman. Driving a Mercedes with a FREE AT LAST bumper sticker, Aunt Jemima tells the writer she " got tired of wearing that rag" and "freed her own damn self." The poem is a powerful representation of the degree to which black women's success has been one of their own making. We have "freed our own damn selves"—largely through education. Over the last 30 years black women have been earning degrees at twice the rate of black men. At some historically black colleges, the numbers are even more stark. At Clark Atlanta University, for example, the student body is 71 percent female. In first-professional-degree programs the numbers are more startling: for women the number of degree earners has risen 219 percent; for men it's 5 percent.[5]

The image of Aunt Jemima driving a Mercedes Benz is also not a throwaway. We may have been underestimated in the American work force for decades, but black women have always been very clear about our financial goals. As far back as 1867, Sojourner Truth boldly declared that "What we want is a little money. I have done a great deal of work; as much as a man, but did not get so much pay. I used to work in the field and bind grain, keeping up with the cradler, but men doing no more, got twice as much pay." By "a little money," Sojourner Truth could hardly have imagined scores of her sable sisters descending on Prada and Gucci, tooling around in Mercedes Benz convertibles, and sipping Cosmos at the latest hot spots. But this, I guarantee you, is what today's young black woman has on her mind. Moreover, she sees it as her right.

Black women are being increasingly recognized as powerful consumers and investors. In 2002, an Ariel Schwab study reported that the percentage of high-income black households that invested in the stock market had grown by 30 percent from 5 years before. Over the same period, stock ownership by whites with similar incomes increased by only 4 percent. In 2001, black buying power jumped to $601 billion, a $58 billion increase over the previous year. In the personal care market (hair salons, cosmetics, manicures and massages) spending by black women topped the $7 billion mark in a single year. An unprecedented amount of college graduates who are moving into professional careers have created a class of black women who, to quote Broadway Books's *The BAP Handbook: The Official Guide to the Black American Princess,* "expect the best and nothing less." Aunt Jemima may still sell pancakes, but the slave isn't in a box anymore.

Breaking the Cycle of Servitude

IT'S EASY TO LOOK at Aunt Jemima and the history created a century ago and declare that today's black woman is a miracle of achievement. But the most critical aspect of this book isn't the difference between 1889 and 2001, but the difference between 1964 and 2001, 1974 and 2001 and even 1984 and 2001. "The news is that in a generation, or a generation and a half, black women who have always been thought of as the lowest on the totem pole are doing better emotionally, financially and sociologically," says Anna Perez, former general manager of communications at the Chevron Corporation. "How did that happen? I think that's news."

The simplest answer is that the Civil Rights Act of 1964 created a wave of opportunities that changed black women's lives. You could also say that each generation builds on the previous generation's success: if black women are doing better than they did 25 years ago, then that's the

natural order of things. However, the real answers are more complicated. For starters, blacks have not had a steady growth economically or
educationally throughout the last century. We have been disproportion-
ately affected by the world wars, by Jim Crow and segregation, by shifts
in government aid and cuts. In 1954, half of the black population was
poor. From 1975 to 1990 the number of blacks living beneath the
poverty line hovered around 30 percent. It wasn't until 2000 that a significant drop to 23.6 percent appeared.[6]

Author and entrepreneur Harriette Cole grew up in an elite black
enclave in Baltimore. Her father was a judge; her mother was an educator. Harriette and her sisters were known as the Cole girls. Yet a generation of wealth has not given her the economic confidence of her white
counterparts. "I think that for black people, for the most part, there's
still that question—is the bottom going to fall out?" she says.

The civil rights movement opened doors, but if that was the primary
reason for the renaissance that black women are experiencing today,
then why are black men struggling? The number of black men in prison,
on drugs or in the drug industry is frighteningly high. Black men have
the lowest life expectancy in the country, and every day young black
men lose their lives to violence on the streets. In the 1950s, black men
didn't have the Civil Rights Act to open doors for them educationally or
professionally, but Lord knows they lived longer.

The seedling of our revolution, the answer to how black women
"freed our own damn selves" lies deeper than statistics. We rarely discuss how the concurrent atmospheres of the civil rights movement and
the modern women's rights movement came together to influence the
black women who came of age in the late 1960s and 1970s. Yes, it's true
that these two movements often battled for our loyalty, but in the end,
they both moved us forward. Today's black woman is a creation of
dreams, ideology and opportunities created by both the civil rights
movement *and* the modern women's rights movement.

The single most important change for black women from a generation ago is not that we make more money, because we don't. Not yet. We
still earn less than white women, black men and white men. What's
changed is the nature of our work and the way we view ourselves. In
1960, 12 percent of the black male population worked in white-collar

jobs. By 1990, that figure had more than doubled to 30 percent. During that same period, the number of black women in white-collar jobs more than tripled from 18 percent to 57 percent. We took what was once a double negative—being black, being female—and turned it into a double positive. As Audrey Edwards writes in *Children of the Dream: The Psychology of Black Success,* "What was different was now not just the nature of these occupations, but also how black women tended to view work: as a career and a profession, and an enterprise that brought not only personal fulfillment but also economic rewards."

It's a critical development in the process of reinventing ourselves that in the 1970s black women began to think about work as more than a tool of survival, but as a means of personal fulfillment. In *Slipping Through the Cracks: The Status of Black Women,* economist Julianne Malveaux notes that, "Work has been so major a part of the black woman's legacy that it is frequently jested that black women are born with a broom in hand." Aunt Jemima is such a powerful touchstone for black women, so painful a stereotype, because for much of the 20th century, black women saw themselves defined through servitude. At the time of Aunt Jemima's incarnation, Audrey Edwards writes, "20 percent of all school-age black girls worked full time and the majority of black women worked either in private households as maids or on farms as share-croppers."

No Choice but to Succeed

DURING THE PAST five years that I've been working on this book, the question that I am asked again and again—by blacks and whites, men and women—is "Why are black women succeeding when black men are struggling?" Implicit in the discussions that followed were the ideas that black women benefit from the "twofer" notion of affirmative action; that we are less threatening to corporate America than black men; that we are somehow stronger or more driven to succeed. These are ideas that I am afraid of assigning too much truth. The black women of my generation are employed in record numbers in finance, advertising, law and medicine. We own more small businesses than ever before and are starting new businesses at such a rapid rate that women of color are, by percentage, the fastest growing group of entrepreneurs in the country. But corporate America is still very much a boy's club.

In the top ranks of the financial elite, black men are still benefiting from gender privilege. No black woman runs a Fortune 500 company and few hold the rank of CEO in major corporations. This is in stark contrast to men such as Richard D. Parsons, CEO of AOL Time Warner; Stanley O'Neal, president and COO of Merrill Lynch; Franklin Raines, chairman and CEO of Fannie Mae; or Roy S. Roberts, who as a high-ranking executive at General Motors oversaw a business worth billions.

Our gains as black women are real, but so are our obstacles. Surely some of our success can be attributed to our role in the community as women. As caretakers of our children, we could never afford to be victims of our pride. In his infamous 1965 report on the breakdown of the black family, Daniel Patrick Moynihan stated that "It was the Negro male who was the most humiliated. Segregation and the submissiveness it exacts are surely more destructive to the male than the female personality. [It is] the very essence of the male animal, from the bantam rooster to the four-star general, to strut." Moynihan (elected to the Senate in 1976) seems to imply that black women weren't humiliated or, somehow, it wasn't as bad for us as it was for our men. The truth is that crying, hungry children have always exerted a more powerful pull on women than they have on most men. If need be, we have always been more willing than our men to wash the dishes, clean the toilets and lick boots. For black women, history and circumstances have required more strength than pride. One of the major generational shifts from the 1970s to the present is that more and more black women are expending that considerable energy—the humility, the inability to take no for an answer, the willingness to work twice as hard—and channeling it toward pursuing our own dreams.

In a 1964 essay entitled "Jim Crow and Jane Crow," Dr. Pauli Murray wrote, "In this bitter struggle, into which has been poured most of the resources and much of the genius of successive generations of American Negroes, these women have often carried disproportionate burdens in the Negro family as they strove to keep its integrity intact against the constant onslaught of indignities to which it was subjected. Not only have they stood shoulder to shoulder with Negro men in every phase of the battle, but they have also continued to stand when their men were destroyed by it. Who among us is not familiar with that heroic, if formidable, figure exhorting her children to overcome every disappointment, humiliation and obstacle. This woman's lullaby was very often 'Be something!' 'Be somebody!' "

The women whose stories I tell in this book are the children who took the lullaby as marching orders.

No Excuses, No Barriers, No Obstacles

AT 41, DONNA AUGUSTE holds four U.S. patents for her ground-breaking engineering work on the Apple Newton, the small personal computer device that was the forerunner of today's handhelds. As CEO and co-founder of FreshWater Software, she's been voted one of the Most Influential Women on the Web and has been honored by the Women in Technology Hall of Fame. The early part of 2000 made dot bombs of many dotcom and tech companies, but Donna's firm is thriving. Her clients include Citibank, Fidelity Investments, AT&T, Lockheed Martin and NASA.

Like many successful women, she is unnecessarily self-deprecating. A religious woman, she is quick to credit all of her success to God. Not that she is naive or weak-willed. Silicon Valley is known for its punishing work ethic, a viper's den of competitiveness that often requires 120-hour work weeks. She thrived at Apple because she knows how to stand up for herself. Donna has never been afraid to speak her mind, even when it meant bruising fragile, white boy, techno-geek egos. "She was a lousy diplomat," Stephen Capps, a colleague and friend from her Apple days, told the *New York Times*. He also said, "This is obviously preferable to the inverse approach that is taken by most managers. They'd much rather think everybody likes them than actually get anything done."

For her part, Donna found that many of the people she crossed paths with were surprised that the software manager was a black woman. "I wouldn't call it sexism," she said. "Just absolute disbelief...

[Discrimination] is very real at Apple. You meet people who do things that are foolish. Sometimes I would have to deal with people who would get my blood pressure going."

Sitting in one of her favorite health food restaurants, I can't help but share in the ignorance of her colleagues. I don't know any black women in technology and, prior to writing this book, never gave it any thought. Before I read about Donna in the *New York Times,* I would also have been surprised to meet a black woman software manager. In person, she is a petite 5'2" with the same honey-toned skin and deeply dimpled smile that her press photos promise. She'd rather talk about her church gospel group (she plays bass guitar) or her latest computer than about racism in the technology industry. When pressed on the subject, she bites into a piece of homemade wheat bread and shrugs, "People can throw race or gender into the mix, but the thing that is overriding is delivery. If you deliver results at a certain point in time, all those other things fall away. Deliver the results."

A soft-spoken woman whose dulcet tones could make a fortune in radio commercials, her voice takes on a steely edge when she talks about work. "When I went to Apple, the same as when I went to Intellicorp, the same thing when I started FreshWater, I stay very focused on 'What does the successful result look like?' Let's get there. Let's understand what our vision is and how that takes shape in a completed form. No excuses, no barriers, no obstacles."

Jemima Gets a Real Job

DAYS, WEEKS, EVEN MONTHS later, that last sentence stays with me. It could be the mantra of any historically oppressed group of people who have fought for freedom and triumphed. But because I am studying the fabric and texture of black women's lives, I hear Auguste's words in the voices of black women who mothered the renaissance that sisters are experiencing today. Harriet Tubman and Sojourner Truth. Frontierswoman and cowboy legend, "Stagecoach Mary" Fields. Civil rights leader Ella Baker and civil rights/women's rights/gay activist Flo Kennedy.

Insurance pioneer Ernesta Procope and CNBC President and CEO Pamela Thomas-Graham. Brown University president Ruth Simmons. No excuses. No barriers. No obstacles.

Certainly one aspect of Aunt Jemima's legacy is the strength born of societal invisibility. The Mammy heritage is one steeped in mockery and servitude, little respect and low expectations. But black women have managed to turn this history of being held down into an ability to thrive in any atmosphere. To quote the old aphorism, "we who for so long have done so much with so little, now feel absolutely qualified to do anything with nothing at all." Within the insulated world of technology where blacks are uncommon, and black women even more so, Donna Auguste benefited from operating beneath the radar. She didn't go to Apple or Intellicorp or even her own company looking for pats on the back or invitations to the celebrity golf tournament. She goes to work every day, focused on the results.

She is successful in a way that is easily measured—she's CEO of a major software company. But like so many women of the post–civil rights generation, she is driven by the ways in which work can fulfill her personally. Donna moved to Boulder, Colorado, because she fell in love with the mountains. She lives in a secluded enclave in a solar-powered home that she helped design. She's particularly proud of the fact that her house runs on solar power given the countless computers she runs from her home. When we first met, I was about to begin a fellowship in Japan. A number of people expressed surprise that my first extended trip abroad was to Asia and not to Africa. I don't have to explain the simplicity of that kind of thinking to Donna. She knows Japan well, traveled there often for Apple. Prior to her tenure at Apple, after leaving Intellicorp, she chose to take a sabbatical in Japan; Donna spent two months there bicycling through the rural countryside. At the time of our meeting she was preparing for a trip to east Africa where she started a major volunteer project that uses solar power and computers to improve the medical system in rural areas. Both at work and in her personal life, she is the quintessential scientist: always tackling a new challenge, confident in both her experiences and her experiments.

Donna's confidence and success represent a lifetime of preparation. Her mother and father divorced when she was a toddler, and her mother raised four daughters alone in West Berkeley. In many ways, the low-income community of West Berkeley is like any other disadvantaged neighborhood in America. However, it happens to be in the shadow of one of the country's best public colleges, the University of California at Berkeley and only a stone's throw away from the heartland of the technology industry, Silicon Valley. This didn't mean much in the 1960s when an eight-year-old Donna was taking apart toasters and radios to see how they worked. But by the time she entered college, the technology boom had started and Donna was ready for it. "I loved figuring out how things worked, that always interested me," she says, her dimples deepening. "I took more things apart than I put back together. But my mother and sisters were always very encouraging. In terms of my family, I was unique in my pursuit of science and math. I loved to do homework. At the beginning of the school year, I'd read all my books cover to cover. I'd be wondering, 'Why should it take me nine months to get through these books?'"

After years of winning science fairs and excelling in a pioneering public high school program called MESA (Math Engineering and Science Achievement), Donna became the first person in her family to go to college. While some black achievers from low-income backgrounds report feeling alienated from their communities and families, Donna didn't have that experience. Her Catholic mother worked two and sometimes three jobs to put her daughters through private elementary school. Her sisters, although not as academically inclined as Donna, made sure that Donna (who describes herself as a "total nerd") had a social life. "Left to my own devices, I would've just stayed in my books and later, in my computers and stuff," she says. "But my sisters always drew me out and made sure that I was at least a little bit social. Which turned out to be wonderful because as a CEO now, those communication skills are really crucial to me."

As a student at Berkeley, Donna was only a few miles from West Berkeley, but the campus, and the newness of university life, made her feel a world away from home. She found community in her fellow MESA alumni from high school. She joined BESSA—the Black Engineering and Science Students Association. "There were not a lot of black students studying engineering, but we all clung together," she says. "We could count on the fact that if you were in 5B Physics on Fridays, there were people in BESSA who had taken all those classes before. They could tell you what to focus on in class, what professors were really good instructors and how to prepare for the exams." Donna became an officer of BESSA her sophomore year and remained involved in the organization throughout her college years.

She was three years into a Ph.D. program at Carnegie Mellon when she caught the start-up bug. She left school without completing her dissertation and joined IntelliCorp, a leader in the field of commercial artificial intelligence technology. "It was very entrepreneurial, very exciting, very much an environment of 'if you have an idea for a technology that solves a real problem, then you have an idea for a business.'"

Almost 15 years after she became the first person in her family to go to college, she is once again a first—the only black woman CEO that she or her peers know of, in the technology sector. "I know a number of CEOs who are people of color," she says. "I know several who are women, but they aren't people of color."

Her sisters helped her develop the social skills necessary to run a large company, but Donna admits that she is still very much a loner. It's less because there are so few black women in her field and more because the solitude suits her early Louisiana heritage. "I choose to live in a very rural area because when I was growing up, we'd go home to Louisiana to visit family. I always loved the country, anyplace where there were cows, horses, pigs, elks, rabbits, snakes, whatever. Mice. Everything. I like the outdoors and wildlife and being able to see the stars at night. Living in the mountains, I can spend time in prayer, in reflection, in meditation, then I can recharge and when I come back to the mix of community, I can hit the ground running."

Even with all that she has achieved, there are times when old obstacles and barriers send Donna running for the refuge of her mountain home. "I've had situations where people have made racist comments to my face," she says placidly, with no hint of offense in her voice. "I've arrived for meetings and have had people refuse to meet with me when they realized I was black and they didn't know that before. It's not that biases don't exist or they don't matter. But I focus on delivering results and that's the most straightforward way to cope with other people's small-mindedness."

None of the black women I spoke to in this book would say that they worked in a meritocracy—they were well aware of the importance of mentors, old boy networks, the nepotism and other subtle systems and obstacles that stood in the way of them reaching the top of their fields. Yet each of them retained an old-fashioned, almost Puritan, optimism about how far they could go on the basis of their own steam. Like Donna, they were each convinced that hard work is the best and only deterrent to racism and/or sexism. And in every one of their cases, hard work had been their most powerful weapon. It was the key to our great-grandmothers' survival in the time of slavery; it is the cornerstone of our empowerment today.

Getting Rid of the Head Rag

WHEN THE Quaker Oats Company decided to give Aunt Jemima a makeover, most notably tossing her much-detested head rag, it was front page news. But a Mammy wearing a flattering shade of Bobbi Brown lipstick and sporting relaxed hair will still be a Mammy to those who lack the imagination to see her in any other way. For black women, the icon has lost its bite because we are no longer a class of domestics and sharecroppers. Young black girls grow up today and know that the world doesn't expect them to be a cook. And if they do aspire to a career in the kitchen, there is dignity, grace and even (courtesy of the Food Network) wealth and fame in that profession as well.

Angela Davis once said that the thing that the black power movement failed to recognize is that you could change the images, but revolution is an inside job. The legacy of Aunt Jemima is that we have learned that the shame implicit in our situation was never really about the head rag, it was about whether the head rag put a ceiling on our brains, our dreams, our ambitions.

We have moved on, yet old stereotypes and old images die hard. With the exception of celebrities such as Oprah Winfrey, many people still see black women, even middle-class black women dressed in Armani, and wonder why they aren't in a position of servitude instead. I was on a business trip, with a colleague, in a chic Palm Beach hotel when someone asked her to bring fresh towels to her room. No matter that she was dressed, as always, to the nines in a designer pantsuit. Like a joke that never ceases to be funny, my friends constantly ask me to tell them about the editorial assistant at a magazine I worked for who was incredulous that I was an editor while he answered the phones. He was young, blond and rich. We were the same age—22. He would walk by my office and whine unabashedly, "But I went to Yale. I went to Yale."

Being mistaken for the help is common for successful women like Anna Perez. As press secretary to Barbara Bush, she was one of the first black women to serve in the White House. After that, she moved on to Creative Artists Agency, where she worked closely with then Hollywood super agent Mike Ovitz. During her tenure at CAA, she often spent her lunch hours shopping on nearby Rodeo Drive. Inevitably, she would be asked a question about the merchandise or ordered to go fetch something. "One guy even had the nerve to get mad at me," Anna says, laughing out loud. "I was reading my *Newsweek* and waiting for the elevator. He asked me something and I said 'I don't know' and I went back to my *Newsweek*. Then he started to hassle me. I didn't feel like I had to tell him that I didn't work in the store." On another occasion, Anna sat barefoot, "obviously waiting for someone to bring me some shoes when an older, white woman turned to me. She said, 'I can't remember where I put my shoes. Can you help?'"

We all agree; the small indignities of racism that still exist are a small price to pay for the successes we now enjoy. The economic strides black families have made over the past ten years are remarkable. This economic growth is due, in large part, to the rising numbers of professional black women. There are more and more sisters living affluent lifestyles, but our image in the media and the mainstream has been slow to change. Accomplished black women have had to chart their courses, professionally and personally, with little support and few role models.

In this book, the key word isn't success as much as it is change. We have changed our educational levels and, as a result, our income levels. We've changed our notions about what makes an acceptable mate. We've changed our relationship to our families and the messages that we send our daughters. Most important, we've changed our perception of ourselves. We're changing America's perception of us, too.

CHAPTER 2

*What We Mean When
We Say Home*

FAMILY   RESPONSIBILITY   RELATIONSHIPS   SUCCESS   MOTHERHOOD   BALANCE

CRYSTAL ASHBY is the textbook image of a sister on the move. At 40, she's an antitrust lawyer for a major Chicago oil company. She enjoys the fruits of her labor—wears designer clothes, drives a late-model sports car and enjoys jet set vacations. A native of Detroit, you could say that oil is in her blood. "I came from a car family," she explains. "My mom worked for General Motors and my dad worked for Ford." A bright student, she quickly outpaced her classmates at her Detroit elementary school. The principal wanted to skip her two grades. Her mother took that as a sign that the public school system wasn't good enough for her little girl. She searched for a school that could challenge and stimulate her daughter—preferably one that offered scholarships. She found it in The Grosse Pointe Academy, a tony private school in the old-money suburb of Grosse Pointe, Michigan.

When it came time to choose a high school, Crystal picked the Academy of the Sacred Heart. By the age of 14, she was well schooled in the art of self-improvement; Sacred Heart had educated Michigan's debutante set for generations. The combination of these two elite private schools gave Crystal a sense of comfort in the mainstream that was foreign to many of her peers in Detroit's inner city. Her education also heightened her sense of entitlement. From an early age, Crystal remembers thinking "Why not me? I always believed that someday I could live in a house like the ones I went to school around, that I could live that lifestyle. For me, it was a reality because I saw it every day. I just wasn't living it every day. But if I was exposed to it, there was no reason to believe I couldn't have it."

She's the only sibling to have attained a professional degree: Crystal's sister works at a medical facility, her brother manages a glass company. While her mother was the architect of her early educational career, mother and daughter inhabit two different worlds. At 40, Crystal is divorced and childless. At the same age, her mother was married with three children and had been working for 20 years. "I probably have more money than my mother ever dreamed of earning," she muses. "I've done things in my life that my mother has never done. And my grandmother? My life fascinates her. Absolutely fascinates her."

A few weeks before our first meeting, Crystal had traveled to London for her company. Her mother, by contrast, spent her entire career in the international division of GM and never once took a business trip. "I travel two or three times a month on business," Crystal says, over cappuccino at an upscale Chicago cafe. "It's nothing for me to get on a plane. I live a lush lifestyle. I have enough money to do the things that I want to do, go to places I want to go, buy the things I want to buy. I live very differently from my family."

Chicago is only a four-and-a-half-hour drive from Detroit. But to Crystal's family, she didn't fly the coop, she jetted away on the Concorde. "My mother lives 20 minutes from my grandmother who lives 20 minutes from my great-grandmother," Crystal tells me when we first meet; it's as if this quick lesson in her family geography should tell me all I need to know about what she's left behind. What surprises me about our subsequent conversations is how much of a comfort Crystal's family is to her, how much she values the fact that theirs is a limited arc of movement and change.

"Part of my job is getting past the color issues, the prejudices and biases," Crystal says. But it's also true that her early years of attending white prep schools has given her a lifetime of training in keeping the peace. "The reality is a lot of my friends are white and a lot of my friends are black," she says. "I work in an environment where my exposure is primarily white. You can either be a loner or assimilate. These are the people that I spend my days with and I like my days to be pleasant."

Her stop-gap against the bitterness and frustration is the time she spends with her family. At work, she says, she is constantly called upon to give the black point of view and to be the bigger person when confronted with a colleague's ignorance. But at home, "I'm just me. None of this stuff goes home. I still bake cakes and cookies at Thanksgiving. I have nieces and nephews to tend to and my mother is still my mother. She still cracks the whip when she needs to. What I do is what I do, it's not who I am."

There's No Place Like Home: the Amazing Career of Sheila Bridges

SHE IS, ACCORDING to a CNN/*Time* magazine survey, the best interior designer in America. Although she has decorated homes for a wide range of clients from Andre Harrell and Puff Daddy to software giant Peter Norton to former President Bill Clinton, it is the type of home that Crystal Ashby talks so lovingly about that prompted Sheila Bridges to embark on her ground-breaking career in residential design. Sheila grew up in Philadelphia with parents whose spirited weekend puttering could have given Martha Stewart and Bob Vila a run for their money. Sheila's parents built with their hands what couldn't be assured for many black girls growing up in the 1960s: a safe haven. When she goes home, even at the age of 38, she sleeps in the same room that she has slept in her entire life. Her mother is a retired teacher, her father still tends to a dental practice he built more than 30 years ago. Bridges says, "This isn't what my parents did professionally, but my parents always really cared about our home. They were constantly decorating, re-designing or building something. My father was always very, very talented with his hands. He would re-tile the bathroom. My mother always had a knack and interest in color. My brother and I gained an understanding that it was important to have a place you call home: to value what you put in it and how you treat it."

As Americans, we've turned into a nation of movers. Extended families that live in the same town are rare; generations that abide under one roof are even rarer still. There's no place like home, the saying goes. Say it aloud and it hangs in the air as quaint and unreal as a needlepoint message hanging on a kitchen wall. But none of us can deny, especially after the September 11 tragedy, the importance of home and how it defines us. What has made Sheila Bridges a pioneer in her field is that in the early 1990s, she watched the growing numbers of middle-class blacks, the civil rights babies who were living the dream, and she figured out that eventually this new elite would get tired of spending their hard-earned dough on nice clothes, nice cars, nice vacations to the Caribbean. With the right guidance, this group could develop a new passion: the desire not only for the right address, but for a truly beautiful home.

After graduating from Brown University with a degree in sociology, Bridges began to work for an architectural firm, which led to her going back to school to get a master's in interior design from Parsons in New York City. She started her business, Sheila Bridges Design, in 1991. "I wanted to perform, for African Americans, the same services I saw at the firms I worked at," she says. "We never had any black clients. We never used any resources, tradespersons or vendors that were African American. And I felt like I knew all these people, including myself, who cared a lot about home. It seemed that there was this huge void. That was something for me, there'd be a lot of personal fulfillment in being able to fill that void."

What she didn't want to do was to swath her clients' homes with the kind of *In Style* meets *Roots* relics that were so popular at the time. Just because her clients were black did not mean that they should lounge on zebra-striped sofas or invest in an array of African sculptures. "People always want to trap us into this box of things looking 'Afrocentric,'" she says, patiently but wearily. "I didn't really grow up with kente cloth, not to say that I don't like it. I think there are other ways for us to represent our culture and who we are without necessarily having to use those kinds of things that I think white people have decided represent us. I really draw inspiration from a range of different things: it may be Egypt, it may be Europe, it may be something out of hip-hop culture. It really depends on who it is."

We are sitting in the living room of her Harlem apartment and office. I keep looking around the room with an uncomfortable sense of déjà vu when I realize that I know these rooms so well because I've pored over them on the pages of design magazines, where Sheila's face would be the sole image of a nonwhite person, of any color. I'm startled because being in her apartment is a little like meeting a movie star. I only think I know these rooms because I've seen and admired them so often. I recognize the details the way people recognize Julia Roberts's grin or Benicio Del Toro's deep-set eyes: there's the unusual Hercules sculpture, the book cases that curve, ever so slightly, like décolletage, on the top, and the fireplace, tiled with the most unusual shade of green. Up close I realize that there are several different greens among the tiles, ranging from leaf to pine. No wonder the fireplace seems to glow: the colors are so wonderfully layered, it's like staring into an amazingly verdant patch of trees. Ten minutes into our interview, I feel unbelievably serene.

When we meet, Bridges has just published her first book, *Furnishing Forward* and is about to begin production on her new television show. Her business has grown so much, and she has become such a well-known arbiter of style, that she only takes on a few clients a year. Still she hopes to continue on television what she has, for so long, done in her career. "It's all about exposure and education," she says. "A lot of the choices we make, as African Americans, are because we haven't had the exposure and because we don't know. I tried to write my book in a way that's very anecdotal and personal. I don't always know what I'm doing. I try to give examples in my homes so people can see. I'm trying to put it out there in a way that's a lot less intimidating."

She hopes that more African Americans will discover what her parents always seemed to know. "My feeling is that wealthy people treat themselves well," she says. "They feel that they've earned the right to have beautiful homes and nice things. My point is that all of us work hard and all of us deserve to treat ourselves well. It doesn't mean that you have to spend a million dollars. It just means that there's nothing wrong with surrounding yourself with things that you love and things that inspire you."

Sheila Bridges has a soft spot for Italy. She studied in Rome during her junior year at Brown University. While completing her master's, she studied decorative arts in Florence. She began to understand what a leap of imagination it takes to choose a career such as hers. "In Italy, kids that are on the school bus pass by the Duomo every day," she says. "Every day they go home for lunch and pass by the Vatican. There's such an incredible level of exposure that starts at a very, very young age. If you can see that someone *designed* this incredible building, you think, that's something I can be when I get older. For us, we don't have those sources of inspiration. The kind of things that little black girls pass by on their way to school don't make them say, 'Wow. I can really do this.'"

It's Not Where You're From, It's Where You're At

FOR SUCCESSFUL African-American women, the definition of home is ever shifting because the places we call home are so stark in their differences. Is home the black neighborhood where you were raised or the white prep school where you came of age? If you grew up an "Only" in a predominantly white neighborhood where you often felt isolated, does home become smaller in scope and represent only your literal house and the people who lived there? Among rappers, there's a phrase designed to put those who boast dubious street credentials in their place. "It's not where you're from, it's where you're at" is the refrain of many a hip-hop song. But for successful black women, the reality of those words can sting. When you find yourself in a walnut-paneled conference room with tufted leather chairs, priceless Persian rugs, a Picasso hanging to your right and a Pollock hanging on your left; when the air-conditioner is running at full blast and nobody at the table looks even a little like you—where you're at can be a very cold, isolated place. At the same time, where you're from begins to take on mythic qualities—when you're a black professional woman in a world as foreign to you as Oz, the 'hood can seem as sweet as Kansas.

In *Flux: Women on Sex, Work, Kids...*, Peggy Orenstein writes about a young medical student named Shay, who lived in the inner city but was bussed to a prep school. Twenty years after that first bus ride, now at an Ivy League medical school, Shay feels more connected with her black world than the white world she travels in every day. "I may have known the kids I went to school with from the time we were seven," Shay tells Orenstein. "But friendship-wise, my real life was always once I got home, with my black friends."

It doesn't help that the very notion of a black world and a white world is steeped in stereotypes and value judgments. Too often, the black world is assumed to be one of poverty and tragedy, the inner-city visions of the local nightly news. Conversely, the white world is held up to young blacks as being a world of academic achievement and financial success, with little discussion of white poverty or illiteracy. The ambitious young person who takes the stereotypes at face value can end up with a fine education, a good job and an unhealthy mixture of self-loathing and cultural schizophrenia.

A generation ago, every black community had a need and a place for black doctors, lawyers, accountants and the like. But with few exceptions, young black women studying for those degrees today don't expect to work in the black community. The highest goal, always, is to conquer the mainstream world. Many black middle-class women find themselves utterly lost, when even after their best efforts they can't make a place for themselves in the mainstream. In her powerful memoir, *Trespassing*, Gwendolyn Parker describes how disillusioned she became with her unrelenting status as an outsider in corporate America. She's moved from strength to strength: an exclusive boarding school, Harvard, the most conservative law firm on Wall Street. Yet after eight years as a director at American Express, Parker had had enough. "These halls were my home now," she recalls. "I had sojourned for over ten years in them—centers of power and prestige in white America. I'd been trained in their very own breeding grounds, made my career at institutions that were overwhelmingly white and male. ... As a black female, I was the perpetual outsider, persistently viewed as a trespasser on private preserves at the same time [that my success] was a role I'd been groomed for since birth."

It's that constant feeling that one is "trespassing" in the white world that makes it so important that we find the place, the people, who represent home. How well professional black women negotiate the spaces between black and white worlds is perhaps the most critical element to their success. It determines how well they will overcome obstacles and how happy they'll be once they reach their goals. Crystal Ashby strikes a very strong balance between her two worlds: clearly successful on paper, but also very self-confident in person. She'll be the first person to tell you she lives in two worlds, but it's a dual citizenship she relishes.

For Aisha Brooks-Lytle, a 27-year-old student at Princeton Seminary, the feeling of trespassing often masquerades as a fear that blacks who are still struggling will mistake her for a person born into privilege. "It's the feeling you get when you're with your white friends and the only people serving you in the cafeteria lines are working-class minorities," she says. "I always want to jump on a chair and say, 'I'm different from them! I remember what it was like to heat up the kitchen with the oven! I've battled roaches! I ate government cheese!'"

Home to the Church

THEY CALL THEM "the generation that forgot God," the more-than-40-million baby boomers that dropped out of churches and synagogues in the 1960s and 1970s. For African-American boomers, the folks in my parents' generation, the exodus was particularly defiant. The black church had, from slavery to the days of lunch counter sit-ins, been the nexus of change and rebellion. But in the late 1960s and 1970s, black nationalists put the church on trial. How long were we supposed to turn the other cheek? What good had nonviolent resistance done when Martin and Medgar Evers had been gunned down in cold blood? Not to mention the Jesus that black men and women had prayed to for so long. How could we kneel down before what the black power acolytes called "a jive-ass white boy"? Former Spelman College president Johnetta

Cole remembers, "looking up at the white faces in the stained-glass windows and thinking, all these people down here are black."[7] When the black power movement gained prominence, she cringed at the memory of being in Sunday school and singing "Jesus will wash me whiter than snow." Steeped in European imagery and a benediction in need of change, the church was yet another symbol of black people's oppression.

It wasn't always that way. During slavery, blacks were not allowed to gather for worship for fear that religious meetings would lead to talk of uprising. Since the beginning of our history in America, the black church has been a political force for freedom—instrumental in many battles up to and including the civil rights movement. "Black women from the 1930s through the 1960s knew how to organize, were accustomed to working together and felt a strong kinship with members of their community beyond their immediate families," Darlene Clark Hine and Kathleen Thompson write in *A Shining Thread of Hope: The History of Black Women in America.* "The church and the community work in which they had been involved for two centuries made them ideal political activists."

In the mid-'80s and '90s, the black church again came to prominence. While their pews may have been emptier during the years following the civil rights movement, the churches never went away. Some had been there for more than 200 years. A classic example is Bethel African Methodist Episcopal Church founded in Baltimore in 1785; a large and influential church, it was known affectionately in the community as Big Bethel. Like many black churches, the 1970s were lean years. But in the 1990s, its flock returned in droves. The membership has exploded: from 310 members in 1975 to 14,000 members in 1999—when the church's biggest problem was finding enough land on which to build. What is even more striking is that its members are overwhelmingly young and middle class, with an average member being only 35 years old.[8]

In New York City, Jacqueline Bazan, the 37-year-old founder of Bazan Entertainment, a marketing and PR company, is one of the thousands of young, middle-class blacks who've returned to the church. "Religion is very important to me," she says. "It gives me a sense of clarity, hope and determination. There was a period in time when I lost my faith for a short while and I can honestly say that it was the most miserable time of my life." "I attend St. Paul Community Baptist Church in Brooklyn's East New York section," says Kencle Satchell-McKoy, a 30-something magazine circulation manager. "I neither live nor work in this community, yet I feel connected based on the work my church has done and is currently doing. My church is my foundation."

For some black women, the faith has changed but the foundation of spirituality has not. "One of the anchors for black people, historically, has been spirituality," says Harriette Cole. "Some might argue that it was an anchor that was drowning us, but I make a difference between religion and spirituality." Cole grew up in the United Methodist church, but for the past 12 years, she's been following a yoga path. "As a result of my Eastern practice, I now have a lot of respect for my Methodist upbringing. It's not separate," she says.

"The church continues to emit a powerful homing signal for African Americans," Beverly Hall Lawrence writes in *Reviving the Spirit: A Generation of African Americans Goes Home to Church.* "For some it presents an opportunity to return to community and people who were abandoned along the road to bourgeois affluence; for others it offers an extended family and a plain old great place to socialize." [9]

For FreshWater Software CEO Donna Auguste, church is a touchstone. She looks forward to her weekly visit to the African-American Catholic community where she can be simply "Sister Donna." In church, she's not "the first" or "the only" or the CEO or the pioneer: she's the fellow member. She is greeted there with love and affection by men and women who are as poor as she is wealthy and by all the people who live in between. They don't ask how much money she makes from her patents. (The number one question whenever she visits math and science classes in public schools.) At church, Sister Donna doesn't have to give the same inspirational speeches about cracking the glass ceiling as she does when she speaks at the Society of Women Engineers.

Her church members know only that she works with computers, lives up in the mountains and plays a mean guitar. Gospel music, she says, is her passion and release. Auguste belongs to a multi-denominational, multicultural organization called "The Gospel Music Shop of America" where she says, "We come together and make great music and what we have in common is that we love the Lord. That is something that is a calling for me and I stay very focused on that as a high priority in my life."

The church and community are synonymous for Donna. I suspect that it is so for many black women. I'm not speaking about individual women's levels of faith, but rather about the idea that the church is perhaps the most prominent means for black women of all backgrounds to maintain a connection to and nurture a relationship with the black community. For middle-class black women, who often work in predominantly white neighborhoods, the need to come "home" even for an hour a week on Sunday mornings can be particularly acute.

When I returned to New York from Los Angeles to work for the *New York Times Magazine,* I became the only black female editor on staff. I lived in Brooklyn Heights, in a predominantly white building where, for the first year, my neighbors refused to hold the door for me if I approached the door behind them, making a point to push the door closed in my face and forcing me to produce a key. This might sound like the unfortunate rudeness of city living, but I live in a small brownstone building with 14 apartments. I knew my neighbors, at least by face, within two weeks.

My sister-friends were scattered from London to Los Angeles and, if it wasn't for the head of research at the *Times Magazine,* I could go whole weeks without face-to-face contact with another black woman during the many long hours I spent at work. Renee Michael Prewitt, my *Times* colleague, tolerated my constantly hanging around her cubicle. I like to think that our quest for advice and solace was mutual. I longed for a place, as Crystal Ashby so powerfully described, where I could just be me.

Several months later, I found it in Reverend Paul Smith's First Presbyterian Church. It was a purposefully multiracial congregation headed by a hip African-American minister who won my heart with an early sermon about a crisis of faith that centered on a metaphor about my favorite basketball team, the New York Knicks. First Presbyterian was a place where on a weekly basis other black people embraced me, a place where no one asked me to give the black perspective or to justify my point of view as a black woman. A place where I could talk about sports, trade recipes and restaurant recommendations, be myself. Miles away from my mother, my aunt and my cousins, I would sometimes find myself close to tears when during the service, when it was time to share the peace, some older black woman would ignore my outstretched hand and embrace me in a tight hug. Church became the antidote to my isolation at the *Times*. It was simply home.

Balance has become the major buzzword in the pop cultural exploration of women's lives—work versus family, the mommy track versus the fast track, being single and professionally successful but sometimes lonely versus the compromises and companionship of marriage. For successful black women, there is another component to this concept. Race makes us a permanent, irrevocable citizen of the black world, but class and experience makes us, with few exceptions, a lifelong sojourner in the white world. These are the muddy waters that Martin Luther King's children of the dream must wade through. It's the next beat of the story that he could never anticipate—that while black and white children may walk side by side, play side by side and study side by side, we do not inhabit the same world every moment of the day. Not yet.

In *Reviving the Spirit,* Beverly Hall Lawrence introduces us to a number of middle-class professionals, like herself, who have returned to the church for community as well as spiritual nourishment. "I went to a white college, grew up in a white high school, but I never experienced what I felt in law school," says a 35-year-old woman named Pam who still recalled, with anguish, her futile efforts to befriend her white law school classmates. Even when she stood right in front of them and waved, she says, they still ignored her. "You'd sit in class with a white person all day, and then you'd walk three blocks away from the school and they don't acknowledge you. I didn't understand this." As Lawrence observes, "What she sensed was not racial contempt from her white schoolmates but an indifference and dismissiveness that she felt was demeaning." For Pam, joining a black church was a quest to regain her humanity, because her classmates' indifference made her feel that she was "vanishing."

The door to racial equality has cracked, but it is far from wide open. For women like Pam who went to all the right schools, got the top grades, went along to get along at prestigious law firms, the daily incidents of racism and sexism are more than mere annoyances. They symbolize the American promise broken: work hard, prosper, be accepted as a valuable member of society. For successful African Americans, unlike any other immigrant group of the 20th century, there is no such thing as full assimilation. There is always someone who will remind you that you are black, that you are different, that you are trespassing. Black churches counteract the hostility and indifference of the mainstream world, providing a place where we can gather and be regarded with respect and pride.

The Only Black Person She Knows Is You

ROSE SALEM KNOWS how to make an entrance. She arrives at the home of her friend Tracie Howard, late and slightly flustered, in a white sweater, black leather pants and a full-length mink coat, that she slips off without a backward glance. A technology consultant at her own firm, Salem and Salem, she's not afraid to speak her mind. "When I got into the computer industry, I was working for a company where I was the only black person," says the 32-year-old mother of two. "I did things that I thought were very normal: going abroad on vacations, going to a Broadway play, going to nice restaurants. My boss sat across from me and would overhear conversations where I would plan my evenings. One day we had lunch and she said, "Rose, you are very different. You aren't like other black people." I said, "No, I'm like a lot of people I know."

All of the women gathered in Tracie's living room nod their heads knowingly. They are all successful women in their 30s and 40s, their ranks include: a VP at a nonprofit agency, two stockbrokers, a former financial executive and a real estate agent. They can all relate to the backhanded compliment implicit in the phrase "you're not like other black people." They wish the people they worked with would accept that it is not uncommon for a black woman to be well educated, capable and successful.

Rose says that eventually she came to see that her boss saw her not only as being an anomaly culturally—scuba diving at luxury resorts, shopping at designer boutiques, attending Broadway shows—but as someone who was too big for her britches. "I was working on commission and my commissions started to rack up," Rose says. "My boss said, 'You know you're making more money than most black people would.' She actually wanted to cut my commission!"

Sandra Rice, the head of a nonprofit foundation that places minority youth in high-profile media internships, sees a different point in Rose's story. If whites tend to see successful blacks as an exception, it's because they don't know enough black people to know better. "I'll bet you were the only black person that she knew," says Sandra. "You and minorities she might read or hear about in the media. She probably never had anyone of color in her home or invited them out socially. Otherwise, her comment wouldn't have been made. It's so important for us to speak up."

It's that lack of familiarity that is the most troubling stumbling block in black women's success. It is also the hardest one to remedy. In 1999, Catalyst, a national nonprofit group that studies women of business, published a report entitled "Women of Color in Corporate Management: Opportunities and Barriers."[10] In a survey of 1,700 women managers and professionals, 47 percent cited the lack of an influential mentor or sponsor as their biggest barrier. Another 40 percent pointed to a lack of networking with influential colleagues. In comparison, only 28 percent cited the lack of high-visibility assignments as a problem. The survey also found that "African-American women are more likely than white women to feel excluded in both business school and business environments." This is at the same time that black women are advancing through the professional ranks at a faster pace than ever before. Between 1976 and 2006, the number of black women in the work force will have increased by 35 percent, this is in comparison with white women, up by 10 percent, and white men, down by 17 percent.

In 2001, Catalyst released a follow-up study, "Women of Color Executives: Their Voices, Their Journeys." In it, half a dozen top minority women executives are profiled. One of them was Cheryl Hamilton, the human resources director for Acme Manufacturing. She points out that "When the company says, 'We want to advance women,' implicitly they're saying, 'We want to advance women with whom we're comfortable.'" Hamilton recalls that a senior manager once told her,

"Cheryl, all of the managers have had a white female in their life. It was their mother, their sister or their daughter. And they have had an experience with a white female that inherently enables them to understand that she's a very capable person. My only experience with an African-American woman may have been the cleaning lady, the nanny or the sales clerk at the store. I don't have a lot of positive experiences that say inherently, 'I'm going to put you in charge of minding the store.'"

As more black women assume leadership roles, the confidence in our ability rises. On a personal level, many black women are uncomfortable with the notion of what it takes to make whites comfortable. I myself remember becoming increasingly dissatisfied at a job and having a white co-worker say, "You don't smile anymore." I could have thrown her through the window. "Is it my job to *smile* at you??!" I wanted to scream; images of happy darky minstrels dancing through my head. Eventually I learned the importance of creating what one executive in the Catalyst study calls "a corporate space"; a place where I could be personable, without necessarily getting personal. It's an idea that many black women resist. "I've had people in my office that have said, 'I ain't gonna do that shit. I'm good at what I do, but I'm not going to sit down and have a cup of coffee with them,'" one senior executive told Catalyst. "They say, 'I am not going to chitchat about what I did over the weekend with them.' I say, if you don't they're going to make up stories. Don't look at it as an infringement on your private space. Create your corporate space. You create a corporate space by giving them the image that you want them to have, not necessarily what reality is."

Finding Our Place in the World

AS A GROUP of women who travel easily between the black community and the white mainstream, I'm curious about where the women I've interviewed feel most comfortable. Where do they call home?

Yvonne Durant remembers the distinct moment she decided to move to Italy. She was an advertising executive in New York and was vacationing with friends on the Italian Riviera. "I was on my friend's boat," she remembers. "And I realized that this didn't have to be my vacation, it could be my life. I was also becoming frustrated with America, the rampant racism. I found that New York was becoming difficult, too. It was taking so much and giving nothing." Soon after her revelation, she moved to Milan—and stayed for seven years.

In Europe, she says, she learned "how to take time to live graciously. The joie de vivre! Life didn't feel so heavy, there was always something beautiful to see, touch, eat, smell." These days, she is back in New York. She lives on the Upper East Side, a neighborhood she chose because it has a cosmopolitan air that reminds her of Milan. "I love roaming through Sotheby's exhibitions," she says. "Discovering blocks I've never roamed down before, even those with the old East Side tenements." She says that living in a wealthy neighborhood gives one "social capital." A neighbor's husband turned out to be the CEO of a huge company and got her resumé to presidents at three major corporations in a matter of days. When Yvonne had a health scare recently, another neighbor turned out to be a prominent specialist in the field. "She made everything that needed to happen happen in two days," she says.

Upper East Side living is not without its down side, however. "Sometimes, for blocks, I'm the only black woman not pushing an elderly white person or a baby," Yvonne says. Waiting for an elevator, a neighbor's toddler kept staring at Yvonne and saying, "Nanny, Nanny, Nanny" while his mother turned several shades of red. Yvonne is often mistaken for another black woman in the building, a woman she describes as "five shades lighter than I." When she first moved into the building, she was very careful of how she dressed when she went downstairs to get the mail or do laundry, taking care to dress "casually chic" in her Gucci loafers and good jewelry. Though she is fierce when she notes, "I wasn't scared about being mistaken for the help. I was more scared for the fool who may have asked."

Sandra, Tracie Howard's friend, has found that in her 40s she feels fully bicultural. "When I was in a predominantly white elementary school and they started addressing slavery in the history books, I was the only African American in the room. There were no other minorities and I was very embarrassed and ashamed," she says. "I should have asked the most questions out of all those kids in the room, but I couldn't speak. Now, when I'm in a room of black people or in a room of white people, I have no problem communicating what I'm thinking. The older I get, the more grounded I feel."

Sandra doesn't speak any foreign languages. "Just English and mo' English" she says with a laugh. But during her years in management at ABC she was able to spend extended periods of time working in France, Greece and Latin America. That time abroad helped her to develop the confidence she displays today. "It's different for women of color abroad," she says. "I feel more respected. Traveling has been of such value to me. One of the reasons I've matured as a woman is because of the traveling that I've done. It's what I want for my daughter and my stepson."

For one corporate consultant, the great pleasure of her work abroad is taking a leadership role where it's least expected for her as a black woman. "Dealing with Japanese men and having to lead meetings and having them give you high regard. That's great," she says. "Even in Africa, in my role as advisor, I'm leading and guiding. The dynamic of that is on one hand, they want to take your advice. But they are also dealing with the emotions of following your lead as a woman." She considers her extensive travels one of the sweetest aspects of her success. "I've been to almost every continent," she says with pride. "When I was a kid, all I wanted was to experience the world. I just went for it. I still do."

When I meet art consultant Kim Heirston, she has just returned from her second trip to India. She was surprised to see a lot of African Americans on Indian TV. "There were a number of black films, Cosby reruns, Fresh Prince reruns," she says. "I think it might be that Indian viewers want to see people of color. It's fascinating. I always feel so at home there. I love India." It's the kind of trip that she points to as being directly influenced by being raised by her mom. Kim grew up on Long Island, the daughter of a single mother who was, in the 1960s, unique among black women of her generation because she was such a free spirit. "She was the original New Ager," Kim remembers. "She did yoga before it was fashionable. She loved to cook international cuisine. She loved to travel. I had a very, very bohemian suburban background."

As a child, Kim and her mother spent hours in New York City

museums. Later, when Kim decided to pursue a career in art, her early exposure helped her feel comfortable in an environment that many African Americans often find unwelcoming. "I know that people say galleries are intimidating. I hear it a lot," she says. "For me, it's like home. When I try to put myself into some of my collector's shoes, walking up to the desk in this completely white room, where there's some really pretty, well-dressed, blonde, slightly snooty person who doesn't want to give you the price list, I could see where that would be intimidating. But as a child, I spent so much time looking at art in museums. From that standpoint, you do feel at home."

CHAPTER 3

*To Whom Much Is Given, Much
Is Expected: Successful Women,
Family and Responsibility*

FAMILY RESPONSIBILITY RELATIONSHIPS SUCCESS MOTHERHOOD BALANCE

TO WHOM MUCH is given, much is expected" was both personal and political to young black women in the 1970s. At the time, Walteen Grady-Truely was getting her undergraduate degree at Michigan State University. She remembers two things distinctly: the culture of black nationalism that permeated her campus and the sense of marriage panic that hung over her heart. "As I reflect over the atmosphere of the 70s, my decisions were overlaid by the sense that the revolution was going to happen tomorrow and that you had to choose sides," says Walteen. "If you didn't make the right choice, you could hurt the whole black community. It wasn't like I could have the luxury of finding myself. I had to choose the right side of the battle lines. My brother who came along four years later felt much freer than I did. His wife is white, yet he had no problems fitting in."

"It took me three years to understand that the countless speeches that all began, 'the black man...' did not include me," writes Michele Wallace of her experience as a teenager in the late 1960s. Like Walteen,

Wallace felt drawn in by the movement that put sisters on a pedestal by declaring black was beautiful, only to discover later all the ways in which black women sacrificed for the community would later make them scapegoats. "I was told of the awful ways in which black women, me included, had tried to destroy the black man's masculinity," Wallace continues. "How we had castrated him, worked when he didn't work, made money when he made no money, spent our nights and days in church praying to a jive white boy named Jesus while the black man collapsed into alcoholism, drug addiction and various forms of despair. The message of the black movement was that I was being watched, on probation as a black woman, that any signs of aggressiveness, intelligence or independence would mean I'd be denied even the one role still left open to me...keeper of house, children and incense burners."[11]

For those women who came of age right after the civil rights movement, life was a mixture of often contradictory rules. You were supposed to say it loud about being black and proud, but to assert your independence with black men was counterrevolutionary. Education was a key component to uplifting the race, but as Stokely Carmichael so famously put it, "the black woman's place in the movement is prone." Black men could, and would, date white women without losing their place in the black power movement. Yet, black women who chose to date white men were nothing more than self-deluded, voluntary chattel, ignorant of 200 years of rape and slavery.

At six-feet tall, with a short salt-and-pepper afro, Walteen is now in her late 40s. At the time of our first conversation she's recruiting mentors for at-risk teens as the Director of the New York Volunteer for Youth Campaign. She radiates a strong, calming presence. As we sit and talk at a Thai restaurant near her New York City office, she is in the process of divorcing her husband of 15 years. Her smooth, dark skin is unlined, but there is a definite furrow across her brow. She has been taking a memoir-writing course, she tells me, and it has helped her as she tries to assess the choices that she has made in her life; there are pieces of her younger self that she misses and that she hopes to recover.

Walteen spent her teenage years traveling with her family; her father was in the military. She lived in Nigeria for four years, attended a Swiss boarding school for another year, then graduated from a high school in Bangkok. One of the memories that her writing course has brought up is that in Thailand, as a high school senior, she asked a white classmate to the Sadie Hawkins dance. Returning to the United States to go to school, she would never have considered such a possibility. "When I went to college, there was such a strong era of nationalism," she remembers. "I felt that I didn't have the right not to marry a black man. I felt I had a responsibility to have a black child."

"I didn't have the right." "I felt I had a responsibility." Those are powerful words to use when discussing one's personal life. How did she end up shouldering so much guilt? "It's guilt and responsibility," Walteen corrects me. "I think the two things are very much entwined. No one ever told me that I could be true to myself and still carry out that sense of responsibility." Yet she is hardly alone in her generation of women, who allowed the politics of the black power movement to dictate who and how she loved.

Guilt was also a factor in how Walteen chose her life's work. "Oh absolutely!" she says emphatically. "I believe it is what drove me in almost all my career choices. I chose to go into education. Before that, I wanted to be a lawyer. It was always with an eye towards creating a world where there would be more people like me, where there would be more people who shared a quality educational background, who had the advantage of having access to the whole world, not just the neighborhood."

This was a powerful notion for Walteen, who felt it was her life's work to bridge the gaps between the blacks who were haves and those who were have-nots. Growing up as a middle-class black girl, Walteen remembers complaining to her parents about her sense of isolation. "I didn't have any friends like me," she says. "I wasn't meeting people. My mother used to say, 'Well, I've been lonely all my life.' I guess she thought that was comforting, but it wasn't." Her mother's comments are clearly a painful memory for Walteen. During our most recent interview, she had moved back home to the Poconos where she's an instructor of education and coordinator for the Learning Support Center at the local Penn State campus. She moved so her son could be near his grandmother and attend better schools, but she worries that while he is now thriving academically, he's also suffering from the same loneliness she once did. "I don't think it's new," she says. "But there's a sense that if you're African American and on the cutting edge economically and educationally, there are not going to be other people like you. There are so few of us. I definitely have that feeling and my son has it, too."

Several years earlier, when she worked in Tribeca, she decided to register her son, Romare, at a nearby school. She knew it would be a marked improvement from the school he attended in their Fort Greene neighborhood. In an effort to ease the transition, she made it a point to continue Romare's play dates with his best friend, Rodney. The boys were both ten when Walteen overhead the following conversation. Rodney asked, "So what's your school like?" Romare said, "Oh, it's a school." Rodney paused, then asked, "Well, do you have gunshot holes in your windows?" It's a painful memory for Walteen, whose face, as she tells the story, displays a mixture of shame and hurt. "It just blew me away," she says. "It was almost as if we had to have a choice between having a community of black people and an environment that was very unsafe or having a safer environment physically and no community. It hurts me to see that repeated over and over again." Even in this day and age, a whole new generation of young people are being offered opportunities that aren't afforded the majority. As far as we have come, there is still a talented tenth—with all the weight of responsibility and guilt that comes along with it.

The Talented Tenth

IN 1903, THE GREAT SCHOLAR W. E. B. DuBois published his masterwork, *The Souls of Black Folk.* DuBois's writing was an intellectual, improvisational pastiche of narrative fiction and social criticism, anthropology and state of the union address—it reads like highly developed literary jazz. In it, he famously declared "the problem of the 20th century is the problem of the color line." DuBois would be hailed as a visionary, again and again. His words resonated throughout almost all of the 20th century's great social struggles and tragedies. Whether it was the Turkish massacres of Armenians, the German slaughter of Jews, or the colonizers' ways with the colonized, it's remarkable how we've been driven again and again into war, massacre and upheaval by the power of racial difference. DuBois, who always meant his quote to address a far greater scale than racial politics in the United States, saw it coming.

DuBois's prophecy was marked not only by the eloquence of his words, but also by the breadth of his scope: what ambitious statesman—black or white—would look a hopeful people in the eye and tell them that racism would last not a decade or two, but 100 years? As bold as it was, his proclamation was hardly a news flash. Even Langston Hughes's fictional colored man on the corner, Jesse B. Semple, could have looked at the masses of sharecropping southerners and northern factory workers addled by poor working conditions and minimum pay and declared "Houston, we have a problem." Any uneducated black man or woman could have told you that Lincoln didn't solve the race problem as they cited the tyranny of hapless, random violence that was a constant threat to their lives. In those fragile years, as former slaves and their children tried to construct a place for themselves within the severe constraints of the northern-mandated freedom, *The Souls of Black Folk* could have been merely a preacher yapping at the choir.

DuBois, however, operated like a jazz musician. For the most part, his book wasn't aimed at black folks at all. Like other great race men and women before him, such as Frederick Douglass and Sojourner Truth, he sweetened the melody for the liberal white audience that he hoped would start swaying in beat to his cause. Yet he knew that blacks were listening and, in order not to lose their attention and support, he would sometimes curve a note in their direction. His theory of the Talented Tenth swung like that. DuBois's Tenth was the segment of the black community who had the wit, social skills and means to uplift the entire race. This Talented Tenth would be the leaders and architects of black achievement in America. Our shining glory.

From the beginning, the theory brewed controversy. At the turn of the century, the problem of entry into the upper echelons of black society was indeed the problem of the color line. Black elites monitored membership in the most prestigious black civic organizations, churches, fraternities and sororities with a paper bag test: anyone darker than a paper bag need not apply. Despite their own intraracism, these people considered themselves sanctioned by birth and skin color to lead the poorer black masses. They beamed with pride at DuBois's notion of the Talented Tenth because surely, they reasoned, he was talking about them.

Conversely, there were those who disagreed vehemently with DuBois. Some of them could care less about the colorism that plagued the black upper classes. These critics simply saw the idea of a Talented Tenth as being inherently divisive and problematic. How could we commit the wealth of our resources and energies to just one-tenth of our community? How could we be sure that once educated and anointed they would uplift our cause? And what happens, generation after generation, to those who are left behind? It's a question that black people struggle with to this day. Cheryl Mills, former deputy White House counsel and current Oxygen Media vice president, put it this way to Lynette Clemetson in a *Newsweek* article: "We're now getting to this place where we have the privilege to decide if we are all going to be on the same bus or whether or not we are going to get off the bus. I think the black community is finding itself now at this crossroads where it has to decide. Are we going to continue to be connected as a community or are the privilege levels and the progress we're seeing going to mean different things for different [people]?"[12]

Take, for example, an anecdote separated from the race issue altogether. Each year, a poor village has ten students that complete the modest lessons taught in its one-room schoolhouse. They pick one young man to continue his education in the big city. They pay for his schooling, his lodging, his expenses—everything, so he can focus on his studies and become a doctor. Obligation, and some might say guilt, would predicate that the young man returns to the village to open a practice, and perhaps one day, a hospital. But who's to say that the young man will? Maybe he will take a job at a research facility; maybe his destiny is not to cure colicky babies and ill farm animals, but to find the cure to some interminable disease. Maybe his aim or intention isn't even as noble as that. Maybe he takes a job with a big city hospital, gets rich and builds himself a big house. What happens to the village then? What good is their investment in the Talented Tenth? Maybe they should have sent two students to college, with partial scholarships each. Maybe they should have truly hedged their bets and sent three.

Shaking Off the Guilt: A Generational Shift

AT 31, ANGELA KYLE feels much less anxious than Walteen Grady-Truely about finding a place in the black community. And she feels none of the guilt. It's the gift that women of Walteen's generation have given to the women of mine: we have the luxury to find ourselves without worrying that our actions are, as Walteen phrased it, "hurting the whole black community." Angela and I meet at the Bel Age Hotel in Los Angeles; she lives nearby in Beverly Hills. Angela is tall and thin with the kind of All-American freshness of a J. Crew model. Today, she's wearing a close-fitting T-shirt, slacks and has a cardigan tied around her hips. Angela's chestnut-colored skin is flawless, without a hint of makeup, and she wears her shoulder-length hair in a fashionable bob. She's just finished her second day in her new job as senior director of business development at Live Planet—a company often in the news because of its two co-founders, Ben Affleck and Matt Damon. The heartthrobs want to bring together old media (film and television) with new media (the Internet) in intriguing, profitable ways.

It's a high-stakes gambit. Other Internet-related companies led by such visionaries as Steven Spielberg and Ron Howard blew through millions of dollars, then failed. Ben and Matt have Hollywood convinced they'll do better. Angela's an anomaly in the office; the executive suite is largely a good young boys' network from Boston and their early days as struggling actors in L.A. She's an Ivy League graduate, with business degrees from Columbia University and the London School of Economics. She's a young, black woman in a business that could care less about affirmative action or the Talented Tenth or diversity. She's at Live Planet for one reason alone—to make deals and making deals is what she loves.

Angela remembers that growing up, "I lived in a predominantly white neighborhood and went to a predominantly white school. In order to balance the whole white thing, I went to a black church." It's interesting to me that even Angela's language is more flippant, more casual, than Walteen's pained confessions. By the late 1970s and early 1980s, "the whole white thing" was not a big deal at all. "I was really active in church stuff so I had a group of black girls my age," she says. "Then at school, I had white female friends. I never really tried to bridge the two or bring them together, I was comfortable with them being separate."

Later, at Brown University, Angela felt none of the social or political pressures that Walteen experienced at Michigan State. At Brown, she joined a group called OUAP, the Organization of United African Peoples. But this was hardly her social center. "I wanted to be in OUAP," she says. "I wasn't really active, but I was at least present and accounted for." The desire to be simply "present and accounted for" is a seismic shift from Walteen's college years when she felt weighed down by her obligations to the movement. Recall that during Walteen's college years, she felt she "didn't have the right not to marry a black man. I felt I had a responsibility to have a black child." In contrast, Angela describes her experience with black groups at Brown to being similar to the way her Asian friends felt about Asian-American organizations. "We were all aware of what was going on in our respective communities," she says. "But what drove my experience was meeting people that I had things in common with. I was pretty comfortable forging this network of friends that was racially mixed."

Similarly, when Angela talks about her career in business development, race hardly enters the conversation at all. She's not pressured to find a black husband, hasn't even begun to think about kids. "My thought is that right now I can't get married and I can't have kids," she says. "For me, the ultimate success as an adult is career success, getting to the top of something, winning awards. This is the arena in which I feel like I'm making my mark on the world. I know that I can't balance my life with family in any way, shape or form so I haven't really tried."

In Angela's conversation, there are hints of so many things, especially the luxury of young black women today to put career first. While back at Tracie Howard's Hoboken gathering, writer Debra Jackson may speak proudly of holding onto her "ghetto card," women like Angela don't feel a need to prove their connection to the black community. There may be so much talk in the public sphere about successful black women and the dearth of highly educated, high-income earning male counterparts, but there seems to be little realization that for women like Angela, marriage and family aren't a priority. She doesn't know or care if there are "enough" black men out there. She's not really looking. It's not that she doesn't value her black girlfriends or that she isn't interested in black men. It's just that right now she's having too much fun and is way too ambitious to worry.

"My friend Suzie was here last weekend," Angela mentions. "She was saying that sometimes it stresses her out to be in a group of all black women. She says that no matter where the conversation starts, be it on the topic of work or family, it always ends on men and how everyone's looking and can't find one. Blah. Blah. Blah. It's not so much that the fantasy of a Prince Charming doesn't apply to me as a black woman. It's more that I'm a workaholic and I have other issues." And on that note, Angela gets up to leave. Her company is throwing a party to announce the winner of a screenplay competition they've been running. It will be one of her first opportunities to get face time with the heads of her company. With a wave, she is off—to gather intelligence, to meet and greet, to make deals.

Even though they live on different sides of the country, I know that Walteen would be proud of Angela. That in some ways, Angela's attitude is something she is striving for herself. Both women represent a vision of DuBois's Talented Tenth, but they embody it in radically different ways. The last time we met, Walteen said that what she has always admired about my generation is that "You've always represented for me the right to have stuff, the right to carve our own space and not just be the banner carrier for the race. You feel a right to be yourself. This is the next level of black liberation: the right to be ourselves, the right to define our own successes. In the '60s, I might have defined success as the right to fight for my people. That was the pinnacle. You are part of a group of women who are enjoying their lives. That's the next frontier."

Who Do We Owe?

IF THE CIVIL RIGHTS ACT of 1964 was our economic emancipation, the open sesame to access to the education and jobs that would level the playing field, then it is a relatively recent freedom. One of the markers of the black middle class is that, for the most part, its members are still closely tied to those in real poverty. The women I interviewed spoke of their concern for the black community in general. But they could also each point to a sibling or a cousin or other relatives who were struggling.

To a certain extent, the problem of the villager who goes off to medical school and feels an obligation to his community is one these women can relate to easily. On a Saturday afternoon in Hoboken, I got together with a group of 30-something and 40-something women. The walls of Tracie Howard's living room were painted a warm golden hue that brought to mind the faded gilt of Renaissance Italy. The chandelier was a 1920s Art Deco find and framed photos of family and friends graced the surface of her baby grand piano. Paintings by prominent African-American artists hung on most walls, while a lighted breakfront displayed her collection of three-legged teacups from Limoges, Japan and Italy. In complete defiance of the old paper bag rule, the women were a rainbow mix from fair-skinned to very dark-skinned. All of them were members of the upper middle class and had ventured to Tracie's from their homes in New York City, Westchester and Greenwich, Connecticut.

The women talked animatedly about their passion for mentoring and community service. For them, it's more than doing a good deed. They see themselves in the young people that they are helping, they believe that their actions are improving the lot not of "poor black folks" but of "brothers and sisters." There's a big difference in the way these women speak about community service and the language their white society counterparts use. By doing good, they feel they are also "doing the right thing," as Spike Lee so aptly called it. Furthermore, their charitable efforts keep them in touch with a home they don't want to leave behind.

I probe a little deeper, and each woman admits that while community service is fulfilling, trying to meet the needs of poorer family members is almost always a losing battle. The women in their 40s have come to terms with the economic disparities in their own families. "No guilt," says one of the guests, an investment banker on Wall Street. Her simple declaration is followed by so many "Amens," the room is almost transformed into Sunday church. But these are women in their 40s, who've made the tough choices and don't take any mess off anyone. I found that among my peers, women in our 30s, there's not always the same confidence. We're not always sure that we don't owe the village every penny in our pockets.

Though I'm not a banker or Wall Street broker, my "Amen" was right there with the others. As the first person in my immediate family to graduate from college, I basked in the glow of achievement. I lived the dream deferred. A year after graduation, I was making more money than my mother was. My role as the family money store began. Siblings and other more distant relatives began to pull a guilt trip on me: I'd been "lucky" to get a scholarship, "lucky" to meet whites who mentored me and offered me jobs. They'd not been so lucky in life. Where they lived, life was hard—or had I forgotten?

Looking back, I could say that I was young and easily influenced. But I know that it was more than that. Despite the hefty student loan bill that I pay each month, I would not have been able to attend college at all had it not been for the largesse of a W. E. B. DuBois scholarship that handled a sizeable portion of my tuition every year. My school, Simon's Rock College, is in Great Barrington, Massachusetts: birth home of DuBois. My reading of *The Souls of Black Folk* at the age of 16 had a powerful impact on how I viewed race and its obligations. I would never have called myself part of the Talented Tenth, but I certainly took my place among its platoons of strivers.

When my summa cum laude degree was rewarded with one good job after another, I knew I had to give back. And as my family laid it out for me: charity begins at home. Throughout my 20s, I buckled under the guilt and pressure and gave out thousands of dollars in "loans" that could never, would never, be repaid. Even when lending money meant draining my savings account or giving away the next month's rent, I jumped at the desperate calls in the middle of the night and the wailing darkness of "I have nowhere else to turn." Like many professional black women, I'm hardly wealthy by mainstream American standards. But compared to the poverty of those I love so dearly, the fact that I even had next month's rent in the bank meant that I was rich. Absolutely loaded. "We have extended family who think we're Rockefellers," says Robin Nelson Rice, a former pharmaceutical company executive now living in London. "We're not even Rock, forget Rockefeller! But from their viewpoint, it's 'Oh yes. Somebody comes and cleans your house. I need that job. I could be that. You could pay me that money.' They're always calculating. 'Oh, the nanny. Do you hear that? They've got a nanny.'"

For Tarin Washington, a 32-year-old finance executive, earning an

MBA roused the jealousy of old friends. As one male friend put it, "You think you're better than me because you're successful and moved out of the hood." It had been a bonanza year for Tarin: she'd recently completed her MBA and purchased a home in Connecticut as well as a used luxury model car. She says, "I realized that his perception of my having reached success was just that, perception. I wasn't anywhere near the success that I have planned for myself. I still have a very long way to go. As a matter of fact, I was still living in the 'hood, just in a new development in a different city!" But like a lot of the women I spoke to, poorer relations and friends thought that the purchase of luxury items, an advanced degree and a healthy income meant that all of your problems were solved, forever and ever.

Soon after I graduated from college I read an article in *Money* magazine that struck a similar chord about the expectations of extended family on young black professionals. The headline of the piece was: "Hunting for the First House." The sub-head read: "Home-buying can be a financial and emotional challenge for any couple. As African Americans looking in Chicago's white suburbs, Trish and Larry Harvey faced special hurdles—but overcame them."[13]

The story went on to introduce us to the Harveys, ages 26 and 29. They were "both MBAs, with fast-track jobs and a combined income close to $100,000 a year." But the article showed this couple to be more than materialistic Buppies. Although childless themselves and still so young, they were raising Trish's 16-year-old niece, Raven. And their "carefully calculated budget" included not only money for rent and insurance, food and a vacation fund, but $500 a month toward assisting relatives. Money that, out of politeness, might be called a loan; but money the Harveys never expected to see again.

Who Is Giving? What Is Expected?

I CAN'T REMEMBER the first time I heard the phrase, "to whom much is given, much is expected," though I suspect I was still in diapers. Nor can I tell you how often the phrase was repeated throughout my childhood; the number would have to be in the hundreds, if not the thousands. I heard it every Sunday that I attended church and every Saturday when our family went visiting. I heard it from my teachers when I received high grades and heard it, underlined, when I brought home Cs. The parents of my friends uttered it during pep talks after school and old black ladies murmured it in my ear when I respectfully leaned forward to kiss their powdery cheeks. Along with the West Indian equivalent of "Walk good" and the also often-repeated "Each one teach one," "to whom much is given, much is expected," was passed down as more than a platitude. It was the knight's code, a secret moral compass that would guide me should I make it through the woods, into the kingdom of higher education and on to the palaces of good fortune beyond.

Though I did not know it then, the reference is biblical. It's in the New Testament, Luke 12:48: "For unto whomsoever much is given, of him shall be much required: and to whom men have committed much, of him they will ask the more." The first sentence of the verse had been passed down in the black community (no doubt by savvy pastors who found their collection plates to be a little light). The second part of the verse may not have been uttered, but was certainly implied. I know that I'm not alone among middle-class women and men who have had to learn that you aren't a traitor to the people when you turn down a relative or a friend for a loan. I also know that as black women continue to outpace black men educationally and financially, more of the burden of helping falls upon us. We pay for our success not only financially, but emotionally as well.

In the work place, the "much is given, much is expected" motto can be a double-edged sword for successful black women. Clearly, our success provides an opportunity for service. "It's about taking ownership," one 30-something programmer from San Francisco told me. "I love going out on recruiting trips and being able to reach out to young black kids. Even if they don't come and work for my company, I can give them the tools and tips they need to get ahead. I feel like I'm helping people."

At the same time, the expectation can be that our success means we should be ever grateful and behave accordingly. We are dealt our daily share of racism and sexism, yet our class—and the means by which we make our living—predicates that we must often bite our tongue or risk being labeled as "angry," "difficult," or even "racist." As

Isabel Wilkerson, the Pulitzer Prize–winning journalist, once said, "It's an incredible burden of living this dual life and being constantly reduced to third-class citizenship and still be expected to operate with a smile on your face after one thing or another."[14]

At home, the challenge can be equally painful. One need only look at the hit film *Soul Food*, the story of three sisters and their families in Chicago. The most successful one is a lawyer named Terry. As portrayed by Vanessa L. Williams, Terry is brittle, caustic and quick to criticize. The message the filmmakers send is that Terry's ambition has drained her soul. She's on her second marriage and, when husband number two commits adultery, it's Terry's fault for working so hard. Her sister Maxine, in contrast, has no loot but a lot of love: she's been married to her husband for 11 years and the two still flirt shamelessly. Maxine has three beautiful kids, while Terry is trying, but childless. Maxine can also cook huge Sunday dinners, steeped in Southern tradition. Terry has no domestic skills, but a seemingly endless ability to write checks. The film sets her up as a bad guy, but I painfully recognized her plight. Who can blame her for being so cranky when she's the one who's got to pay her mother's hospital bills, fund her youngest sisters' business ventures and bail her brother-in-law out of jail? With not so much as a thank you, mind you. It's little wonder that when Terry explodes, she says, "As far as you know, I'm an ATM. It's always Automatically Terry's Money." My generation is getting better at shaking off the guilt, but for those of us who come from families that were born poor and have stayed poor, balancing the weight of expectation is never easy.

What We Owe Ourselves

AS CHAIR OF THE African-American studies program at Princeton University, Valerie A. Smith is a high-profile figure in a high-pressure job. She is the Woodrow Wilson Professor of Literature and the author of many critically acclaimed books, including *Self-Discovery and Authority in Afro-American Narrative* and *Representing Blackness: Issues in Film and Video*. Among certain passionate circles of Afro-Bohemia, she is known as the woman who brought Andrea Lee's *Sarah Phillips* back into print, a novel about race, class and identity that is now taught in hundreds of colleges nationwide. She is smart. She is powerful. But what I hear more than anything about Valerie Smith is that she is physically fit. I mean really fit. I begin to hear a rumor that while she was a professor at UCLA, she would only hold student conferences during her daily hour- and-a-half hike up Runyon Canyon. I hear that she is known for urging her black women colleagues, students and friends not to give so much of themselves that they don't take time for themselves. It's when this last comment drifts back to me that I decide I have to meet her.

We meet for tea, at 4:00 at Sally Lunn's in Princeton, an old-fashioned teashop that looks like a scene out of *Mary Poppins*. I ask Valerie, who is indeed fit and who looks barely old enough to buy alcohol, much less chair a university department, about her fitness journey. "In junior high school and high school, I really wasn't athletic at all," she tells me. "For a variety of reasons. Mostly I was this high-achieving academic kid, who couldn't get into competitive sports. Then I began running in graduate school. There was a group of us who got together and running was a social thing."

As a young professor at Princeton, in the early '80s, she got into aerobics. Princeton was a very different place back then. There weren't many women faculty, and the few that made it on staff worked very hard to be taken seriously. Valerie saw her lunchtime aerobic classes as a sort of rebellion. "It was important for all of us to be as intellectually rigorous as possible," she recalls. "The institution didn't know what to make of younger women. Aerobics were seen as a flaky kind of West Coast thing. To take an aerobics class instead of having lunch with a senior person who could further your career was unheard of. But I felt I was being defiant. That's one of the reasons I felt so emancipated when I moved to California."

I ask her about the student conferences held during grueling canyon hikes and she laughs out loud. "I'm notorious for that," she says, mischievously. "I'd get my grad students to have conferences with me during my 6:30 A.M. hike. I felt like I was sending a message: channel your anxiety into this exercise. I also felt like this was a way for them to have my full attention. They certainly were not going to get an hour and a half of my time while I was busy in my office." Not only did some of her students begin to exercise on their own, but a number of them also quit smoking. "They didn't have enough wind to talk, going up those hills," Valerie says with a smile.

More recently, she's become passionate about Pilates, which she first tried while teaching a summer session in Santa Fe. "I found that it worked me in ways that I'd never been worked before," she says. "It was both physical and highly cerebral. It helped me to gain flexibility and abdominal strength." Adding Iyengar yoga to her Pilates routine has not only made her stronger, it's kept her sane during a time when the kind of work she does is constantly under attack. During her first year back at Princeton, Cornel West famously abandoned Harvard's powerhouse of African-American studies to join Smith's department. It was only seen as a feather in Smith's cap to some. "It's a spectacle. My heart goes out to them," neoconservative Shelby Steele told the *Yale Herald* in April 2002. "American society sees black studies as fraudulent and always will." For her part, Smith likes to joke that if she had her druthers, she would begin each department meeting with a yogic breathing exercise and a prayer. She isn't joking when she says that she schedules all of her meetings around her exercise schedule.

Smith believes that if we are going to continue to thrive as black women we need to take care of not only our minds and our spirits, but our bodies as well. The week before we meet, thousands of black women had mourned the death of the poet June Jordan. She was 65. For me, as for others, it had echoes of the deaths of Audre Lorde, Virginia Hamilton, Sherley Anne Williams. "We're beginning to see how many of our successful sisters are dying young or suffering from chronic illness," says Smith. "We've got to pay attention to what we eat, what we do physically. We take responsibility for so much. We've got to take responsibility for ourselves."

CHAPTER 4

The Mommy Track:
How It's Different for Sisters

FAMILY RESPONSIBILITY RELATIONSHIPS SUCCESS MOTHERHOOD BALANCE

IT USED TO BE that for most black women, there was no choice. You had a baby and you went back to work. These days, black women are making new choices. "A good percentage of the black women I know believe that they can have it all," says Erika Clarke, a 27-year-old producer at MTV. "Personally, when I choose to have children, I don't want to feel the pressure of having to juggle career and family. As I get older, I belive that being a parent is a career in and of itself." If Erika does eventually choose to stay at home, she'll have the kind of company and support that just did not exist even as little as five years ago.

By all accounts, these middle-class black women who choose to stay at home with their kids are a sign of a growing trend. In 1998, three African-American women founded BEAMoms, a web community of "black, educated, at-home moms." The site offers a chat room and articles on such weighty topics as child-rearing, relationships and adoption, as well as fast, easy recipes and fitness tips. Other groups and websites are popping up all over the country. Mocha Moms started four years ago when a handful of black women found themselves in the relatively new role of being stay-at-home moms. Now the group has four chapters nationwide and 175 members.

In 2000, 29 percent of white women and 22 percent of black women with children under 18 were full-time moms. For sisters, that's the highest number ever. It's a historic step for black women. One that's made all the more interesting because these black full-time moms are, overwhelmingly, college-degreed.[15]

One might argue that black women have been stay-at-home moms for generations. The dramatic difference being we weren't in our own homes. The children we spent our days raising weren't our own, they were white. In the years after slavery and throughout most of the 20th century, black women worked outside the home by necessity. It was an economic imperative; a black family needed two incomes to make ends meet. While college-educated white women felt pressure to remain at home and be the good mother, college-educated black women were pressured to use their degrees to "uplift the race." It wasn't that we didn't want the best care for our children. Working outside of the home offered the best opportunities for black women to insure that our children had a future.

We have raised generations of men and women in this country, but we've never been revered for mothering skills. Negative stereotypes classify us as sexually loose and overly fertile. Some of the most nefarious media images of the last 25 years are tied to our inability to be good mothers: the welfare mother, the crackhead mother who sells her body and her kids. President Ronald Reagan's first lie, that of the Cadillac-driving, welfare-cheating, birthing machine, was so tenable to the mainstream press that it went unchallenged for months. In comparison, as Patricia Hill Collins writes, "The cult of true womanhood, with its emphasis on motherhood as women's highest calling, has long held a special place in the gender symbolism of white America. From this perspective...women gain social influence through their roles as mothers, transmitters of culture, and parents of the next generation."[16]

Black women were never put on a pedestal in the cult of true motherhood. Mothering was simply what we did, without applause or special appreciation. Though we weren't with our kids during the day, this doesn't mean we didn't take their welfare seriously. It's important to remember that while we always worked, we also relied on a much larger community of extended family and neighbors to help us care for our children. Hence the African-American tradition that novelist and playwright Shay Youngblood describes so evocatively in *The Big Mama Stories*. We had our big mama, but we had other mamas too: Mama Hilda, Mama Jane, Mama Clara. Besides all the women we may have called mama, there's a small militia of women we'd call aunt, who aren't any blood relation at all. Hillary Clinton may have written a book called *It Takes A Village* but the phrase comes from an African proverb—it takes a village to raise a child. In the Reconstruction South, in the Midwest and even in northern cities, black mothers relied on a network of support. In *Double Stitch*, a domestic worker describes the importance of the community-based childcare that a neighbor offered her daughter: "She kept Vivian and she didn't charge me nothin', either. You see, people used to look after each other, but now it's not that way. I reckon it's because we all was poor, and I guess they put theirself in the place of the person that they was helpin'."

To this day, the emphasis on early infant care is different among black women and white women. For example, black women are much less likely to breast-feed: a practice that one doesn't begin if she expects she must leave her child in another's care almost immediately after giving birth. Women like the Mocha Moms are working to change that: lobbying for better childcare for poor women and giving seminars on the pluses of breast-feeding. Yet even the Mocha Moms know that they are at the front of a changing wave of motherhood; even for black professional women, being a stay-at-home mom is an unimaginable luxury. "Among whites, there's still a strong strain of those who frown on mothers who work," writes Bart Landry, author of *Black Working Wives: Pioneers of the American Family Revolution*. "For many white women, the question is how do I stay at home after having a child? Where with black women, the question is how do I make sure my child is well cared for while I work?"

Black women have outnumbered white women in the workplace since the 1940s. Even when black women achieved a middle-class family income, they continued to work. Sociologists say there wouldn't have been a black middle class if sisters hadn't entered the workplace and stayed. In 1940, 40 percent of black middle-class wives worked versus 17 percent of white middle-class wives. In 1970, that figure escalated to 70 percent of black wives versus 45 percent of white wives. By 1994, the gap wasn't so dramatic, but it was there all the same: 87 percent of black middle-class wives worked versus 78 percent of white middle-class wives. [17]

In a new book called *From Stumbling Blocks to Stepping Stones,* two sociologists studied 50 black professional women between the ages of 53 and 87. This is the generation that opened the door to white-collar work for me and my peers. The researchers found that even as far back as the age of June Cleaver, black middle-class women were committed to working throughout motherhood. An idea, they point out, that makes the older generation of black women strikingly similar in attitude to today's working woman. "These women went into the work situation and stayed," says Kathleen Slevin, co-author of the book. "They had been taught as young girls that they had to be economically independent, even if they married. Their parents knew it was going to take two incomes to get by." [18]

Black women are the linchpin in the astronomical growth of the black middle class; but our economic triumphs are hard won. It's long been said that blacks have to work twice as hard to get half as far. "The State of Working America 2001," an annual study published by the Economic Policy Institute, shocked the media by revealing that the old maxim was true. Americans are working harder than ever before, but black Americans are working twice as hard to make ends meet and get ahead. The average white middle-class husband and wife work 3,885 hours a year, a figure that's up 237 hours or six more weeks than a decade ago. The average black middle-class couple works 4,728 hours a year, up nearly 500 hours or twelve weeks from ten years before.

Perhaps this is why black women are so dismissive of tomes that purport to tell women how to "have it all." We've been doing it all, being all things to all people (employers, husbands, children, family and friends) for a very long time. In order to achieve our middle-class and upper-middle-class status, we've had to work even harder than the norm.

Out of the 200 women Peggy Orenstein interviewed for her book, *Flux,* the woman whose life stood out as a model of balance was Denise

Littleton, an African American. "It would be easy to make Denise's life sound perfect," writes Orenstein of Littleton, a vice-president of legal affairs for a multi-billion-dollar hospitality services company. She has a beautiful home in a wealthy neighborhood, she co-owns a summer home with her best friend in an affluent black beach community. "It is, after all, pretty close to what the younger women I interviewed wanted—and expected—to attain," Orenstein writes. "She has achieved not only success, but a sense of authenticity as a woman and an African American in a white male world—and she does it four days a week, for a six-figure salary. She has a loving marriage to a man who's also a fully engaged parent; she has time to spend with her two daughters, who are each bright and happy."

Denise's life was hard won. As Orenstein makes clear, she is no Cinderella. There was no fairy godmother, no trust fund, no magic wand. "I've had to work really, really, really," and here she pauses for emphasis, "really hard to get here." Yet how is it that in a generation, we've not only gone from the kitchen to the boardroom, but been able to achieve, at least sometimes and for some women, a level of success that even white women find enviable? If black women have been juggling for a long time, then what's the message for the greater population of women? What do we have to teach? Certainly, some piece of that is in how we approach the mommy track and how we balance work and motherhood.

We love our children, but the fact that we tend to work throughout their childhood means that we have to allow them their independence. We have to trust that while everybody needs and wants a piece of us, there's only so much to go around. Martha Beck, a white author who writes a regular column for Oprah's magazine, has a child with Down's syndrome. In an article for *Real Simple* she remembers attending a conference for parents of kids with Down's syndrome. She was so proud of the fact that her seven-year-old son could do everything at mealtime except pour his own milk. She was surprised when the other mothers rolled their eyes. "Well, duh, put the milk in smaller containers," they told her. "He's seven—he should be cooking for himself. You won't be around forever, you know."

It was a powerful lesson for Beck. "These mothers, pressed by unusual circumstances, had rediscovered what other species have never forgotten: mothers are not servants, they are teachers," she writes. Pressed by the unusual circumstances of our race and class, it's a lesson that black women learned a long time ago. Guilt just isn't a currency in our lives the way it is in the lives of white women. "Perhaps this is the difference between black and white women," Julianne Malveaux wrote in *USA Today* at the start of Hillary Clinton's senate campaign. "White, female baby boomers see Hillary Clinton as having broken new ground, helping us define gender roles in the 21st century. Some African-American women want to yawn at the angst about shouldering multiple burdens and juggling multiple roles. Been there, done that, got the T-shirt so long ago that I recycled it." [19]

Yet the undeniable fact is that just because we've always worked doesn't mean we wanted to. "Usually when people talk about the 'strength' of black women they are referring to the way in which they perceive black women, coping with oppression," writes bell hooks. "They ignore the reality that to be strong in the face of oppression is not the same as overcoming oppression, that endurance is not to be confused with transformation." [20]

In a study of how women develop identity across racial lines, Temple University psychologist Suni Petersen found that, "Childbirth added a new role to the African-American women's lives and provided an impetus to change their priorities. However, none of these priority changes forced them to reject any part of their identity. The women merely added a new role—returning to work assisted by their connections to their community. Many of these women had helped in raising their siblings, and the interruptions of childcare were not as unique an experience in their lives as it was for the Caucasian women. The polarities of working or mothering, marriage or career, self or others, as seen in the Caucasian culture, were absent, both in the language and the stories of these African-American women who blended new roles into their established identities." [21]

The Choice to Stay at Home: You're Going to Catch It, Baby

WHILE THERE ARE those among us who think that white women would do well to emulate how well we juggle, there are also those among us who don't want to do it anymore. Having never had our turn at being June Cleaver, we'll take it now—thank you. For sisters, though, making the choice to stay at home doesn't mean you can claim the role of "the good mother" who's sacrificed career for children. Black women who stay at home have to answer to their husbands, their parents, their family and their friends. Cheli Figaro, one of the founding members of Mocha Moms, has an undergraduate degree from Yale and a law degree from Columbia.

A civil rights baby, her parents are absolutely stunned by her decision to be a full-time mother. "It's hard for parents because it's not expected," she told me one afternoon at her home in Bowie, Maryland. "Anything not expected is hard. 'Anybody can raise a baby.' That's the response. Because for generations, anybody has been raising us. Any old body, aunt so-and-so twice removed, because we had to go up north to work in the factories. That's our heritage. Or if you're from the Caribbean, it's 'I'm going to leave my children. Go to America and strike it rich over there.'" Her friend Teresa Gardner-Williams pipes in, "And I'll send for everybody." Cheli turns to her and smiles, "And I'll send for you. But if I can't send for you, you will wait a year, two years."

The two women have a back and forth that is equal parts good humor, tenderness and venom; it's a repartee born of the fact that outside of their Mocha Moms circle they are constantly at battle: justifying their choices, defending themselves from the criticisms that they've let their husbands, their families, the entire race down by staying at home with their children. In Prince George's County, known for a powerful community of affluent African Americans, the pressure is even more intense. The trappings of materialism surround us: from the sprawling town homes in Cheli's bucolic development to the late model luxury cars that line every driveway. Cheli says that all around her, she sees middle-class black people applying dollars to psychological wounds. "We weren't given any respect by white society so what we drove, what we wore, became badges of self-worth," she says. "Badges of success meant everything and still do. That Mercedes. That fancy Chanel suit. That three-karat rock. So when you, as a black professional woman, come home and say, 'I'm not going to contribute to what would be the family's disposable income. We're not going to be able to buy that fancier car, that fancier house, that fancier *whatever*...' Sure, you're going to catch it. You're going to catch it, baby."

The black middle class is thriving, but there haven't been enough affluent generations to build a great deal of sustained wealth. A Census study found that black households had a net worth of $7,073 in 1995, while the average white family was worth $49,030. Black women who stay at home find that the missed paycheck is valued more highly than the more attentive childcare she provides. "Being a parent is the hardest thing you'll ever do and you don't get a second shot," Cheli says. "I'll get another shot at being a lawyer, if I live long enough. I'm certainly not going to close the door on anything. But right now, I am where I'm needed the most. I am not replaceable here. They could find another attorney, any day. Anybody can write a brief. But my kids can't find any old mom." She says the best moments are the ones that sound absolutely inane to her friends who don't have kids or who don't understand her decision not to practice law. "My daughter and I sometimes take her little baby stroller and we'll go out on the deck and blow bubbles," she says. "Now that sounds like maybe a sort of boring thing to do with a bright and brilliant mind like myself, but you know what? It's priceless. And I'll never see it again." She looks at her daughter, playing contentedly on the living room rug and she whispers it, as if the words are a spell that will keep her children as they are this day, close, safe and happy. She whispers, "I'll never see it again."

The irony is that what drove Cheli to full-time motherhood wasn't some belief that she could raise her child better than a professional care-giver. The commitment to being there for every moment—to see the first time her son would sit up, take his first steps, say his first words —that only came later. A lawyer at the Commerce Department in D.C. when eight-year-old Brandon was born, she fully intended to go back to work full time. But Brandon was a high-need kid who cried constantly. "My son *whupped* us," she says. "It was beyond colic or anything normal. My husband would leave for work in the morning and I would be sitting in the bed, with Brandon screaming on my lap. He'd come back from work and I'd be right there. I wouldn't have moved all day. I truly believed that if I put him in day-care, he'd be abused. So we tightened our belt and I stayed home."

The changing way we approach motherhood is a critical part of how professionals are inventing our own lives and changing the history we've been handed. For one, it means that we are no longer defining ourselves solely through work. It also means that we are, to some degree, divesting ourselves of the strong black woman mantle. Our foremothers may have been unsung heroines in the art of having it all, but it doesn't mean that we have to keep up the juggling act.

Professional sisters who give up their professions are finding that full-time motherhood presents new challenges as well as new rewards. Teresa Gardner-Wiliams left a nonprofit job she loved to stay at home, and what surprises her is how much she enjoys her work as a mother. "My husband wanted to have children from the moment we got married and I was like, 'No, I don't think so,'" she says, with a grin. "Now, I can't believe how much I'm enjoying this. What a wonderful experience it is, I just can't get over it. It's to the point where I like to joke that I'm going to need a new set of friends. My friends with children didn't tell me that being a mother was this great, so clearly I need new friends!"

Cheli Figaro says that she knows that her kids won't necessarily turn out better than the kids of her many friends who have chosen to go the nanny route. What she does know is this is the way she wants to live. "Women are going to feel guilty," she says. "If you stay at home, you feel guilty for not working. If you work, you feel guilty about not staying at home. Women who work from home feel guilty when they're not playing with the baby. Then you play with the baby and you feel guilty for not doing more work. You have to choose your poison. You got to choose it. What's going to matter when you're 60. That's it in a nutshell. Because you're going to feel guilty about something." It's a brutally honest appraisal of the choices she's made and what they mean to her, choices many black women just 30 years ago could have never imagined.

You Know You Have It All…
and You Give It Up

LYNETTE HALL was turning 40. Among all the ways she was assessing that milestone her career stood out as a great source of pride. She had worked hard to build a name for herself at television networks. At the time, she was director of on-air promotions for ABC daytime. Her husband, Paul, had his own film and television production company. They were living in Los Angeles, but had bought a condo in Santa Barbara for weekend escapes. Her two daughters were six years old and six months old and her parents lived close enough to happily provide childcare. She was healthy, wealthy and wise enough to know that she had a good thing going.

Why then was she having fantasies about being a stay-at-home mom? Could she really give it all up? How would her family continue to grow economically—she had worked like a demon to move them into the upper middle class. Without her paycheck could they stay there? Dare they imagine moving forward into the territory of real wealth? There were no inheritances to count on, no wealthy parents to lend a helping hand. She knew that the loss of her income would put more pressure on her husband, another concern. Black men simply do not earn what white men do, even in the upper middle class.

As Dr. Beth Davis Phillpotts, a 34-year-old physician, says in the book *Not Your Mother's Life,* keeping up with the Joneses is more than a full-time job for black folks. Phillpotts bore the brunt of the childcare responsibility in her marriage. Her husband never even considered taking the flextime that some white men have chosen. "It's so hard to change those patterns," she told writer Joan K. Peters. "Especially right now in the middle-class African-American community where everyone's riding around in Land Rovers and buying their first house before they're 30. The men are driven."

Money was definitely an incentive to continue working for Lynette. "I had a lot of separation anxiety with Jordan, when she was younger," Lynette remembers about her oldest child. "It was hard for me to see other nonworking mothers. I was able to deal with that by taking a lunch and going to the mall and buying special things for Jordan that I could afford to buy because I was working. School tuition was never a problem because I was working, trips were never a problem because I was working. I was able to subsidize and rationalize because of the monetary contributions of my brilliant career—as I call it."

She also felt the pressure of being one of the Onlys to keep being successful. Coming of age in the '70s, she remembers all the women were on point, moving forward with a purpose. Her friends let her know that she was living the African-American dream. "There were moments when it was very powerful, I felt very powerful," she says. "I had it, I was working it. I'm on the car phone, my secretary's calling, there's a breakfast, there's a campaign meeting, we're in edit rooms, we're in mixing rooms, we're designing graphics. We've got this beautiful child who's at home with my parents. I've got a great marriage. *You know* you have it all. It may be just for an hour or a day or an afternoon. If you're lucky, it could last a week."

Lynette didn't feel guilty about working, but she genuinely missed her child during the day. Her husband would take Jordan to her parents' house in the morning to lessen Lynette's daily dose of separation anxiety. Lynette picked her up in the evenings. "I had the joy of picking her up," Lynette remembers. "Which was always a reward for the day. But the juggling act and the fast track and the mommy track and all the other politically correct terms that come about all came into play."

With both her pregnancies, Lynette went back to work after exactly six months' maternity leave. After having her second daughter, Kendall, she began to make some serious choices. "During that period I got real organized," she says. "Paul and I made our financial decisions and goals." This is a critical part of the puzzle. If Paul had not been supportive, if he hadn't been as confident of his ability to earn a hefty paycheck as a black man in the predominantly white movie industry, Lynette wouldn't have been able to leave her job. If she insisted, it could have put her marriage at risk.

A University of Illinois study found that black marriages are three times as likely to end in divorce. Black men's financial insecurity is one prominent reason. "A major factor in marital risk among African Americans is the anxiety felt by many black husbands about being able to provide adequately for their families," reports sociologist Shirley Hackett, author of the black marriage study. "Moving out of marriages where they feel inadequate may be a way of escaping a feeling of failure or establishing a sense of competence." [22] It's a phenomenon Lynette is familiar with. These days, she and her husband refer to themselves as a dying breed. "We don't know many people like ourselves," she says, "that are African American and married for 25 years."

As it turned out, Lynette left ABC, made the decision not to work full time and turned 40 all in the same month. Initially, it was very difficult. "It was interesting when people would say, 'do you miss work,'" Lynette remembers. "Originally I didn't because it was one less thing to worry about because I had four or five producers reporting to me...so to miss work—no!" Like women of all races, what Lynette found most difficult was figuring out how to gauge her success when there are no deadlines, no promotions, no raises and no end-of-the-year bonuses. "Being a stay-at-home mom, particularly when the kids are school age, can be a very solitary experience," she says. "And it was really hard for me to define what a productive day is. It could mean getting to the grocery store, getting to the car wash, taking the kids to and from school, getting some homework done and making a few phone calls. That may be one scenario. If the kids are home sick from school that day and you stayed at home with them, you probably got nothing done. Is that a non-productive day? I'd try to translate a productive day in my job to a productive day at home. Is going to the grocery store greater than, less than or equal to cutting five promos? For a long, long, long time, I pretty much thought it was a 'less than' and there was no value in what I was doing. That hurt a lot."

Lynette says it's taken a full seven years for her to get comfortable with what is now her job. Then, she didn't have the benefit of an organization like Mocha Moms to help her along. Just as it's taken a century for black women to develop a sense of pride in the workplace, to seek and find work that not only sustains but fulfills, it is a challenge for black stay-at-homes to find value in their work when the community doesn't necessarily reward their choices. "I can say to you now that the value is in my children," Lynette says. "I look at my girls now and Paul is eternally praising me for what I've done. I don't think you realize it when you're doing it because as I've said, you're flying blind."

Ultimately, Lynette says the biggest pay off in full-time motherhood is in the pacing of her life—and her life lessons. "I worked for 18 years in television and at every turn, it was about becoming a better producer, a better director," she says. "You don't get the same opportunity when you're raising children. If you take 18 years to get really good at it, they'll be gone. So you have to look at the work you're doing every day, you can't be passive. You don't want to miss the opportunities, you don't want to miss the asked questions by saying, 'I'm too busy' or 'I'm too tired.' I look at my daughters and how comfortable they are in their own skin, how openly they talk to me and I know this is what happens when you work really, really hard at the job of mothering."

Coming All the Way Down

LIKE LYNETTE HALL, Robin Nelson-Rice began to consider staying at home full time after her second pregnancy. She had been on the fast track at a major pharmaceutical company. Both she and her husband had senior executive positions in the London branch of their company. They had a toddler son, Solomon, and the best childcare their local nanny agency could provide. Then Robin became pregnant for the second time—with twins. "My husband defines success through his career, family is a given," she says. "As we get older, women start to incorporate other things because women have so much more to think about than men do. Should I work? Should I stay at home?" Eventually, Robin decided to stay at home.

It was a soul-shaking decision because Robin's entire adult life had been shaped by her ambition. She grew up in Indiana, raised by her grandmother and aunts. Everyone within yelling distance worked at the local factory, and the lives of all the adults around her were broken into a never-ending stream of shifts. She would visit her parents and her father was especially encouraging. "He instilled in me that I could be anything," she says. "I just knew I wanted to dress up to go to work. I did not want to wear a uniform. I did not want to wear dungarees. I wanted to wear a suit."

She earned her undergraduate degree from Indiana University, then worked for a year in Chicago before returning to Indiana for her MBA. When she joined her husband at the pharmaceutical company, they mapped out a plan for their careers that would allow them to work abroad. A post in Toronto was first, followed by the coveted London slot. Her professional life was a world away from the one she grew up in, and for a long time, that's what she wanted. "It's only an opportunity for someone who is interested in having it," Robin says, philosophically. She is, as always, well dressed, confident and composed—the very definition of what they used to call good breeding. "When I talk to my grandmother, she says, 'When are you going to stop this nonsense?' Because this is not her framework. I'm very close to her, and when I call and say, 'I'm in Germany or I'm in France,' she says, 'I feel so sorry for you. That company just won't leave you alone.'"

While she loved her work, what Robin found trying in the corporate environment was the juggling between black and white worlds. "I don't really have any white friends that I would say that I'm close to," she says. "If I had an issue that I would want to discuss, I would think of ten other people before a white person would come to mind, unless it was corporate or work-related. My friends are black people, not necessarily all in corporate America."

It was to the black world of her family and friends that Robin retreated when things got stressful. "It's so hard sometimes day to day," she told me, while still working full time. "When you're away from that, you want to calm down. You want to come all the way down because you've had such a day being all the way up in that world. What I've found is that I can come down with some white people, but not as boldly as I can with my other friends. You just want to drop them and be with some people that say 'ain't.'"

A year later, when I hear that Robin has decided not to return to her corporate job, the conversation resonates in my head. I wonder whether for some middle-class black women, maternity leave is a sabbatical from the daily race-and-gender isolation in their corporate lives. Do some of the women who choose to stay at home find that in motherhood they can, as Robin says, come all the way down? And does the degree of comfort that comes from not having to put on a corporate mask become so tantalizing that one would rather give up the paycheck than put on the armor of the Onlys? Robin says it didn't motivate her choice, and certainly having twins, with a toddler running around, proved to be more than a full-time job. But I can't help but wonder if there's not a small bit of relief in not having to be the strong black woman who can do it all anymore.

The Lady of the House

ROSE SALEM'S HOME in the bedroom community of New Rochelle is a large bi-level ranch-style house. The sitting room is outfitted with skylights, Italianate furniture with Versace-style leopard-print chairs and gold records from her husband's career as a music producer. She's thinking about removing her backyard deck and putting in a pool. Black-and-white portraits of her children and stepdaughter line the living room wall. They stand out by virtue of the photographer Lyle Ashton Harris, whose work is in the permanent collection of the Whitney Museum. Her shiny black Jaguar sits in the driveway, another symbol of her success.

At 33, Rose is the president of Salem and Salem, a computer consulting firm that she started in the family basement four years ago. The company is now housed in a downtown New Rochelle complex and boasts eight full-time employees and sixty-five contract workers. Her clients include such massive accounts as Chase, Citibank, Deutsche Bank and the government offices of New York State. As a small business owner, Rose is part of the growing number of black women entrepreneurs. The computer company is Rose's baby; she worked in the field for close to ten years before venturing out on her own. Her husband still produces records underneath the banner of Salem Entertainment.

She has two children: Norelle, age two, and David, age four. Unlike the Mocha Moms, Rose is committed to working full time and wouldn't have it any other way. "My mother was the breadwinner in the house. She worked, took care of the kids, had a nanny. That's what I saw," Rose says. She is 5'7" and curvaceous, dressed casually in a V-neck white T-shirt and hip-hugging jeans. "I knew when I grew up, I would never stay at home with a child. I love my kids. But I think I have the same mentality that a man does, that a job is who I am." She pauses and then tries to explain another way. "Steve and I go out a lot and I'm so used to telling what I do," she says. "Imagine if I didn't have a job. It would be 'yes, I'm Steve's wife.' I'd talk about my kids, but the goal-oriented person that I am would be taken away. My poor kids would be neurotic because I'd be trying to plan their whole lives. Now I do different things so I feel more balanced."

Her son attends a local Montessori school where most of his classmates have at-home moms. "Those teachers expect me to be at everything," Rose huffs impatiently. "What's with the 9:30 A.M. meetings? I'm not like these other mothers who come running to the school because they are so happy to have something to do. I'm running a business. I don't have time for it." Like many African Americans in the upper middle class, Rose's income helps support the family's lifestyle. In fact, Rose says that her black girlfriends, without exception, live a more glamorous lifestyle than their white neighbors in Westchester. "We all live really affluent lives," she says. "We work and we can afford to wear Fendi, Gucci and Versace. We buy the Chanel and Oscar de la Renta dresses for our functions. We travel to the south of France—we love the south of France. We go to the Hamptons and the Vineyard and Italy and we do all the shopping that goes along with it. None of us would dream of going to Europe without an empty suitcase to fill up." Furthermore, she says, "the black successful couples I know aren't living beyond their means. They've got the stocks and the bonds. It's just that two incomes make a difference. We can do more than the white guy who lives across the street who makes $200,000 a year but his wife stays at home."

Rose grew up in New Rochelle and, more specifically, in the North End where she and her husband live today. It was then and is now a predominantly affluent Jewish area. "There's a synagogue within walking distance," she quips. "That's always a clue." It's a joke she feels comfortable making not only because she's been in the North End for so long, but also because her husband is Jewish. In many ways, he's an interesting opposite to her. Rose grew up a black girl in a Jewish neighborhood. When they met, Steve was living in the Fort Greene section of Brooklyn and had been a hip-hop and R&B producer for more than 15 years. He'd produced a number of old-school classics like

UTFO, Full Force and Roxanne Shante. Rose says, "I understand his Jewish background, and we like to joke that he knows more about black culture than me. We clicked."

Rose grew up in the North End, but her family wasn't wealthy. As a child, Rose and her sisters lived in the South Bronx while their single mother worked in the New York City school system as a principal. When her mother's best friend became a widow, the two women decided to merge households and look for a place in Westchester. Rose says they didn't know the south end of New Rochelle from the north, they picked a house they could afford on the prettiest street they could find. Theirs was the extended family community that Patricia Hill Collins writes about in *Double Stitch*. Rose grew up calling her mother's best friend "Aunt Beryl." She knew Aunt Beryl's kids as her cousins. And when the two women needed full-time childcare, they hired a nanny. "I grew up with a nanny, but it was my mom's older sister," she explains. "To me, a nanny was a family member."

Sitting in her living room, sipping a glass of red wine, Rose looks embarrassed at what she is about to say. "The problems I have with nannies are what we used to think were white women's problems," she says. "With black people, you don't think we have problems with the help. If you have a nanny, then lucky for you. But you get issues." Like most of her neighbors in New Rochelle, Rose hires her nannies from a local reputable agency. They have all been, without exception, West Indian. They share a cultural bond with Rose's mother and Aunt Beryl who were born in Jamaica. It's because of that cultural bond, not to mention the shared skin color, that Rose says the nannies find it so difficult to respect her. "Every nanny I've had calls my husband either 'sir' or 'Mr. Salem' or 'boss,'" she says. "They call me Rose, even when I ask them to call me Mrs. Salem. They want to tell me their personal problems. They want to tell me how to raise my kids. I've even had a couple tell me, 'You know, no one likes working for a black woman.' All of my black friends that have help treat them like family. We've learned not to, which is really messed up."

Although her computer consulting company is a much more stable business than the music industry that her husband works in, Rose's nannies assume that he is footing the bills, especially because he is white. "They all thought I was poor!" she screeches. "They all thought my husband was the most successful man in the world and that I was living off of him. Finally, I said, 'Where do you think I go when I leave the house every morning at 8:30?'" Rose says the nannies will admonish her to keep the house neat for her husband. "Don't mess up the bed. Mr. Salem has to sleep there," they say, "I just cleaned up Mr. Salem's bathroom." It makes Rose furious, but she knows they aren't the only ones who have a hard time imagining that a young black woman could buy a nice house, earn a six-figure salary and own her own company. "It's not just the nannies," Rose admits. "I guess it comes with living in a white neighborhood. Whenever people come to the door they say, 'May I speak to the lady of the house?' It never fails and it's soooo irritating. I just look at them and say, I am the lady of the house."

Priorities and Choices

LONG BEFORE JANET HILL became known to basketball fans as Grant's Mom, she was a trailblazer. A 1969 graduate of Wellesley College, she was a suitemate of former First Lady, Hillary Rodham Clinton. A math major, she spent the early part of her career as a scientist. Her many projects included environmental assessments of various Navy intelligence units and the development of computer programs that managed Soviet submarine surveillance. Since 1981, she has been vice-president of Alexander and Associates, a corporate consulting firm in Washington, D.C.

When I ask her how she has balanced work, marriage and motherhood so successfully and for so long, she says that for one, she doesn't waste time on feeling bad about the sacrifices that come with the territory. "I do think that my advice to young women, all women, but certainly African-American women is not to stress about any sense of guilt when they leave their children," she says. "Now, there are some women who have to and some who choose to. We should differentiate. If you're leaving your children, make sure that they're well taken care of. But don't feel guilty, what good does that do you or your child?"

One of the ways that Janet kept the family strong was that she and her husband, Calvin, decided that they would rarely accept dinner invitations. Throughout Grant's childhood, the family dined together almost every evening. "You have to be highly organized and you have to prioritize," she says. "We weren't part of the political scene and the social scene. I'm constantly meeting people who say, how long have you lived in Fairfax County? I say since 1978. We didn't socialize. We didn't know people."

Despite the fact that they no longer have a child at home, the Hills still tend to be homebodies. During the Clinton administration, they were invited to the White House for dinner. At the time, Grant was playing for the Pistons, and the Pistons were playing their long-time rivals, the Knicks. When Janet came home and told her husband about the invitation, Calvin replied, "That's the night the Pistons are playing the Knicks. Why are they having a dinner on that night?" Janet just shrugged, "I don't know. They're *not* terrible people." To which, Calvin declared, "Well, we're not going." Janet agreed.

She called the next day to decline on the RSVP line and said, "Janet Hill and Calvin Hill will not be able to make it. Our son, Grant Hill, and his team will be playing the New York Knicks. Thank you very much for your kind invitation. We hope you will invite us again." When Janet relayed the message to her friend, the woman was incredulous, "Janet! Did you tell the Clintons you didn't even have tickets to the game? That you were staying home to watch Grant on TV?" Janet just laughs with delight when she tells me the story, "What can I say, I'd rather sit at home with my husband and watch my son on TV, than dine at the White House." She adds, sheepishly, "Of course, we could have taped it…but we like to watch the games live."

While many young women see marriage to a professional athlete as the dating equivalent of winning the lottery, Janet Hill has never allowed the talents of her husband or her son to cloud her own ambitions and ability. "During part of the time when Grant was a child, my husband played football for the Cleveland Browns," she says. "I moved into a situation where my husband was a professional athlete and I didn't have to work. But what was I going to do home all day? Grant was in public school every day and when he came home, there was a sitter."

Part of Janet's commitment to working, despite a level of financial security, comes from her mother. "I joke with Grant that if I'm doing what my mother is doing at the age of 85, then he needs to put me in a nursing home—just make sure that my husband is in there with me."

Janet's mom, Vivien McDonald owns and operates a dental lab in New Orleans. It's a business she's owned since 1946. Janet's father ran the business with Vivien until he passed away in 1976. "She's run the business for 26 years alone, which is staggering," says Janet. "She's 85 and she goes into the office every day. She doesn't work a full day, but she's there every day. Now this business is extremely lucrative and successful. She doesn't work for financial reasons. I'm always asking her, why don't you retire? The first thing she says is, 'What would I do?' The second thing she says is, 'Who would hire me?' Which means this business gives her a reason to wake up every day. I so admire that. She's a tremendous role model."

I ask her about the famous 4:00 P.M. phone call. My friend Elizabeth Alexander, whose father is Janet's business partner, told me that Janet had a standing appointment to talk to Grant every day after school. As a working mother, those calls were more than obligatory check-ins, they were a lifeline. Janet smiles when I mention the call. "At 4:00 P.M., he called me," she says. "It started when I was working at the Pentagon, and I would walk out of meetings with generals in the army and the Secretary of the Army to take his call. We'd discuss what happened at school that day. I'd hear it again when I got home that night, but I wanted to hear it when he got home from school. We would also discuss what he might have for dinner, if he was going to order Domino's pizza for himself or for himself and the sitter. That 4:00 P.M. call was incredible. We talked every school day at 4:00 P.M. until he went to Duke. And I wasn't going to accept just, 'Hi Mom, I'm on my way to the mall.' No. Tell me about everything, start at the beginning, I've got plenty of time."

During college, the calls stopped. Then when Grant started in the NBA, he began calling Janet every day again. When he got married, to the R & B singer Tamia, the calls stopped for a little while. But recently, Grant began calling his mom every day again. The call time has shifted. It's now 9:30 A.M., when the basketball player is on his way to practice.

"We talk about what's going on in the world, what he read on the Internet that morning," she says. "He's 29 years old and we've talked almost every day, all of his adult life." For Janet Hill, it's proof positive that the 4:00 P.M. call, all the turned-down dinner invitations—along with the career she insisted on maintaining—are all choices that have, in the long run, earned her son's love and abiding respect.

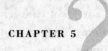

CHAPTER 5

At Home in Her World:
Empowerment and Entitlement

FAMILY   RESPONSIBILITY   RELATIONSHIPS   SUCCESS   MOTHERHOOD   BALANCE

THE OLD SAW ABOUT the tragic mulatto was that her dual bloods—
black and white—led her down a path of doom. Neither a part of the
white world nor part of the black world, she was pummeled between
them both, until she fell, to her literal or psychological death, into
the chasm in between. For professional black women, there has been
a variation on the tragic mulatto myth—maybe less dramatic, less of a
paper-thin caricature of life and death, but a foreboding tale of possible
doom all the same. Stories abound about those women who are young,
gifted and black who, like Red Riding Hood going to visit her grandmother, are accosted by wolves along the way.

When I arrived at *Newsweek* magazine in 1996, I was warned that
black women hadn't fared well at the magazine. There were rumors of
Harvard-educated sisters who'd lost their minds on the job, who'd been
forced to quit, who'd sued or, the worst fate of all, had been banished to
a forgotten cubicle in Siberia, collecting a paycheck, but never seeing a
byline in the magazine. As it was, this turned out to be far from my

experience. I thrived at *Newsweek* and was able to seek out any number of mentors—male and female, black and white. I joked that I'd already gone into tragic black woman mode at another magazine, I wasn't going to be scared by the monsters underneath the bed at *Newsweek*. But in my years there, I could also see how it could happen, how if I'd been younger, greener, less enterprising, more unsure, maybe the stories would've gotten to me. Maybe they would be telling stories about me.

Yet the notion that middle-class black women live their lives between two worlds is one that persists. Testimony about women who travel comfortably in both the black world and white world are hard to come by. At the library, I did a search for the terms "African-American women" and "entitlement." What I found were hundreds of references either to the entitlement politics of welfare or to the rape of slave women being considered the "entitlement" of the white slaveholder. When I added "middle-class" to the search, I came up with nothing at all.

The mythology of the tragic black professional woman was also reflected in my early research for this book. I knew that there were African-American women who were born into privilege, who had wealth that went back for generations, but I dismissed them as exotics, whose experience was far from the norm. When I chose to focus on middle-class black women, I quickly learned that while the term "middle class" tends to connote a singular perception in the mainstream, something akin to the idea of "middle America," for African Americans it's a particularly loaded term. There are middle-class African Americans whose parents were the first to take part in the benefits that the civil rights movement offered. These are men and women who are now, for the most part, in their 30s or early 40s. There are also middle-class African Americans whose family lineage includes generations of the educated elite—the teachers and small business owners produced by schools such as Howard and Spelman. Then there are those in their 20s and 30s, the first generation middle class, who might be the only professional in their immediate family, such as lawyer Crystal Ashby.

I was often asked to put a dollar figure on the amount of money someone made or the title they had, in order to be interviewed in my book. But soon, salary and family legacy began to take a back burner to how these women felt about money, privilege and their own successes. I began to interview women for whom an integrated life had happened rather naturally; women who negotiated the boundaries of race, gender and class without a great deal of guilt, frustration or angst. It wasn't that they weren't aware that distinctly black worlds and white worlds still exist, but they didn't value one over another. They never seemed to doubt their right to be wherever or whomever they wanted.

For Angela Kyle, 31, moving abroad after completing an MBA and a Master's degree in journalism helped her develop an individual identity outside the realm of traditional American racial politics. "When I moved to London and was looking for jobs, it was a totally different environment," she says. "When I was talking to people at the *Economist,* I don't think they were thinking 'Oh gee, we really want a black woman.' Maybe if I would've been interviewing for the same kind of jobs at Time Inc. I would've thought that. But London was a different cultural setting without all that as a backdrop." Kyle went on to land a position in international business development at CNN in London. And after a stint at CNN in Atlanta and as VP of development at an internet company, she's now Senior Director of Business Development at Live Planet. In many ways, her experience—the travel abroad, the top-notch education, and the satisfaction in her professional path—epitomizes the experience of the women that I interviewed.

I began this book with the deep belief that the civil rights movement and the women's rights movement had forged a powerful dual legacy in black women's lives, empowering us in ways that we have barely begun to articulate and explore. When I began to interview women who said they felt as much at home in Harlem as they did on Park Avenue, as comfortable in South Central as they did in the South Pacific or South Africa, I knew I was entering rich territory. There used to be a saying in the South that no one was freer than the white man and the colored woman; the idea behind this being that he had everything to gain and she had nothing to lose. At the turn of the century, young black women seeking to uplift themselves out of slavery's legacy sought education and empowerment at black-run technical schools. At one such school, the Nannie Helen Burroughs National Training School, the students espoused a motto that could well have been the motto for 20th-century African-American women's lives: "We specialize in the wholly impossible." That could well be the motto of 21st-century African-American women's lives as well, but in this century their role models are much more prominent—women like Oprah Winfrey, Condoleezza Rice, Brown University president Ruth Simmons—and their goals even loftier than their mothers or grandmothers could have imagined.

In her study, "Multicultural Perspectives on Middle-Class Women's Identity," Temple University's Suni Petersen theorizes that, "By being outside of the dominant culture, African-American women are provided a vantage point from which they can evaluate and interpret messages of that culture without adopting these messages as truth." By 2001, black women had managed to leapfrog over the antiquated, but culturally persistent, equation that put them perpetually at the bottom of the race/gender totem pole. It was as if we, in a single generation, had miraculously reached the point where we felt like we had everything to gain, too.

The Cocoon of the Black Middle Class

IN THE 1950S, before the guarded enclaves of suburban New York opened up to successful black folks, there was Queens. Dizzy Gillespie lived there, as did Nat King Cole. Lena Horne and her kids moved in, alongside the brothers Adderley, Nat and Cannonball. It was into this community of black upper-class wealth and privilege that Thelma Golden, a museum curator, was born. She is, in a word, a dynamo. Barely five feet tall, she somehow manages to demand attention—always dressed in stylish designer clothes. Her hair, cut in a closely shorn Afro, is as no-nonsense as her attitude. When she speaks, it's with a crisp intelligence that brings to mind a BBC announcer with an American accent.

Of course most of the people in her neighborhood weren't celebrities or even truly wealthy. Thelma's father owned an insurance brokerage business. Her mother was a stay-at-home mom—a rarified position for a black woman in the 1960s and one that spoke volumes to their neighbors and friends about the Goldens' lot in life. From kindergarten, Thelma and her brother attended Buckley Country Day School, a Long Island institution that's dedicated itself to the education of the horsey set since 1923. She was the first black girl to graduate from Buckley.

Fifteen years later, at the age of 30, she would complete a cycle of firsts by becoming the first black curator at the Whitney Museum of American Art in New York City. When we first met to discuss this book, Thelma struggled to explain that despite the fact that the media kept their eyes trained on her as a first in a tightly woven community of curators, she never felt anything but at home within the museum's walls. In direct contrast to Gwendolyn Parker's experience at white-shoe law firms and American Express, Thelma never imagined herself as a trespasser in this world. Some of the museum's most powerful patrons were men and women that she'd known since childhood—the parents of her classmates at Buckley. Years before her high school internship at the Metropolitan Museum of Art, she'd set her sights on a career as a curator and had never imagined she couldn't achieve it simply because so few blacks had done it before.

She recalled her childhood as one in which her parents pulled off a dicey parenting trick—empowerment without the burden of expectation. She was raised to have a sense of entitlement, to feel that she had the same life chances as anyone else, white or black, male or female. Yet at the same time her parents managed to avoid imparting to her the all-too-common feeling that she carried the mantle of her race. As I mentioned earlier, many African-American achievers are raised with a clear message that in order to succeed they have to be twice as good as their white counterpart. Add to this the notion of legacy—the idea that a young person's opportunity to attend a top-notch school or to achieve a professional career is not only the embodiment of what their parents had fought for in the civil rights movement, but is at the very core the dream of their ancestors in slavery. The pressure can be immense. Black parents impart these messages to their children in order to instill a sense of pride that will help protect them against the racism of the mainstream culture. But the tactic of expectation has a practical side as well—when a black parent fears that the world won't give their child a fair shot, encouraging the child to work harder, to be twice as good, is an attempt at leveling the playing field. This sense of duty can be particularly acute in black women. Among professional black women, one might well call this phenomenon Negress Noblesse Oblige.

In Queens, that world of black celebrities, self-employed business people and other strivers was an unusually sheltered arena for the children who grew up there. "It was an extremely, boringly, stable middle-class household and success was defined by a society of black people," Thelma remembers. This point, especially, is key. For many professional African Americans, success is defined by entree into a society of whites, where there is almost always a sense of otherness, a sense of trespassing and, all too often a feeling that no matter how hard one tries, there's always a limit to how much you can achieve. "Young African Americans like Shay," Peggy Orenstein writes in her book *Flux*, "who are groomed for mainstream achievement, are tacitly taught that the white world and the values associated with it represent success. But if that's true, where does that leave Shay's 'real' life? How much of the world she grew up in is she willing to leave behind in order to succeed?"

The children of middle-class black communities sometimes have a different struggle. They enter the white professional world both expecting more and expecting less than their parents, or kids from less privileged backgrounds, may have. They expect more because they have been raised with a sense of entitlement that has ingrained in them the belief that they have a right to anything the world has to offer. At the same time, they expect less of the white professional world. Their lives, since childhood, have been defined by what Thelma Golden calls "a society of black people." The children of this world grow up with a sense of acceptance among other successful blacks, which makes them less likely to look to the white community for validation or a sense of self. "I guess I grew up with certain assumptions," Thelma says. "It was never a question of whether I would go to college. I went to private school my whole life. It was never a question that I wasn't exposed to culture in some way—I went to camp, I had skating lessons. I would say that my aspirations in childhood were relatively trivial, just because there was a certain level of comfort already there."

For their first few years at Buckley Country Day, Thelma and her brother were the only black students. In her private high school, there were ten black students (including a woman who is Thelma's best friend to this day). When she arrived at Smith College and discovered that there were 17 African-American women in her class of 600, she practically threw a parade. "Most of the black women were complaining that there were so few black people. I was in heaven. I'd never been in a school with 16 other black people altogether. I kept telling my friends from high school, there are 80 black women at Smith!"

At Smith, sisterhood—especially among black women—was powerful. But class was a very real wedge. For first-generation college students, the emphasis was on pursuing professional, lucrative careers—medicine, law, finance. In Temple University Professor Suni Petersen's study of middle-class black women, she found that "Work far overshadowed education in the importance it held for these women. Education was a commodity to be used to enhance career options. Success meant self-sufficiency, independence of thought and leadership."[23] As an art history major, Golden stood out as a black woman who had the luxury to make a different kind of choice. "Other black women from different economic backgrounds were supportive, but it was hard for them to understand," she says. "Where did I get this mental sensibility that made me feel that I didn't need more insurance in the world?"

It was that sense of internal security fostered in her household and her Queens neighborhood that allowed Thelma to feel so at home at Smith. It was, after all, a collegiate replica of the schools she had been attending all her life. But the fact that she wasn't experiencing the same culture shock as many of her African-American classmates didn't go unnoticed. "Somehow this college, that for so long had been the province of rich white women, felt very much my own," Thelma says. "It wasn't because I thought I was white or rich, it was because growing up no one had ever told me differently. Perhaps to my own detriment, I always had that feeling of entitlement as part of my inner life. So as an adult, I had to work that out a little bit because it made me understand the world in a better way."

Even after becoming a pioneering force in the art world, Thelma found that her career choice baffled many black people. In many ways, she was an ambassador of black art: increasing the amount of African-American artists that exhibited at the Whitney, discovering and supporting emerging black artists and wielding the ultimate curatorial power by acquiring a landmark number of paintings and photographs for the museum's permanent collection. "To the world of my extended

family, my mother, my cousins—my success would be more understandable if it were more specifically validated by the mainstream
culture," she explained. "I work in a world that's not title conscious at
all, and I think that black people do put a lot of value on titles as a
marker of success. In the art world, it's more important to have a certain
kind of power, to go minimally on titles. I'm a curator—it's not chief curator, head curator, big curator. We just don't do that in the art world.
The fact is that I work in one of the most powerful museums in the city,
all of my status is implied in a kind of low-key manner."

What about that sense of being one of what Lynette Hall calls
"the Onlys." I was curious how Golden, who at the time was still at the
Whitney Museum in New York City, felt in her day-to-day professional
interactions. What was it like to look around museum board meetings,
exhibition openings and the countless gallery receptions that are so
vital to her work and be—so often—the only black woman there? Her
answer, like her situation, was complicated. "I'm not happy about it,"
she said. "But I haven't figured out how—beyond my personal efforts to
change it—the world I'm in will change. It doesn't make me uncomfortable though, in my working day. It has never made me feel that I cannot
do the work that I do."

While Golden's specialty at the Whitney Museum was African-
American art, she was careful to emphasize that it's her passion for art,
not politics, which drives her professional life. Moreover, she seemed at
a loss to explain how she'd gotten so far, so fast. And why, when every
indication of race and gender suggested that she couldn't do something,
she continued with her work, undaunted by the challenges. "I wish I
had a clear story, but I don't," she said with a shrug. "Often, it means
admitting to a certain amount of my childhood where I assumed certain
things outright. I never considered, with any seriousness, that something I was doing—hadn't really been done. I never went to the Whitney with the idea of being the first black woman at the Whitney. When
people look at me and ask what it's like to be the first, I tell them I don't
have an answer for that. Not a good one. I just relay the chain of events.
Strung together, they become what my career is."

"It Was the First Time I Ever Felt Profoundly Underestimated as a Black Woman."

A YEAR AFTER OUR initial interview, Thelma Golden's life had changed dramatically. David Ross, the director of the Whitney, departed and was replaced by Maxwell L. Anderson. The administrative shift left the museum's curatorial staff fearful, and rightfully so, about the status of their jobs. For Thelma, the timing could not have been worse. At 30, she was a rising star, fast-tracked for greatness. Artists that Golden had championed were winning awards and solo exhibitions that validated her role as an influential cultural taste-maker. Most notably, one of her protégés, 27-year-old Kara Walker, had recently won a MacArthur "genius" grant, due in no small part to Thelma's celebration of her work.

She had brought lucrative patrons to the Whitney, infusing the venerable institution with previously untapped sources of cash. This was important to her future as a potential museum director, a job that includes a great deal of fund-raising. The success of her biggest exhibition, the Black Male show, had given her an international profile in the art world, which she followed up by launching a retrospective of the little-known, but highly acclaimed, Beat era artist Bob Thompson. To top it all off, she had recently been named the curator of the 2000 Biennial. The Whitney's Biennial, with its bold exploration of the best and the brightest new artists, always shook up the New York art scene. Millennium fever was sweeping the cultural world and the 2000 Biennial was sure to get more attention than previous shows. Despite the fact that she had neither a Master's nor a Ph.D. (the lack of which drove her critics to distraction), Golden had outlasted those who'd tagged her as an affirmative-action hire. To use basketball parlance, she had game at the Whitney—and everybody knew it.

When the new administration came in, she found herself on shaky ground. Eventually, she and five other curators, all forced into sideline positions by the new regime, would resign. They departed as a group, but Golden felt terribly alone. The sense of entitlement and assuredness that had carried her, seemingly effortlessly, from Buckley Country Day School to Smith to the Whitney was shattered. "I, perhaps more than most of my coworkers, was nervous," she says. "I felt that it was going to affect me more not just because of race, but the combination of race, gender and age."

She was stripped of her title as curator of the 2000 Biennial and offered the much lower role of "coordinator" under a team of new curators that would be brought in. These curators, Golden was told, were experts in the field of contemporary arts. She, her new supervisors informed her, was not. The very work that had made her a star—the solo exhibits of African-American artists and the Black Male show—was cited as evidence that she did not have the chops to be a full curator at a museum with such a broad national profile as the Whitney. On a personal level, Golden got a glimpse of the discomfort, fear and weariness that had been the rigid backbone of her poorer black classmates at Smith. "It was the first time I ever felt profoundly underestimated as a black woman," she says. "Moreover, I began to know what it was like to be thought of as a 'black woman,' they had this image of her and what she could do, and it created a great deal of friction."

It was telling that Thelma felt so disassociated from this image of a black woman who could be underestimated that she didn't say "this image of me" and "what I could do." Instead, she used the third person: "her," "she." Born in 1966, she was the very embodiment of what Martin Luther King called "children of the dream." Not only had she never expected to be judged by anything but the content of her character, but she refused to see it as something that was happening to her. Her new bosses' mentality, she insisted, was a reflection not of her, but of an image of her. An image she refused to accept.

As a child, her parents had protected Golden from what could have been a crippling sense of racism and sexism. At the same time, her largely effortless passage through one elite circle after another hadn't prepared her for a time when the doors would not open—not just because of racism, but for any reason at all. "I grew up with this incredible interior world," she says. "I kind of assumed certain things, that there's no way I should have believed." Things like what? I ask, pressing her to be specific. Then she smiles, "Things like...I would always be able to do whatever I wanted."

It took a while, but eventually Thelma came to see her experience at the Whitney as not only critical to her development as a black woman, but as key to her growth as a person. None of us—regardless of race or gender—live in a world where we get whatever we want. This is a crucial point. We live in a country obsessed with race, which has made it difficult for African Americans to judge their experiences without studying them through a racial lens. To the extreme, this has created a victim mentality among some blacks who, when pressed, will always reach for the race card.

At the same time, the paucity of African Americans in the top ranks of almost any field—law, medicine, publishing, science, technology—necessitates that those who attain the top ranks will be perceived as ambassadors for their race. The position of ambassador is, by nature, one rooted in duality—measuring the social mores and political climate of the country you inhabit with the rules and expectations of the people that you represent. As African-American ambassadors in white professional circles, it's difficult to develop an individual identity, one that can sustain ups and downs without the undertones of race. It's also difficult to allow yourself the opportunity to view certain failures or setbacks as a maturing process, when those incidents are always tinged with race.

Her resignation from the Whitney may have opened Thelma's eyes to the fact that race would and could touch her life, but it also forced Thelma Golden to grow up. "I felt genuinely, ironically, liberated," she says. "In many ways, I'd never really been called into question, asked to put my politics out there as to who I was as a black woman. I'd never really had to make a stand for what I believed in. Prior to the changes at the Whitney, I moved comfortably around a lot of people who knew what I believed in and supported that."

For the first time, Golden was forced to defend her abilities and the carefully nurtured sense of entitlement that she'd worn like a cloak since birth. It was the kind of experience that is seminal in the life of any young professional. "I was being asked to change how I thought about myself and my job in a way that was completely undermining my sense of self," she says. "In a very trivial way, I know it was personal and little, but I felt that I was making a stand. Do I have to take this shitty job that I was being offered? No. Did I know what I was going to do because I wasn't taking the job? No. That was my Rosa Parks move, you know?"

Golden's mentor at the Whitney, David Ross, had hired her and been her boss throughout her tenure at the museum. After her resignation, there were those who chalked up her previous successes as nothing more than the fortunate by-product of her being favored by the influential Ross. Talking about him, it's clear that her respect for him runs deep. She brightens at his name and speaks of him with a quiet confidence that suggests that she trusts him absolutely. "When David left the Whitney, I was devastated because I knew that it was the end of something great for me. I hardly ever write letters, but I wrote him a letter to thank him for what he had created for me there. David never bent the rules for me. He taught me what the rules were and gave me the rare experience, as a black curator, to operate within those rules. I wasn't some angry black woman yelling and screaming for newness. I was given a portfolio like everyone else and I could play it out the way I wanted."

David Ross is, by all appearances, the kind of white man who makes the most powerful ally for a young African-American professional. He was, by Golden's estimation, "really committed to all the things that the late 1960s were about. He really believed that multiculturalism didn't just happen, that it had to be an agenda. An agenda meant that you had to invest people with the power to have their voices heard. So David, more than any other museum director that I can point to in this country, didn't give lip service to this idea of inclusiveness. Often that means you invite a few black artists to show on what is clearly your turf."

As one of a handful of black curators at major art museums nationwide (some estimates put the figure at fewer than half a dozen in 1999), Golden enjoyed an unusual level of autonomy and visibility. "David allowed me to operate at the Whitney as any curator might," she says. "So if I wanted to do a show of Gary Simmons, that wouldn't be any less legitimate than Julian Schnabel or Bruce Nauman. David supported me emotionally, but he put money behind it. He allowed me to do Black Male at a budget level that made the show important on an international scale."

Golden knows that there are those in the art world who saw her as nothing more than Ross's puppet. "Relationships between black women and powerful white men are often seen as suspect," she shrugs. "There are just as many people who understand my relationship to David as there are those who feel that David controlled me, that David set up an agenda that I was playing out. Some people thought that the controversial images in the Black Male show had to do with his negative feelings about black men and black masculinity. Even now, in the art world, it's all so suspect."

She pauses for a moment, and her face is a mixture of sadness and regret. She pushes her shoulders down, then leans across the table and speaks carefully into the tape recorder that has played for two hours between us. "With the white man in a position of power, ours is a friendship that is hard for some people to see."

Home to Harlem and the Truly
Interesting Thing

FOR THE YEAR that followed her departure from the Whitney, Golden went through all the emotional changes that unexpected unemployment can bring. She worked as a special projects curator for her former Whitney patrons, Peter and Eileen Norton, who resigned from the Whitney board when Thelma was forced to step down. When we meet again to talk about the changes in her life, she's as vibrant and confident as ever. She's dressed in a bright red business suit and, as always, heads turn when she walks into the restaurant at the SoHo Grand Hotel. I take particular notice of her walk—part fashion-runway strut, part general leading her troops into battle.

She tells me that she considered, but eventually passed on, several offers from mainstream museums where she might continue the work that she began at the Whitney. "I interviewed with a really important interesting exhibition space in SoHo," she says. "Twenty-five years old, a stellar history. They offered me the job, but I just felt like right this second I wanted something radically different. Quite honestly, my life has been spent in this bastion of the mainstream culture."

She was wading through offers from the mainstream when an interesting thing happened: she was offered the job of deputy director of the Studio Museum in Harlem. For a young African-American woman who'd spent her entire educational and professional career in exclusively white enclaves, a job in Harlem was a very radical move. It helped that her new boss would be Lowery Stokes Sims, a woman who had served as a curator at the Metropolitan Museum of Art for 27 years. Just days before, Sims had left the Met to become director of the Studio Museum—a move that had sent ripples through the art world.

At 51, Sims could not only relate to Golden's experience, she had been there, done that. While Golden's rise had been meteoric, even by art world standards, Sims had had a slower, more considered ascent. While Golden held no advanced degrees, Sims had a doctorate in modern art. Golden began her career at the Whitney as director of the Phillip Morris branch, a job that gave her the power to mount her own shows from the beginning. Sims had worked her way up to curator from the Met's educational department. By all accounts, including Golden's, the women's strengths complemented each other, and together they made a powerful pair. More than that, by joining the Studio Museum, Golden relinquished—at least for a while—her status as the only black curator at her place of employment.

Between them, the two women brought to the Studio Museum 40 years of experience from two of the most venerable museums in the country. As the *New York Times* noted in a lengthy two-page profile, "The arrival of Ms. Sims and Ms. Golden in Harlem comes at an interesting and difficult moment in the museum's history. To a museum named for a specific community, they bring the glamour of high-powered institutions elsewhere. Their hiring marks a potentially far-reaching break in the Studio Museum's pattern of training and promoting its curators from within...Their move uptown also leaves a significant gap in the art world. The departure of Ms. Sims from the Metropolitan and Ms. Golden from the Whitney has taken black curators from two of the city's leading museums, which might well be seen as a step backward in the far from resolved battle to break the art world's color barrier."[24]

While Thelma's move to the Studio Museum might seem natural for a young black curator, I knew that for her it was a bold move, one that represented a kind of cultural reintegration into the black world of her Queens youth. The professional challenge that the Studio Museum presented—to take a marginalized institution with slender resources and put it on the art world map—only sweetened the draw.

I suspected that the job would raise personal challenges for

Thelma, ones that she seemed eager to embrace. In the 1920s, young writers and artists, eager for inspiration, had flocked to the Harlem neighborhood that would later house the Studio Museum. Their passion had created some of the most vibrant work of the 20th century, spawning writers like Langston Hughes and Zora Neale Hurston, painters like Aaron Douglas and Romare Bearden, sculptors such as Augusta Savage and photographers such as James VanDerZee. A popular saying of the time was "Better to be a lamppost in Harlem, than governor of Georgia." But Harlem had never been home for Thelma in the way that it was to Langston Hughes and Romare Bearden. Buckley Country Day School was home. Smith was home. The Whitney was home. Harlem was a foreign territory.

When we first met to begin talking about this book, Thelma said something that stuck with me. "If we had met in high school," she said, "you would've hated me, because it would've been easier for me to talk to the white kids than it would've been for me to talk to you." I thought that was a strong assumption, not that we might not have been friends, but rather that I would have "hated" her. But I understood that she was trying to explain the degree of comfort she had grown to feel not only around whites, but specifically whites of privileged backgrounds. Now I wondered if the Studio Museum might not raise those old feelings— working every day with blacks who she suspected might have hated her at another time and place.

In her new job, Thelma hopes to bring all that she has learned along the way to make the Studio Museum a world-class institution. Of course, before she accepted the job, she consulted her former boss, David Ross. He reminded her that at places like the Whitney, you may make a mark, but you never bring the walls down—or put them up. For better or worse, museums like the Whitney and the Metropolitan will always reflect their many years of history. At a young museum, he explained, she would have a chance to not only learn the rules, but to make them. Ross took on a similar role, early in his career, at the Institute for Contemporary Art in Boston, a place that at the time "had no profile whatsoever," Thelma tells me. "David is thrilled. He keeps telling me that this is what it's about, this is the moment, when I have a chance to build a landmark. For the Studio Museum, this is going to be the defining time that gives it its institutional stability. That makes it stay forever."

It occurs to me that she is attempting to give the museum a taste of the cosseted upbringing that she herself enjoyed. This is also her opportunity to bring together the white world of her youth and early career and the black world that has sometimes viewed her experience and life choices as an anomaly. Only a year before she had said, "In the black community, my life's work doesn't really fit in at all." Now her work was in the community and whether or not she could attract large numbers of African-American audiences to the museum, whether or not her work fit would be one of the markers of her success. Minutes before we finished our last conversation, she looked away for several moments and smiled to herself. "David says, 'This job is going to kill you, but it will be the truly interesting thing.'" The words "truly interesting" roll off her tongue like sugar, and I know that this, more than anything, is what pleases her.

Hi. My Name Is Thelma Golden: Art, Celebrity and the Politics of Fame

TWO YEARS INTO her tenure at the Studio Museum, Thelma Golden was the subject of a long, and some say embarrassing, profile in *The New Yorker*. At the age of 34, such attention to her work, life and influence is a definite testament to the iconic status she is achieving in her field. At the same time, the piece revealed two things that made people uncomfortable: the extent to which she is, despite her Harlem perch, completely piped in to some of the most rich and powerful people in the world. In one part of the piece, the writer describes a trip that she takes to Aspen with collector Fred Henry and artist Glenn Ligon. For those people, black and white, who perpetually insist that the diminutive curator is nothing more than a walking, talking black girl puppet of liberal-minded white male powerbrokers, the *New Yorker* piece was, in some circles, black-and-white proof that Thelma Golden was not down for the people, but only down for herself. As one of the many hate letters she received put it, "Thelma Golden is the biggest sellout known to man."

Sitting on a banquette at Balthazar one rainy Friday morning, months after the *New Yorker* piece first appeared, she is still stunned at the extent of the criticism. Mostly because, as she says, she's always made it clear that what she wanted was to be an art world powerhouse, *not* an art world rebel. She believes that while the world of outsider art may seem like a noble democracy, it rarely is. For Thelma, to work within the structure of the mainstream may indeed mean working under the dictatorship of the mainstream. But, as she found during her tenure at the Whitney, to adopt the *lingua franca* of the mainstream can be subversive and effective. "While there are many people much smarter than I am, much more diligent than I am, who have been able to work effectively from the outside, I could never do that," she says. "I felt like if I was going to do the kind of work I wanted to do, at the level I wanted to do it, I had to get deep inside. And not just get deep inside, but be able to galvanize those resources deep inside."

At the Studio Museum, she has succeeded in not only creating critically acclaimed shows, such as Freestyle, but in creating an atmosphere very different from the one she encountered when she interned as a college student. Back then, the museum steeped itself in formality and bureaucracy, much of it an imagined parroting of what the administrators thought took place at the white-run museums downtown. "Not that I don't believe in respecting your elders, but everyone had to be addressed as Mr. or Mrs. Somebody," Thelma remembers. "There was a lot of that old colored formality." Fresh out of Smith, Thelma came to the museum, brimming with enthusiasm and ideas that were seen as threatening by the old guard of black curators. "I'd spent my whole life in private schools and private colleges where any sense of initiative was rewarded," she says. "It wasn't just about doing what you were told, but about challenging and taking initiative. So I got to do the Studio Museum with all of that in mind, for my little $11,000 a year stipend, and my enthusiasm wasn't necessarily welcome. As a museum, it was an incredibly nonartful place."

She acknowledges that some of what she felt had to do with youthful naiveté; college hadn't really prepared her for the business side of running an artistic institution. At the same time, she knew enough from her life outside the museum to know that there were important things going on with black artists that the Studio Museum was ignoring entirely. "Basquiat was still alive then," she recalls. "There was a moment there. It was huge, and there was no connection to that and what was happening in the museum."

For a while, she really struggled with the question of how she might be able to maintain a vision for black art and culture while working outside of a major black museum. Then she met Bill T. Jones in the museum gallery and through their friendship began to envision a place for herself outside of the staid, conservative black arts institution. Shortly thereafter, she landed a job as a curatorial assistant at the Whitney, where even the head curators were called by their first names, where her boss, Richard Armstrong, encouraged her to read the mail that she opened and to follow up on the things that interested her.

This time around, she is aiming to make the Studio Museum a place where young staff members don't have the experience that she had. She's gotten rid of the militarylike schedule of sign-in sheets. "There are 20 people here, they don't need to be signing in 50 times," she says, rolling her eyes. "Yes, we need to know who's in the building and who's not, but the bureaucracy!" She was horrified to find that there was actually no art hanging in the museum's reception area. On her first day, she took the revolutionary step of hanging pictures in the reception area of the museum's offices. "Those are the kind of weird things that we laugh about now," she says. "But for me, having remembered what it was like to walk in there with my great Smith college education and all of my good Girl Scout initiative, I remember how it was so dysfunctional. I didn't want it to be this way."

Golden values working with Lowery Stokes Sims and together they have eliminated the hierarchies of senior staff and junior staff, partially because the limited resources of a place like the Studio Museum mean everyone needs to be able to be good at everything. "At the Whitney, the resources are huge," she says. "I am really not wedded to any kind of deep, hard-core managerial bullshit, because frankly, there's no time for it. My work has become very project-centric. I feel like we have very little resources, all of it needs to go into the work." Thelma believes that the environment of the museum is changing and she hopes her legacy will be not only artistic, but have a human impact as well.

"Last summer, we had two wonderful little interns from Barnard and Columbia," she says, smiling broadly. "I worked really hard to make them feel that yes, you can thrive in a place like this. You can work with older women of color and we are going to encourage you. We are going to help you. We are going to show you what it is we do."

Increasingly, Thelma is getting comfortable with the fact that while the eyes of the black community are now on her more than ever, she's not going to make everybody happy. After nearly 15 years in the art world, she knows what she likes, what she believes, what she is trying to create. "I'm very confident, which I've taken a hit for," she says. "Because my confidence is read within certain quarters as a certain arrogance." One of the letters that came to me said, "Oh, I saw you at the Black Fine Arts Fair and you barely looked at any of the work." Well, that's because most of the work was bad, I didn't have to look. At the end of the day, I've learned that I have to have confidence in what I believe in as opposed to making people think I'm a nice girl, because that's not going to get the work I really believe in forward. Someone knows if I do something I believe in it."

The confidence that is read as arrogance also has to do with her awareness of just how well known she is in the art world. Recently at the opening of the Tate Modern in London, Thelma attended with the husband of one of her good friends. He was in London on business and Thelma invited him to accompany her. It was a celebrity-studded affair, with guests that ranged from Mick Jagger to the Queen of England. Thelma remembers telling her friend's husband. "Look, it's going to come to pass that during this evening, people are going to talk to me and I'm not going to introduce you because I don't know who they are, but they all know who I am." Naturally, her friend's husband thought that Thelma was being incredibly arrogant. "We're walking into this place and there's 5,000 people," she says. "And it starts happening. It's not even that they know what I look like. It's a process of elimination. Well, if she's a black girl and she's here, that must be Thelma Golden." Even when she tries not to take her celebrity for granted, she's reminded of how well known she is. "A few weeks ago, I was working on an architecture show and I called several architects," she says. "One of them got on the phone and I said, 'Hi, my name is Thelma Golden. I'm a curator at the Studio Museum and I do contemporary...' and he just started laughing. I stopped and he said, 'I hope you're saying that as a joke. Don't tell me that you think I wouldn't know who Thelma Golden is.'"

It's a challenging balance to strike between confidence and what some might call arrogance, but one that Thelma is becoming increasingly comfortable with. "Having worked all these years, I have a sense that my reputation is a testament to the fact that what I'm doing is at the center," she says. "I've never been on the margin and I've never been ashamed to say that. I know there's a politically correct way in which I'm supposed to adopt a certain kind of marginality as a badge of *something*. But I'm not interested in it, never have been. That is my great failing, I'm sure, on a certain level. But I'm not interested."

CHAPTER 6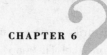

Taking Sides Against Ourselves:
The Push and Pull of Race
and Gender

FROM THE MOMENT OF our emancipation from slavery, black women have been caught between the push and pull of race and gender. In the late 1800s, white suffragettes who had supported the abolition of slavery during the Civil War began to demand their own rights. It was time, they argued, that white women should have the right to vote. At the same time, black men were pressing for their own enfranchisement. Black women? Not even a consideration. Men saw the white women's cause as a dangerous liability; the suffragette movement had far fewer supporters than black men's bid for equality. Even longtime women's supporters, such as Frederick Douglass, had decided that race trumped gender in this sprint to the voting booth. "This is the Negro's hour," Douglass declared.

Black women fell into the chasm created by the split between white suffragettes and those who supported black male enfranchisement. Left alone, they were forced to fend for themselves. "There was a great stir about colored men getting their rights, but not a word about the colored women," said Sojourner Truth, the former slave and great orator. "If colored men get their rights and not colored women theirs, you see the colored men will be masters over the women and it will be just as bad as it was before."[25]

A powerful danger lay underneath Truth's warning—if black women didn't speak up and act up, they would find themselves in slavery again, with their husbands as their masters. For all its inhumanities, slavery had forged a special bond between men and women. Black men had little opportunity to display machismo when their very survival depended on black women being partners in every way. In her groundbreaking text, *Women, Race and Class,* Angela Davis writes, "In the cotton, to- bacco, corn and sugar-cane fields, women worked alongside the men...In the words of an ex-slave: 'The bell rings at four o'clock in the morning and they have half an hour to get ready. Men and women start together and the women must work as steadily as the men and perform the same tasks as the men.'"

Slavery created a perverse equality between black men and women, an equality that would, ironically, erode as freedom grew. For the next century, the concerns and needs of black women were kept weighed down under the double yoke of racism and sexism. It wasn't until after the civil rights movement and the women's rights movement that any generation openly challenged this system. And while it still remains true that many black women still earn less and have fewer opportunities than their white female or black male counterparts, it's no longer the rule. The cycle and the stigma of the double negative of being part of a minority race and minority gender have been broken.

In her seminal novel, *Their Eyes Were Watching God,* Zora Neale Hurston gives a powerful rendition of how black women are raised to see their place in the world. Janie's grandmother, Nanny, wants her granddaughter to have a better life. But she also wants her to be aware of how powerless she is, having neither the privilege of race or gender. A former slave, Nanny warns:

> "Honey, de white man is de ruler of everything as fur as Ah been able tuh find out. Maybe it's some place in de ocean where de black man is in power, but we don't know nothin' but what we see. So do white man throw down de load and tell de nigger

man tuh pick it up. He pick it up because he have to, but he don't tote it. He hand it to his women folks. De nigger woman is de mule uh de world as fur as Ah can see. Ah been prayin' for it tuh be different with you."

Zora Neale Hurston captured the depth of our struggle, the ugly truth of our subjugation when she called us the mules of the world: it's a metaphor that is brought up again and again in the field of black women's studies as well as popular cultural perceptions of who we are. Like Aunt Jemima's mammy baggage, it's a treasured yet painful part of our history. It is not, however, part of our present or our future. We've been able to break a cycle of marginalization in white women's organizations as well as black organizations. Because women like Sojourner Truth refused to be swayed by a myopic version of our existence, today's young black women don't feel a need to choose allegiance between race or gender. We wake up black and we wake up female every single day. We've learned not to take sides against ourselves.

In My Sister's World, It Was a Different Time

THERE'S AN OLD SAYING about the timeless quality of black skin that says, "Good black don't crack." Amina Thomas and Asali Holland are the living embodiments of this. Both women are in their early 50s yet they could easily pass for ten years younger. Asali is petite, with fair skin and delicate features recalling a young Lena Horne. Amina is tall and almost photo-negative opposite—she has smooth ebony skin and deep-set large brown eyes. The two women met more than 30 years ago as 19-year-olds, newly married and members of the militant black revolutionary party, the "US organization." The party wielded a considerable amount of power in Los Angeles, as respected, and feared, as the Black Panthers. A young Maulana Karenga, who went on to found the African-American holiday Kwaanza, headed the group.

They've been dancing around the subjects of race, politics and gender for more than 30 years. They can finish each other's sentences and still call each other by their '60s movement names. At 52, Asali tells her co-workers at the post office to call her Diana, her Christian name. But to Amina, she'll always be Asali, the Swahili word for honey or sweet. Amina is Swahili for faithful or loyal. To Asali, she's the very definition of the word. They've seen each other through revolutions of civil rights and womanhood, through childbirth and divorce, self-discovery and friendship.

I was excited to interview them for this book because I saw within the scope of their families radical shifts in views of race and gender. Amina and Asali joined me in a Culver City conference room with their daughters Liba Daniels and Makina Hopkins, as well as Asali's step-daughter, Funeka Koboka. Before I turn on the tape recorder, the women gather and stitch like thread through a needle. They admire each other's outfits and finger each other's hair. Between the five women, their skin tones range from the lightest caramel to the deepest black. Even the way they introduce themselves has an air of ceremony: the elders first, followed by the daughters in age order. Like the African names Amina and Asali chose for themselves, their daughters' names were purposefully selected as talismans of protection in a world hostile to their race and gender. Liba, short for Libalele, means "the sun that shines at night." Makini means "regal" or "well-reserved." Funeka means simply "desired."

I've invited them to talk about their lives as black women. As products of the 1960s, Amina and Asali still very much identify as black first. But their daughters lead different lives and enjoy a different view of the world. They don't take marching orders from any black power organization. They've arrived at what educator Walteen Grady-Truely called the next frontier: the right to be themselves, to think of themselves as women—individual women—first.

Amina and Asali begin by explaining to the group how irrelevant feminism seemed at the time they were in the movement. Asali married just a year out of high school, joining the US organization at the same age her daughters later picked college majors. Her primary concern then was not herself—her life or her dreams—but the advancement of the civil rights movement. "What about your rights as a woman?" I ask. Asali shrugs and Amina answers for her. "In my sister's world, it was a different time," she says, her voice so rich and powerful it brings to mind the contralto of James Earl Jones. "The social consciousness of the time was completely different. You stood for something. We saw Malcolm X get killed, saw Dr. King get killed, Kennedy—killed. It was a whole different time."

Amina wants me to understand that it wasn't that they didn't care about their rights as women; it was simply that they never separated black from female. Ever. She asks me to imagine what it was like to be "a teenager and watch black people running from dogs and fire hoses." How could she and her sisters believe anything but the black power agenda when her salvation, and the salvation of everyone they knew and loved, depended on their toeing the racial line? By joining the US organization, which organized itself around nebulous principles of African heritage, Amina and Asali hoped to restore to the African-American people all the strength and dignity they once had in the motherland. Amina says she doesn't regret the sacrifices she made. "At the time, I believed the role of the woman was to inspire her man to participate in the social development of the community. As a woman, my job was to educate and protect the children." Both women insist that this was a vital role—the revolution could not be sustained without the strength of future generations. In Swahili, they called the caring and teaching of children "kaida." It is a sacred word. But neither woman was allowed to be a leader in the US organization; that was the work of men.

At 32, Asali's daughter, Liba, remembers that as a child she saw the women as leaders. Liba says that it was by their example that she's become a successful production designer in a field dominated by men. "On Sundays, the women and children of US had 'soul sessions,'" she explains. "The women voiced their ideas and organized for change. Those were powerful meetings to witness." Although feminism was a four-letter word, sisterhood was a powerful component of Amina and Asali's world. "When my children were small, I had to help the sisters in the organization," Asali explains. Consequently, "It wasn't just me who raised them. It was a community. If Liba needed an outfit sewn, there was a sister who would do that. If she needed a special tutoring class, there was a sister who would take care of that, too."

She turns to me and once again tries to explain the choices she has made. "When you say that women couldn't be leaders that sounds bad," she says. "But it wasn't as bad as people make it out to be. It was different, but I knew my rights. I do believe in the feminist movement to a certain extent."

This Bridge Called Her Back: The Defining Moment of Anita Hill

DURING THE FIVE YEARS that I spent researching this book, I asked women to try to recall the first time they thought of themselves as women first, black second. Some women mentioned trips to Europe and the experience of being called a "beautiful girl" as opposed to a "beautiful black girl." For other women, it was the experience of having a best friend who was not black; the unique experience of looking at a woman of another race and loving her as a sister. Overwhelmingly, though, the majority of the women pointed to the Clarence Thomas hearings of 1991 and Anita Hill's public stand on sexual harassment.

The episode is, by now, well known. Following Supreme Court Justice Thurgood Marshall's retirement, President George Bush nominated a conservative African American to replace him. A District Court Judge, Clarence Thomas was a Republican dream candidate: an African American who opposed affirmative action and other federal civil rights initiatives. At the same time, Thomas's up-from-poverty story gave him a Booker T. Washington quality that liberal blacks and whites found hard to tear down. Thomas's confirmation hearings were the dull and drawn-out programming that late nights on C-SPAN are made of; until October 6, 1991, when the allegations of a law professor named Anita Hill were broadcast on NPR. Hill testified that Thomas sexually harassed her throughout her tenure at the U.S. Department of Education and the Equal Opportunity Commission. The Thomas-Hill "he said, she said" became a national scandal that Americans tuned in to watch day after day.

In the black community, Anita Hill was considered especially suspect. It had long been an unspoken rule in the community that in the never-ending quest to "uplift the race," black women should not speak out against black men in public. Before Anita Hill, generations of black

women had been mute about the rape, domestic violence and sexual harassment they experienced at the hands of black men. Thomas was
eventually confirmed, but the ripple effect of the hearings continues to
this day. The case was a wake-up call to corporate America on the issue
of sexual harassment, and thousands of women, of all races, benefited
from Anita Hill's breaking the code of silence.

According to law professor Kimberle Crenshaw, the hearings did
more than pit a black woman against a black man in the highest court in
the nation, it gave the world a rare view of black women's dueling allegiances. "It was no *Twilight Zone* that America discovered when Anita
Hill came forward," she observes. "America simply stumbled into the
place where African-American women live, a political vacuum of era-
sure and contradiction maintained by the almost routine polarization of
'blacks' and 'women' into separate and competing political camps." [26]

When I talk to Amina, Asali and their daughters, Anita Hill strikes
a similarly conflicted chord. As women who had devoted their 20s to a
black nationalist organization, Amina and Asali's initial reaction is to
come down against Anita Hill. "I was a little torn," Asali says. "My first
thought was 'Darn, why is she doing this to this black man?' It was a bad
thing to see these two black people fighting against each other. We
never want white people to see that." Eventually, though, Asali decided
she supported Anita Hill's claim. "She had every right to speak out
against him. I think she did the right thing."

Amina raises a provocative question. What if Clarence Thomas
wasn't the second black to be confirmed to the Supreme Court, what if
he had been the first? Would we still have supported Anita Hill? "Who
could have stood up and made those accusations against Thurgood Marshall?" she asks. "Maybe no one. It was the early days of civil rights
then. Black people were trying to get places." She would never have
tolerated an Anita Hill in the 1960s and 1970s. "Stuff like that didn't
mean anything to me," she says. "It would've been like 'Why are you
talking about that when we can't even vote!' It was a sacrifice because
women didn't have the say so. Throughout our history, women have been
put on the back burner. It's just recently that things have changed."

The change is as close as Amina and Asali's own daughters. Liba
and Makina were literally born into the black power movement. They
spent their formative years attending community-run schools that

stressed an Afrocentric curriculum. But their stance on Anita Hill couldn't be clearer. "She's a black woman who became an icon for all women who experience sexual harassment today," says Makina. "She gave us the will. She gave all women the will to stand up for ourselves," says Liba, her voice brimming with pride. To this generation of black women, Hill is a symbol of strength and self-definition.

Laying Claim to Ladyhood: White Women and Black Women in Conflict

THE SEXISM OF THE black power movement, and previous race-based organizations, is only part of what kept black women from fully identifying as woman first. On an even deeper level, we have—for generations—been in conflict about what our womanhood means. During slavery, being a woman meant that you were sexual chattel, a breeder and a plaything for the white men on the plantation. Black women were either Mammies or Sapphires—the latter a rather pejorative term for a loud-mouthed, abrasive, bossy woman. There were few positive images of femaleness that white women hadn't laid claimed to first. We were always defined in opposition to white women: if the white woman was pure, we were sullied. If she was a wit, we were ignorant. If she was gentle, we were brutes. If she was delicate, we were workhorses. It was a double yoke that would affect generations of black women, including young women my own age.

You could fill a small library with the number of books that examine black women's aspiring to a beauty standard based on white women; from Toni Morrison's *The Bluest Eye* to *The Skin I'm In*, the 1998 award-winning novel by Sharon Flake. In *A Black Feminist's Search for Sisterhood*, Michele Wallace writes, "On rainy days, my sister and I used to tie the short end of the scarf around our scrawny braids and let the rest of its silken mass trail to our waists. We'd pretend it was hair and that we were some lovely heroine we'd seen in the movies. There was a time when I would have called that wanting to be white, yet the real point of the game was being feminine. Being feminine meant being white to us."

During Chicago's monumental Columbian Exposition in 1893,

Fannie Barrier Williams, a college professor and activist, spoke before the World's Congress of Representative Women defending the virtues of black women. It was specifically aimed at white women who pointed to an alleged moral weakness in black women as the reason they would not accept and respect black women as peers. "The accusations are false," she began. "It ought not to be necessary to remind a Southern woman that less than 50 years ago, the ill-starred mothers of this ransomed race were not allowed to be modest. There was no living man to whom they could cry for protection against the men who not only owned them, body and soul, but also the souls of their husbands, their brothers and alas, their sons. But in spite of this dark and painful past, I believe that colored women are just as strong and just as weak as any other women with like, training, education and environment."

Williams's eloquent arguments opened some doors, but not many. In 1895 she became the first black woman admitted to the Chicago Women's Club, a prominent society group, as well as to the Chicago Library Board. But throughout the first half of the 20th century, black women would continue to aspire, mostly in vain, to regain the virtue and feminine respect they had lost during slavery. "A colored woman, however respectable, is lower than the white prostitute," one anonymous black woman wrote in the *Independent* in 1902. "The Southern white woman will declare that no Negro women are virtuous, yet she places her innocent children in their care."[27]

White men may have run the country at the turn of the century, but white women continually denied us the respect we so passionately sought. By the time the civil rights movement and the women's liberation movement began competing for black women's attentions, many black women had come to think of the white woman as her enemy. "I charge the white woman with complicity," said Dara Abubakari, a New Orleans activist in 1970. "When things went down with the black woman, if we had gotten together then, we would have been able to change things. But the white woman, up to now, chose to be a china doll. Even the woman's suffrage movement, after they got the vote, they did nothing else. They acquiesced."[28]

While the modern women's rights movement was driven by white women's entry into the work force, black women saw "the problem with no name" as an irrelevant middle-class problem. "We had worked throughout our entire history in America, often in white women's kitchens and homes. Some white man wrote this book about the black matriarchy, saying that black women ran the community," said Margaret Wright, a Los Angeles mother, active in several 1970s organizations including Women Against Repression, a black feminist group. "Which is bull. We don't run no community. We went out and worked because they wouldn't give our men jobs. This is where some of us are different from the white women's liberation movement. We don't think work liberates you. We've been doing it so damned long." [29]

Inherent in the civil rights movement was a hope, at least for a certain population of women, that equal rights for black people meant that they would get their shot at being the prototypical 1950s housewife, the very role that white women were so anxious to shake. "[During the 1960s] many of the black women in the movement used to joke—but it was partly serious—that part of why they were fighting was so black men would be able to get good jobs and they would be able to stay home like white women and have their men take care of them," said Dr. Alvin Pouissant, a Harvard professor and psychologist. "I think there was always more ambivalence about the women's movement on the part of some black women. It meant that they were losing out on their chance to be in this dependent role." [30]

Making Our Peace with White Women

ALL THE WHILE, the majority of white women in America were hardly aware of how large they loomed in black women's psychology. Elizabeth Taylor probably never thought twice about the fact that Cleopatra looked a lot more like a sister than she did. Farrah Fawcett never thought her blonde 'do tormented black women with thick, nappy hair. And Bo Derek definitely never gave us credit for her braids. It must have seemed that black women's anger and suspicion had nothing to do with them at all. But we had been taught, for generations, that white women were not to be trusted. Not until white women scholars and activists such as Gloria Steinem and Gerda Lerner listened to our anger without defensiveness that a level of honest, substantive communication began.

Young white women today are well aware of the ways that the old boy network is still in place, but they have a harder time copping to the fact that white privilege still exists. As the income gap closes between black and white women, we have become more than peers; we are also, sometimes, rivals. When one black woman I interviewed was promoted in her last job, she felt a definite schism from white women who had once been supportive. "I felt as if I took the job away from them," she says. "It was their job to have and somebody gave it to me. A lot of white women are not aware that they still feel entitled to certain things. The belief was I didn't earn it." More and more black women are finding themselves in the position of outpacing their white female friends in the workplace. In management positions, white women still earn more. But in fields such as sales and administrative support roles, a 1998 Census survey found that black women are beginning to earn slightly more.

The flip side to this competition is that we are no longer strangers. Black women no longer suspect that white women look down on us, morally or professionally; white women no longer expect us to be in a position of servitude. We have deeper emotional bonds than any other generation before us. African-American women today are more likely to have close white female friends that date back to college, high school or even earlier. "My best friend in the whole word is a black woman," says Walteen Grady-Truely. "But numerically, I have more white women friends than black women friends. Just this past weekend, I called some women I went to college with. They're white and I wondered, 'What does this say about me that I'm calling these white women?' But I found it was really valuable just to have this conversation with women who knew me at a particular stage of development."

When and Where We Enter

AS BLACK WOMEN continue to achieve, educationally and in the work place, we are finding that we hit the glass ceiling of gender before we hit the glass ceiling of race. "I don't feel it's necessary to say that I'm black. It's obvious you can see that," says Liba Daniels. "So definitely, I'm a woman first."

We are back in the conference room in Culver City discussing race and gender with Amina, Asali and their daughters. Liba knows that it was because of her mother's strong racial allegiances that she has the strength to be her own woman. "I feel that I can go wherever I want to go, that I can do whatever I want to do," says Liba. "You can decide how you're going to treat me, but know that I'm going to treat you accordingly. If you're going to base it upon race, then fine. I grew up among people who were very focused on black consciousness, I don't let racism define me." Asali looks at her daughter with a proud, but curious wonder. "When I was her age, I was nowhere as mature as she is," she says. "She has a strong sense of herself. When I was a girl, we'd go around saying every day 'black is beautiful.' Liba doesn't have to; it's a natural truth for her. It's a given." While Asali still lives in a predominantly black neighborhood and moves only in black social circles, Liba's network of friends is decidedly multiethnic. Asali sees this as one of her daughter's many strengths, "I don't think she has any problems associating with whites, Asians, Hispanics, whatever. As a matter of fact, in high school she went to a prom with a white boy." The whole group laughs while Liba looks a little embarrassed at the memory of it. "That was something, huh?" Liba says, with a grin. You can only imagine the eyebrows that were raised when a girl who was raised in a black power collective turned around and took a white date to the prom. Asali turns and gives her daughter a hug. "I was a little bit shocked but I got over it. It was no big deal."

What's still a big deal for Liba is succeeding as a woman in a profession where women rarely make it to the top. She has more black male role models in her field than women of any color. "I'm very concerned with gender issues in my industry," she says. "For instance, there was a film that was based on a script about men in the navy. They distinctly did not want a woman production designer for it. They wanted a man. Probably someone who had liked ships as a child. They simply weren't interviewing any women."

The conversation turns to role models and a number of names come up. Amina mentions the Reverend Vashti MacKenzie, the first woman bishop in the A.M.E., the largest black church in the nation. Not surprisingly, Maya Angelou is mentioned. Makina says she likes B. Smith, the restaurateur and Food Network host. "It's funny that Martha Stewart became so famous for domestic stuff because for years, black women played that role. She can cook, clean, decorate. For years, white women hired us to do that and because we thought it meant we were a stereotype, we stopped."

For Funeka, now a teacher in a Los Angeles area charter school, race and gender are equally puzzling issues. She knows that she is coming of age in a time of unprecedented success for black women, but she worries about what is happening with black men. Her guilt isn't as great as the burden women carried in the 1970s when the black power movement "put black women on probation," as Michele Wallace put it. But anxiety and fear tear at her. She worries about whom she will share her success with if there aren't enough black men sitting across from her at the top. Wherever the top may be. Even before graduating, she felt isolated because the black community on her campus is 90 percent female. "I don't think we've succeeded in any way if there's no balance," Funeka says. "I don't know what it's about, but there are no black men on our campus. If it's mostly black women in college then it follows that it's going to be predominantly black women that will get those good positions. If there's no black men in college, they're not going to be in the professional places."

Midsentence, Funeka does something that shocks the women in the room. She bursts into tears. Later, the women will tell me that they can count on one hand the amount of times they have seen her cry. As the group breaks up to comfort Funeka, I stare in wonder at the pure emotion in her shaking shoulders. Her body rocks back and forth as if to say no. No, no, no. Her sorrow seems to echo a primal loss, a sorrow that has nothing to do with wanting a man, not being able to find a man or hoping the man that left you will come back. This sorrow, as Maya Angelou once explained it, has precious little to do with individual black men at all. "There is a schism which exists between black men and women, and it's really painful and frightening because we were taken together from the African continent," says Angelou. "We lay spoon fashion, back to belly, in the filthy hatches of slave ships and in our own and each other's excrement and urine. We stood up on the auction block together.

We were sent to work before sunrise, came back after sunset together. We have been equals and we are in danger if we lose that balance. Our people will have paid all those dues for nothing."

The women in the group gather around Funeka as they have gathered together for more than 30 years. Amina and Asali offer comforting embraces, but they do not tell her she is wrong about the dearth of black men in her present or her future. Makina, who is only 19, tells Funeka that we are lost if we begin to see our strength as our weakness, if we blame our successes for the black man's burden. "Black women are going to be the ones to take our people forward," Makina says. "The men are not able to do it, so we're going to have to be the ones to do it. You know how the Bible says the last shall be first? Black women were always last after white women, after black men. But I think we're going to be the ones."

Her words echo the rallying cry of Anna Julia Cooper, who in 1858 earned a doctorate from the Sorbonne. "Only the black woman can say, when and where I enter, the entire black race enters with me." More than ever before, Cooper's words ring true. It's not about what black women have been given or even what we have survived. Our hard work and the difficult truths we've been willing to tell have brought the black community to unprecedented levels of economic and educational success.[31]

CHAPTER 7

The Onlys:
Success and Isolation

FAMILY RESPONSIBILITY RELATIONSHIPS SUCCESS MOTHERHOOD BALANCE

THROUGHOUT MY CONVERSATIONS with successful black women who had overcome tremendous obstacles to achieve so much, there was a persistent tinge of loneliness. It wasn't that they didn't have loving families, partners and friends. It was that for some part of the day, they were in a sphere where no one, or almost no one, shared their perspective as black and female. It could be the black woman who worked at an up-scale realtor who had to turn a blind eye to the very real redlining that went on at her company every day (*redlining* being the defacto system of not showing apartments or homes in certain neighborhoods to blacks). Or it could be the black woman who told me she has plenty of interactions with blacks during the day, but went home at night to a neighborhood where all but her closest neighbors were white. One too many times to be funny, she was mistaken for a live-in domestic.

Growing up in Los Angeles in the 1950s and 1960s was Lynette Hall's first schooling in multiculturalism. Her parents lived near the University of Southern California (USC), in the neighborhood now known as South Central. Back then, it was an experiment in integra-tion—an experiment that worked well. Great African-American artists like Jacob Lawrence depicted the migration of blacks from the South to the North. But the migration to the west was just as significant. Whites may have come to California in the 1880s seeking gold, but the blacks who traveled to Arizona, Nevada and California hoped to stake a claim to a way of life that was as free as humanly possible from Jim Crow and its dehumanizing practices.

Lynette's father left Louisiana in 1941; her mother joined him not long after. It was during my first interview with Lynette that I first heard the term "the Onlys." We were sitting at the bar in Gabriel's, an Italian restaurant near Manhattan's Central Park. I asked her how often other blacks are present at the professional and social events she attends in California. She just laughed. "Are you kidding?" she asked. "It's so rare that Paul [her husband] and I started calling ourselves 'the Onlys.'" Yet, when she tells me about her childhood in Los Angeles and the life her parents left behind in Louisiana, it occurs to me that she lives in an odd parallel universe to the one of her parents' youth. They grew up in a world of whites only and as Lynette describes it, "My father escaped segregation, the humiliation and frustration. He needed to leave that world and he made sure I never experienced it, because I was raised in California." Lynette's life, while sweeter in so many ways, is tinged by the realization that the signs may have come down but the world is only half changed. Often, if she or her husband isn't in the room, then it still is whites only, not by mandate, but by habit, and sometimes by preference.

When Lynette's father left for the war in 1943, her mother and aunt lived in San Francisco rooming houses with other women: sharing childcare duties, traveling to day laborer jobs on the train across the Bay Bridge. When her father returned home from the war, he bought a house in Los Angeles through the help of the G.I. Bill. She speaks lovingly of the opening sequence of the film *Devil in a Blue Dress* where South Central Los Angeles is not depicted as a ghetto, but as a commu-nity of white clapboard houses and well-tended streets. "There was such pride of home ownership," she remembers. "When I saw Denzel Washington mowing the lawn, I thought, 'That's my dad!'" The moment expressed so many things: the hope of the civil rights movement, the pride of home ownership, a black man's pride in being well employed, all wrought through the single gesture of mowing the lawn. If, through her success, Lynette has come to experience life as one of the Onlys— one of the only black woman producers at NBC and later ABC, one of the only black families in the exclusive enclave of Montecito, the only black face at the horse-riding championships or at a wine-tasting in Tuscany—then hers is an isolation crafted by her parents' hard work and vision.

It's a little-discussed fact that our history as black Americans has ill prepared us for the ways in which class isolates us and sets us apart from our people. We are, despite the legacy of stereotypes and racial profiling, no strangers to achievement. From Reconstruction through the modern civil rights movement, we've operated as a community with a very prominent sense of "us" versus "them." We are, however, struggling to sustain ourselves in an environment where our communities are often in peril. It's our privilege as individuals that makes what is happening to black people so stark.

What the women in this book are experiencing is an unprecedented battle. Not "us" versus "them," but "me" versus "them." For many of these women, to think of a "me," separate and apart from the black community is unsettling and confusing. The macro issues of race and segregation in the 20th century—separate schools, "whites only" lunch counters, Rosa Parks's historic stand in the front of that Montgomery bus—lent themselves well to the notion of group protest. But the microinequities of 21st-century racism are battles we must fight largely on our own. If you're a black professor denied tenure, a lawyer earning six figures who's turned down by a co-op board on the Upper East Side or an advertising director whose boss won't give you the big Nike account, you can cry yourself a river or throw yourself a pity party, but the masses of black people are not going to stand with you. Al Sharpton won't go to jail for you. Jesse Jackson won't organize a boycott. You're on your own, sister.

High-Class Problems

IT WOULD BE EASY to underestimate the historical psychological benefits we've derived from having both the support and the sympathy of the black community. Recently, I sat down to watch *The Original Kings of Comedy*, Spike Lee's hit film about one of the most successful comedy tours ever. The documentary features four top black comedians: Steve Harvey, Cedric the Entertainer, D. L. Hughley and Bernie Mac. After watching the film, my fiancé, who is white, said, "It was funny, but almost every joke was about how black people do things one way and white people do things one way. That gets tired after a while."

It was true. There were 100 jokes about how black people drive/dance/make love/get married one way and how white people do things quite differently. Some of the jokes were at the expense of black people, such as the riffs about the "ghetto weddings" and brides who do booty-shaking dances down the aisle. Other jokes were at the expense of white people, such as the comedian who joked that when black people get fed up at work, they go into chill mode taking extra-long lunch hours and telling you to photocopy those documents your damn self. In contrast, the comedian said, a white man who's unhappy with his job is coming back with a gun. The joke being, "And they say we're violent."

The jokes may not be uniformly funny, but they play on the deep need we have to be validated in a country that continues to mistreat and misunderstand us. The underlying tenet of these jokes is to create an atmosphere of total acceptance. So maybe the white girl that you trained at the bank is now your supervisor; maybe you're 50 years old and making minimum wage; maybe your phone's been cut off for the umpteenth time and you haven't seen nor heard from your baby's daddy in over a year. You go to a show like *The Original Kings of Comedy* and the message is "no matter how hard it is, we've been there." Moreover, the show reinforces a familiar and comforting sense of community. At the end of the day, even in the year 2000 when the movie debuted, it's "us" versus "them," black folks versus white folks.

I want to say that there are no jokes about the Onlys on these comedy tours because, as Eddie Murphy would say, "this shit ain't funny." But of course, it is. Every successful black woman I know can spin a tale about being mistaken for a salesperson, a domestic or a secretary into a humorous ditty about ignorant white people. Once, when I was senior associate editor at *Premiere* magazine, I had a long-running phone relationship with a movie publicist from Los Angeles. She asked if she could visit me in New York on her next trip to the East Coast. It's the law of the magazine jungle that editors are higher on the food chain than publicists. Publicists are trying to pitch stories about their clients, editors have the power to either get the story in the magazine or to turn the publicist down. Meeting an editor at *Premiere* was a big deal for a young publicist and the woman called me several times to confirm, thanking me—in advance—for taking time out of my busy day. When she showed up at the office, my assistant called to say that she'd arrived and I went out to greet her. "Lauren," I said, extending my hand. "Hi!" she said, brightly. "Are you Veronica's assistant?" I didn't stop smiling, "No, I'm Veronica." It wouldn't have been much of an incident if, when she and her colleague got back to the lobby, they didn't begin blabbing right away at how shocked they were to find out that I was black. "She didn't sound black on the phone," Lauren told the colleague that accompanied her. "Are you sure?," her coworker asked. "I wonder how she got this job?" Lauren continued. And so on and so forth, for a good ten minutes while they checked their messages on their cell phones and gathered their winter coats from the hall closet. Five minutes after their departure, the receptionist—who was black—called me out to the lobby and gave me the blow-by-blow. We had a good laugh and enjoyed the way their ignorance seemed to grow exponentially—first, in assuming that I was my assistant, then in assuming that because she was black, the receptionist was also deaf.

However, the camaraderie I was able to share with some of the support staff I worked with was the exception and not the rule. For the most part, these interactions were built on superficial encounters that could draw on the dynamic of "us" versus "them." The more subtle moments of isolation had to be endured on my own. No assistant could commiserate with the pain of having story ideas turned down because they were "too black" or the frustration of finding out that I was being grossly underpaid compared to a white colleague who shared the same job. These kinds of incidents fit underneath the banner of what my friend Lise Funderburg calls "high-class problems." It's a basic theory of mental health that if something is a problem to you, then it's a problem. But for successful black women, these high-class problems can become regions of guilt, shame and isolation. Often, we bite our tongue for fear of seeming too angry to our white peers or of seeming ungrateful and elitist to the blacks we hold dear.

We are the baby boomers of achievement, the largest group across the board to gain significant professional and financial recognition in the years since the civil rights movement. At the same time, we are often the Onlys in our immediate families and among childhood friends: the only one to go to college, the only one to attend graduate school, the only one to own a second home and so forth. Despite their own financial success, few black comedians are going to risk a joke about the racist at the Jaguar car dealership or the white law partner who thinks he's hip with the brothers because he never misses a Knicks game. The common argument is that the jokes don't reach a wide enough audience. But it's also true that to the vast majority of black people who are struggling to make ends meet, if you are at a Jaguar dealership or a law firm in the first place, you're no longer part of the community. When you've got high-class problems, you're on your own.

The conversations I've had with successful black women over the past three years emphasize that they feel this invisibility and isolation acutely. They don't feel represented on the pages of black magazines and, to a large extent, on television or in film. The women I spoke to were so eager to participate in this book because it's rare that they are able to speak freely about their problems. But they were not interested solely in complaining. They know their lives are sweet—they've worked hard to build careers, homes and families that they can be proud of. It seemed to me that what they longed for, more than anything, was to find role models where there are so few.

For the most part, the women I interviewed were all confident that they could do the tasks they were being paid so handsomely for and displayed an extraordinary amount of pride in their professional lives. What they were curious about was life outside of work: how other women maintained friendships and romantic relationships, spent and saved their money and dealt with the deep chasm of being haves in a world of have nots. They also hoped to be mentors, so that the next generation of Onlys had a blueprint that would make them feel less alone.

A Place She Could Call Home

AS A CHILD, LYNETTE HALL never expected that achievement would set her apart from the black community. Even as an only child, she had felt embraced by the tight knit neighborhood of folks that she grew up in. Blacks in California in the 1950s who came from the deep South held onto a certain kind of neighborliness. The Butlers down the street may well have attended church with your relatives back home. And on New Year's Day, every kitchen on the block cooked their variation on Hoppin' John: baked ham and cornbread, along with black-eyed peas for luck, rice for health, greens for good fortune. The few Mexicans who lived in the lower-middle-class neighborhood were welcome, as were other Latinos. Lynette's mother became a life-long friend with the Panamanians who lived next door. The white families who chose not to move to the valley when blacks moved in didn't have to go out of their way to be friendly. They showed their penchant for racial tolerance by staying put. "It was a wonderful heterogenous neighborhood, where we lived next door to the Gonzales, the Smiths and the McClanahans," the 40-something Lynette remembers. "It was a great time. The best of the best. It was a better Los Angeles than the one I moved away from five years ago."

Fair-skinned with pale blue eyes, Lynette could be a cousin of the actress Vanessa L. Williams. A century ago, an ambitious black woman with her complexion might have considered passing for white. In California, in the 1960s, when light-skinned women such as Angela Davis and Elaine Brown were proving that the revolution would not only be televised, but colorized as well, passing was the furthest thing from her mind. As a freshman at USC, Lynette remembers hanging out with other African-American students on what were jokingly referred to as "the ghetto steps" and sometimes getting a double take. "People would see me, and not knowing my ethnic origin, they would be puzzled," she says.

Lynette's father, a contractor and carpenter, did well during the postwar years, and her mother was one of the few black women of her era to have the luxury to be a stay-at-home mom. Both parents instilled in their daughter, their only child, the absolute necessity of attending college. For blacks of their generation, a formal college education was one of the few weapons a talented young woman would have against the dual challenges of racism and sexism. "College was just the assumption," Lynette says. "The career wasn't as important as going. My daughter knows what she wants to do, but doesn't necessarily know how to achieve it. I was the opposite. I didn't know what I wanted to do careerwise, but I knew I had to go to school. This was true for all of my friends. Everybody was motivated, everybody was doing something."

In many ways, Lynette's experience epitomizes the transition of black women who always considered themselves black first, to a generation of women that considered themselves women first. In her lower-middle-class black community of the 1950s and 1960s, the smart black women became teachers. "In high school, they were my role models," Lynette says. "We also had a Big Sister program in high school, and I remember being enamored of some of the senior big sisters in high school." Then, at the age of 19, she made the biggest decision in her 'woman first' transition. She transferred from USC to Mills College, a tiny women's college in northern California. At Mills, in the 1960s, Lynette found her groove. "I was so happy to be again in a very, very culturally and racially diverse group of people," she says. "The ratio of students to teachers, at the time, was 11 to 1. I really found my voice there at Mills. I loved being in San Francisco and being around all of those very strong women."

Having grown up an only child, Mills was an opportunity for Lynette to adopt 900 women as sisters and role models. "I had grown up alone and I had my own drill," she says. "I was so curious about how other women kept their rooms, how they studied, when they did their laundry, what they ate. What did other women do? I would walk down the campus sometimes and just be in a dream world. I had come to this great place and I was happy. I had great, great friendships and I had a really clear feeling of who I was. There's something about going to sleep at night in a dorm with 99 other women and realizing that we're all completely different and we're all cool. I would lie awake sometimes thinking, 'I can't believe I'm here. I can't believe I'm me!'"

It was also at Mills that Lynette first developed the confidence that would help her deal with the isolation of being one of the only black women in her field. "Being there, I knew that I was going to be successful, I just knew," she recalls. "I was around too many people who had it going on. We were all on task. We were all in the same direction. There wasn't anybody in my college who didn't have a dream, who didn't have a goal."

The 1970s were the golden era of black television. Flip Wilson had his own variety show and *Sanford and Son, Good Times, The Jeffersons* and *Fat Albert and the Cosby Kids* were all Top 20 shows. Lynette got a job as a page and found her calling. "All these great shows were there and I was there with a great group of people," she says. "We led tours by day and worked on shows by night. We got to know production and that's how I fell into on-air promotion." She spent six years at NBC and another eleven years at ABC, where she eventually rose to the position of Director of On-Air Promotion.

It's noteworthy that Lynette made her career in the field of on-air promotions where her responsibility was to sell programming to viewers of all races. If she had been responsible for content, pitching the network shows that did or didn't feature black characters, race might have been more of a daily issue in the work place. Angela Kyle, the 31-year-old senior director of business development for Live Planet, sees her transition from content to the business side as being significant in her life as an Only. "When I was the only black in a setting where I was making editorial judgments, people looked to me as the spokesperson and that's exactly what I did," she says. "I remember being at Simon & Schuster when we looked at Jill Nelson's manuscript for *Volunteer Slavery*. A lot of the comments at our editorial meeting were 'Oh, we don't like her tone' or 'She's too angry.' Then they would look at me and ask whether or not I agreed. There wasn't an explicit mandate, but I was the person that was going to look out for the interests of black writers. Because I was there and I could and I was in the position and I had a responsibility." After attending business school at Columbia University and doing postgraduate work at the London School of Economics, race became less of an issue. "In business development, you're looking at projects and judging them solely on their financial viability," Angela says. "You're evaluating companies with pretty objective criteria."

For Lynette, her work at NBC was the fulfillment of the dream that began with her parents' migration from Louisiana and crystallized in the all women environment of Mills College. "I felt very powerful," she says. "I'm at the network, working on the affiliates campaign, planning the fall season, picking out music, designing graphics. I've got these beautiful children, a loving marriage, a handsome husband." In 1992, her life changed drastically. The Los Angeles riots decimated the multi-racial community where she and her husband were raising their daughters. For many of LA's citizens, the three-day civil unrest was a shocking news story that confirmed their worst fears about the realities of racial harmony. For Lynette, the fear and the hurt cut much deeper. The riots were the denouement in the breaking of a covenant that the City of Angels had made with her father some 60 years before. The safe, clean, multiracial neighborhood of her childhood had become prime territory for drug dealing, gang violence and the glorification of a gangsta lifestyle in rap videos. Instead of becoming more accepting and more integrated, Los Angeles was becoming increasingly striated racially, a collection of separate and unequal neighborhoods. Her husband's television production company was thriving, as was her own career, but they had not worked for so long to raise their children in a gated community, where they suspected the gates were really meant to keep out unruly blacks and Latinos.

Exclusivity and Isolation

FOR YEARS, SANTA BARBARA had been a special place for Lynette Hall and her husband, Paul. When they married, they were working too many hours to truly get away, so they drove two hours north and spent their honeymoon in the charming city of old-fashioned Spanish haciendas and cobblestone streets. They returned as often as they could, planning romantic getaways to the city when they were childless and later bringing their children to play on the city's pristine beaches. As their careers advanced, they decided to buy a condo in the city and it became their home away from home—a place to spend holidays and every weekend they could squeeze in the drive from LA. It had been their refuge during the riots, and in their aftermath, they asked themselves a question that had long been churning in their hearts and minds. Could they move to Santa Barbara full time? They loved the mountains of Santa Barbara and its beaches. But how would their daughters fare—as African-American girls—in a city more enriched with do-good liberalism than any actual diversity? After much soul-searching, they decided the up sides outweighed the downsides.

"We just felt the need to be in a wonderful, safe, clean, healthy environment that was near the ocean so the girls could breathe deeply," Lynette explains. In the mainstream media, blacks are rarely depicted as environmentalists, but of course we care about the environment and the quality of air we breathe as much as any other people. Lynette and Paul are not alone among African-American parents in wanting their kids to grow up in a pastoral environment. Not many African-American families have the luxury to make these choices. "We wanted a place where the girls could feel..." Lynette begins. We are sitting in the living room of her house, the fireplace roaring on a chilly February afternoon and I can see as she hesitates that she is taking in all the material possessions around her. "Safe" is the word she comes up with, and I can tell that she doesn't like the notion of equating wealth, and proximity to it, with safety.

Lynette and Paul purchased a beautiful home in Montecito, an exclusive enclave of Santa Barbara where their neighbors include Jeff Daniels the actor and Sue Grafton the best-selling mystery writer. Oprah has just purchased a $50 million home blocks away. You arrive chez Hall by an idyllic side street, shaded by sycamore trees. The Spanish-style house is landscaped with gigantic aloe plants and other tropical varieties, a gate offers a peek into a large parking area where the familys' myriad cars, including Paul's prized mint-condition BMW 513, are housed. The inside of the three-bedroom house is like a spread for *Elle Decor:* slate marble floors, paintings and sculptures make the living room come alive. The girls, Jordan and Kendall, each have their own bedroom with private baths, decorated to suit their personalities. Kendall's is a shrine to her hero, Teresa Weatherspoon, and the women of the WNBA. Jordan's room reflects the love of movies she shares with her producer father. There are fireplaces everywhere: in the family room, in the master bedroom, on a deck outside near the swimming pool. The library features first editions by Langston Hughes and James Baldwin. The Halls's extensive art collection includes a drawing of their daughter done by the award-winning painter, Lois Mailou Jones. For

Lynette, the house and the life she has built for her family are part of the vision she developed for herself as a student at Mills. Recall when she talked about her time at college being the point when "My voice was very clear and I knew that I was going to be successful. I just knew." This house and being part of this community is, at least in part, an embodiment of Lynette's early dreams.

But this is also where the notion of the Onlys begins to take on another dimension in Lynette's life. She and Paul are the children of black southerners, who moved to California to escape the "whites only" limitations of the Jim Crow south. As a successful woman, who benefited from the civil rights movement and the women's right's movement, who found her voice at a women's college, Lynette spent much of her personal and professional life being one of the only black women in any given room. Now her daughters, Jordan and Kendall, are sixteen and nine years old, respectively. As the Halls are the only black family with children living in Montecito, Jordan and Kendall are the Onlys every time they leave their front door. The critical difference is this: life underneath the magnifying lens of race is the only life the girls have ever known. And as Jordan would sometimes remind her mother in fits of adolescent pique, it's not like she had any choice about whether to live among other black people. "The thing about being Onlys is that for Paul and me it happened to us as adults," Lynette explains. "Our being able to handle it and to assume whatever posture we needed to get through that feeling was kind of an unconscious thing. I can be 'the Only' and not even think about it anymore. What's hurt the most for us is how it's affected our teenage daughter. She's been confronted with the Onlys much sooner than we were. Sometimes we questioned the move." She pauses and speaks slowly as if to disguise the wavering in her voice, "We think we did the right thing."

Lynette's held onto the belief that Los Angeles isn't the answer, though she's worked to facilitate trips back to the city so Jordan can keep up with her elementary school friends. "There's a girl Jordan has known since kindergarten," Lynette explains. "She's Korean American and goes to a great high school in Los Angeles. I think Jordan envies the diversity of people that her friend was seeing. I try to stress to her that it's important to cultivate not only a racially diverse circle, but an economically diverse and culturally diverse circle as well."

While Lynette lives in Montecito full time with the kids, Paul commutes to Los Angeles, where he has transitioned from producing for television to pursuing feature films. Lynette admits that in some ways this move was easiest on her. "I walk between two worlds easily," Lynette says. "I always have. I think I honed that skill at ABC where you have to be able to walk into a Century City programming meeting and get real comfortable, real quick. I can be here, I can be in New York, I can be on a farm and I don't have to think twice about it anymore. When she reached middle school, Jordan grew very, very weary of the lack of cultural diversity. Paul as a black man grew very, very weary early on."

Black women are a rarity in Montecito; black men are even more exotic. Paul would grow frustrated when storekeepers and other service personnel treated him like a visitor. Sometimes, he'll have to say, "Excuse me, I live around the corner, I don't need that to be delivered." At times, Paul wants to order a book at the local bookstore and they explain that he shouldn't because it will take a few days and perhaps he should order it when he gets back home. He is acutely aware of the reaction when he says, "Oh, I can come back for it. I live here."

This is a phenomenon I am acutely aware of myself. When I went to vote in the most recent election, the woman at the desk looked up at me and said, "You're in the wrong place, sweetheart. This here is for people who live in the neighborhood, not for people who work here. You've got to vote where you live." When I explained that I did live in the neighborhood, she could barely contain her surprise. Did I mention that the woman was black? My own experiences as well as the stories the Halls tell are anecdotal footnotes to the growing black middle class and what Harvard economist William Julius Wilson calls the declining significance of race. This is not to say that race doesn't matter. But rather to say that race as any sort of telltale sign of education and financial success is misguided at best, faulty and myopic at worst. The brother wearing hip-hop clothes and ordering whiskey at an up-scale bar could be a multi-millionaire record producer, a stockbroker or a design firm CEO. But every middle-class black person has one, if not many, stories to tell about being mistaken for the help, or a criminal, at some horrific, now humorous, point.

Making Connections as an Only:
And the Importance of a Sister Fix

IT WAS IMPORTANT for me to include Lynette Hall in this book for several reasons. One because she is a woman who, while clearly successful, has never been part of the public eye. She's not an on-air reporter, nor has she appeared in the pages of *Black Enterprise* or *Essence*. While clearly exceptional, she's not the exception. Even in her self-demarcated status as one of the Onlys, she represents the vast number of black women who are the heart, soul and backbone of the black middle class. I was also impressed with her attitude. Lynette regards this journey between two worlds, black and white, as an adventure rather than a political mission. At times, she seems equal parts Amelia Earhart and Fannie Lou Hamer. "I think it's a great opportunity for me to live my life in this kind of environment to let people see who I am," she said of her move to Montecito. "To let people see a black person and 'Hello! We live like you do.'"

It's easy to emphasize the challenges of being the Only, but it also has its advantages. There's an enormous amount of creativity that one develops when you are set apart from a group. Because whites represent the mainstream, blacks are far more intimately aware and comfortable with how things operate in the white world than vice versa. A black woman who is the Only in her company or her community has a chance to not only blaze new trails and dispel stereotypes, but to set new standards because she is the standard. When I became an editor at the *New York Times Magazine*, many of my black colleagues in journalism expressed surprise that I was able to land such a senior position when I wear my hair in dreadlocks. The idea being that my hair would be too bohemian for white folks. It may have been different if I worked at a law firm or a brokerage house where there is a strict conservative dress code for whites and blacks, men and women alike. But what I found at the *Times* was that most white people knew little and could care less about all the dynamics of hair that the black community is so often obsessed with. My colleagues didn't know the difference between "good" (read straightened) hair or "bad" (read kinky) hair. James Baldwin once said that what the oppressor does to you, you eventually learn to do better and more effectively to yourself. Certainly, there was a time when whites held out special opportunities for blacks whose features most closely resembled their own. But from a heritage of an imposed preference for fair skin and straight hair, we've had nearly a century of holding up those standards on our own—with little pressure from the mainstream world. Darker skinned women (including some with natural hairstyles!) have scaled every height. Whoopi Goldberg wins an Oscar, painter Kara Walker wins a MacArthur "genius" grant, Ruth Simpson is president of Brown University and still, in our own communities, we've got the dying old bag of colorism on life support.

A few years ago, I attended a conference for black women in the law. I was especially impressed with one of the keynote speakers, a lawyer at a white-shoe firm in New York. She herself wore a straightened conservative hairstyle, yet she described a situation where a white partner asked what she thought of a summer associate's Afro. "I think it's quite elegant," she told the man. "Don't you?" He paused, looking at the young woman with new eyes, then agreed, "Yes, I do." The moral of the story, the lawyer explained, was that we who are among the few in our work place have the opportunity to help or hinder the blacks around us. "We teach white people what to think," she says. "Because for the most part they don't know." A century ago, as domestics, black women wielded a tremendous amount of power—especially in the lives of the children they raised and the white women whose homes they ran. These women who were nannies, cooks and maids taught generations of whites about sensitivity, humanity and the dignity of our race. Now we're operating on a different playing field, but the pioneering level of intimacy remains the same. In the boardrooms, at power lunches and Sunday brunches, we have, as peers, an even greater power to banish stereotypes and broaden perspectives.

Seeing her role as the Only as an opportunity to serve as a cultural ambassador of sorts has become a pleasure for Lynette. One of the first things Lynette did when the family moved was to join a local book club. She takes great enjoyment making traditional New Orleans gumbo to share with the white women in the group. "Everybody had gumbo!" she said. "That's tremendous to me, at my age, to share and acknowledge culture, to answer questions. I can answer questions, at 48, that being an African-American woman in Los Angeles I might never have been asked. Women living in a smaller community have a lot to say, which is amazing."

There have been awkward moments. Because Lynette is so fair-skinned, people sometimes forget that a black woman is in the room. "I can remember being in meetings where a joke was about to come out of somebody's mouth," she says. "Then they look around the room, look at me and catch their tongue. But maybe what helps me is that I'm not afraid to talk about it when I need to. I'm the first person to pick up the phone and leave a message for any of my sister-friends when I feel the need to connect."

This ability to reach out and connect to other black women is key for women who work in predominantly white companies and live in predominantly white neighborhoods. It's not that these women don't develop friendships with women of other races. But one gains sustenance from a friend who speaks your language, who doesn't think you're too sensitive when you describe a subtle racial snub and who can be your Kwesi Mfume, your rallying civil rights squad, when you're feeling like it's you versus "them." Perhaps it's because women are more open to discussing their problems, more unafraid of reaching out to another woman when as Lynette says, "they feel the need to connect," that black women are achieving to the extent that they are, while black men continue to struggle. Corporate America is still a difficult world for blacks to negotiate; if black women form and maintain stronger friendships, then that is certainly an advantage.

Even in the predominantly white neighborhood of Montecito, the Halls had striven to make their home a bastion of African-American arts and letters. At the ages of nine and sixteen, Kendall and Jordan are familiar not only with the dancers of the Alvin Ailey company, but the choreographers as well. Although theirs is a hip-hop generation, they can play name that tune with music by anyone from Miles Davis to the Stylistics to Stevie Wonder. But both girls, especially Jordan, longed for more personal connections to other African Americans, outside of their family. "Initially when we first moved here, the girls were younger and we were busier," says Lynette of their efforts to keep in touch with the black community they left behind in Los Angeles. "But we're crafting more time now to do more visiting and make more phone calls, to do more of the inclusion stuff so they don't feel so isolated and they have a clear perspective of who they are."

As an avid basketball fan, nine-year-old Jordan has found a world of black women role models in the WNBA. "Her passion for basketball is so great," Lynette explains. "If she could be anybody right now, she'd make herself Teresa Weatherspoon. She has an image, she knows who she wants to be. She has that much earlier than I ever did." For Jordan, it's been more difficult to develop her identity as a young black woman. Years of being the Only among wealthy, white peers gave her the feeling of being a perpetual outsider.

When Jordan began making the painful transition from childhood to adolescence, Lynette began to organize informal gatherings of black women that she called a "sister fix." One year, the fix took the form of a surprise birthday party for Jordan. "I invited my four great friends from high school, some cousins and some family," Lynette remembers. This was during a difficult time in Jordan's school life, when she felt isolated from the other girls at school. Sensing that a party with class-mates would only emphasize that isolation, Lynette reached into her own circle of friends to provide Jordan with the sister fix she so clearly needed. "We yelled 'Surprise!' and within ten minutes my friend Brenda was in Jordan's room, on her bed, and the two of them were engrossed in a major conversation," says Lynette. "The time we have with other black women isn't daily, but it certainly wasn't daily in LA because you get caught up in the rat race of life and driving and so on." Sitting in the living room of her home, a fire blazing inside and outside the window the pool and grill and all the sweet promises of summer visible, Lynette says, "The time we have here tends to be very memorable. We have these great conversations, make food, take pictures and capture the moments. People enjoy coming up here and we enjoy having them." While the impetus for a "sister fix" began with an impulse to be a good parent and fill the hole in her daughter's life, it was also tremendously self-nurturing, providing a high that Lynette could feed off of for weeks.

Last year, Jordan matriculated at Cate, a prestigious private school in the area. While it's not the booming cultural metropolis that LA is, it's been a vast improvement, not only in Jordan's life, but in Lynette and Paul's as well. During one of my interviews with Lynette, Jordan was visited by two upper-class black women who attend the school. Lynette pauses to chat with them and the four of them—Lynette, Jordan, and their guests—make plans to visit again. Only a few years before, it was Lynette who worked hard to create a community of black women that Jordan could reach out to, if not in person, then by phone and e-mail. Now it's Jordan who brings the sister fix home, sharing the time she spends with her black girlfriends with her mom.

A few weeks after my last visit with Lynette, I spoke to her husband, Paul, on the phone. "It's so cool," he says, his accent a mixture of Berkeley baby boomer and Miles Davis bebopper. "I had a couple of brothers from Jordan's school over at the house. One is this amazing history professor; another works in admissions. We were just watching the basketball game, talking about life. It was great." For Paul as well, Jordan has opened up a new social circle where he doesn't have to be the Only.

CHAPTER 8

Black Swans: Women of
Privilege across the Generations

FAMILY RESPONSIBILITY RELATIONSHIPS SUCCESS MOTHERHOOD BALANCE

TRUMAN CAPOTE CALLED THEM his swans: Slim Keith, Babe Paley and all of those elegant, sophisticated society girls that he admired so. But black America had their swans, too. There was the classic beauty Lena Horne—the original Black American Princess—descended from a family that had, despite the limitations of race, enjoyed generations of wealth and success. And after her, there were others: Constance Baker Motley, Dorothy Height, Diahann Carroll, Eartha Kitt, Josephine Premice. These were women who looked at the stone wall of Jim Crow and, like Michelangelo with a block of marble, saw not an impenetrable mass, but potential images that were beautiful, intelligent and transcendental of racial limitations.

All of these women weren't to the manor born. Even for those that came from comfortable financial backgrounds, theirs was a lineage that white America neither acknowledged nor accepted. When racism prevented them from getting their due as ladies, they upped the stakes and rolled the dice. Each, in her own way, set her sights on a Renaissance-style education. The performers were all triple threats: singing, dancing and acting. Connie Baker attended an Ivy League law school in 1943, a feat that was unusual enough at the time to make headlines in the Negro papers. Baker and her contemporaries traveled boldly—whether it was abroad to Europe or to the depths of Mississippi. They went where they were not invited and they were unafraid. Among them, they spoke a half-dozen languages. Needless to say, they were always impeccably coiffed and decked out in the finest clothes they could buy. They cast themselves as larger than life. If society didn't think of them as ladies, they would be queens.

Regardless of whether or not they were acknowledged by the mainstream, these women became our royalty. Role models that we could idolize, but even better, because often they were close enough to touch. Karen Moore, a 34-year-old legal assistant, lovingly refers to her husband's grandmother as a "black queen." A single mother for much of her life, Karen has spent the past ten years taking courses at night to complete her bachelor's degree. She plans to continue next year with law school. She looks to women like her husband's grandmother for inspiration that she can do it, she can become an entertainment lawyer despite her background. When I attend Karen's wedding, she makes a point to introduce me to the "black queen," Mrs. Frieda Greene. She is, as Karen described her, Lena Horne beautiful, a retired school principal and matriarch of the family. Later, Karen tells me, "she is the epitome of class. She's incredibly intelligent, always elegantly dressed, very committed to her church community, an active socialite. I just love her."

These days, there is a new generation of black swans—black women who regularly show up on the pages of *Vogue, Town and Country* and the society pages of the *New York Times*. Women like art consultant Kim Heirston, whose purchase and renovation of an Upper East Side apartment landed her on the cover of *Elle Decor.* As it is for the young white women who sit on the committees of costume balls and hospital fund raisers, some of these swans are legacy: second generation. Perhaps best known among these second-generation doyennes of style is writer-producer Susan Fales-Hill, daughter of Broadway performer Josephine Premice. Harvard-educated—with a body that mimics her mother's tall, thin lines and a wardrobe that is filled with vintage

Yves Saint Laurent and couture pieces—Fales-Hill has become a familiar face on the party pages of the *New York Times, W,* and *Town and Country.*

In May 2001, *Harper's Bazaar* named her one of the best-dressed women in America. Her portrait was totemic: a honey-colored beauty with a long, slim neck, wearing her own Azzedine Alaia dress and her own jewels. Her long, black hair is blown out and frames her face like a lion's mane. But what is truly startling is her smile and all that surrounds it. Her head is thrown back with mouth wide open, as if caught mid-guffaw. It's an expression that can be read in so many different ways. "Ha!" she might be saying, "Finally, a black woman gets her due." But her expression could just as easily represent an altogether different message. "Ha," she might be saying, "You can't expect me to take your silly lists seriously." In either case, the portrait displays an unmistakable mixture of confidence and joy. As the only black woman pictured in the portfolio of glamour shots, Susan Fales-Hill does not seem a lonely Only. She is comfortable, ebullient even, to be in her own skin.

When I invite her to talk about her mother's generation, their struggles and triumphs, as well as her own, she suggests tea at the Mark Hotel. The hotel, a quiet, opulent New York institution that radiates the aura of old money and those who wish to draw upon this aura, is just a few blocks away from Fales-Hill's Park Avenue apartment. She arrives at our four o'clock meeting, nattily turned out in slim black pants and a lovely ruffled blouse that opens at her much-photographed neck to reveal strand upon strand of pearls. It's a look that would be stuffy on a dozen other women; somehow she manages to give the impression that this is a perfectly comfortable outfit for an afternoon of running holiday errands and taking a quick meeting along the way. The waiter greets her warmly in French and Fales-Hill responds in kind, ordering her tea in French as well.

She admits that style and elegance are important to her. It's part of her heritage as the daughter of a black swan. "My mother and her friends were cut out of so many things," Fales-Hill says. "There were jobs they couldn't get, there were places they couldn't go because of their color. The one area where they had complete freedom was the way they looked—their glamour." As she explains it, the glamour was the ultimate expression of their freedom, which Jim Crow or racism could not prevent them from enjoying. Even long after Jim Crow, their careers were limited because of their color. "But no one could control how fabulous they were, how fabulous they looked, how glamorous they were," she says. "That was a very important expression of their freedom and inner dignity. That's what my mother taught me. That's why I care so much about how I dress."

For Fales-Hill, her appearances in the society pages serve two important functions. They broaden the cultural image of black women and they carry on her mother's legacy. Josephine Premice passed away in 2001 and Fales-Hill says she knows her magazine appearances, "made my mother very happy. So that makes me feel proud. She loved it." Several years ago, *Essence* magazine ran a cover package about "It Girls." Premice and Fales-Hill made the only mother-daughter appearance in the issue, a fact that didn't go unnoticed. "There was a sense that there's a legacy here," says Fales-Hill of the many compliments she received on being in the same issue that heralded her as an It Girl and her mother as part of a generation of black divas that paved the way. "It's important because black people have been deprived of our legacies; our legacies have been denied and buried. I run into a lot of her friends when I go out and they feel like, 'Okay, the legacy continues.' To some people, it may seem completely silly. But to me, it seems it's carrying on a tradition of dignity and having black women, and women of color, perceived in a different light. I happen to think this is important. There aren't enough varied images of us. It's great that we have Lil' Kim and those girls out there, but we need other images, ones that represent education and elegance."

While there may have been black swans in the 1950s and 1960s, for many young black women their lifestyle was neither attainable or, at times, politically relevant. The sea change of achievement that black women are experiencing means that more young black women have the time, money, energy or desire to lead the lifestyle of what Susan calls "a social girl." More than just appearing in newspapers, the social girl lifestyle represents a Holly Golightly mailbox full of invitations to the swankiest parties in town. "I run into a lot of girls who say they're happy to see me in the social pages," says Susan. "One young woman who works at *W* said, 'I was so excited to see your face in our magazine.

I work at the place and I never see anybody who looks like me.' To the extent that it makes people think 'This could be you,' it's important."

Although she has spent her career as a television writer and producer, Fales-Hill is now writing a biography of her mother. "My mother was a performer and started at the age of 17," she explains. "Diahann Carroll was her best friend, so that was Aunt Diahann. The two of them turned into goofy little schoolgirls together—they'd be laughing and doing silly things. Eartha Kitt, she knew from the time they were both 19 years old. They traveled together to Paris and were roommates there." Lena Horne was slightly older, but Josephine Premice did two shows with Horne. The first was a 1957 Broadway production called *Jamaica*. Of Premice's performance in that production, the *New York Times* critic wrote that Premice was a "razzle dazzle lead performer who was hot flame to Horne's cool fire." Later, in 1978, the two women joined forces in Los Angeles for a production of *Pal Joey*. Premice's circle also included Tony-winner Gloria Foster and Carmen de Lavallade, perhaps the most famous black ballerina of her generation. Susan remembers them as a glorious circle of role models. "I grew up with these extraordinary, glamorous, accomplished, sophisticated, funny, raunchy, crazy, creative, women who were real fighters," she says. "Their whole attitude was 'Nobody was going to keep us down.'"

The black swans of the 1950s, Premice, Carroll and Kitt, knew that their blackness made them unique. Rather than turn into shrinking violets, they became klieg lights. "They walked into a room and eclipsed everybody else," says Susan. "They were just stunning to look at. Even the women in my mother's family were very independent—some of them chose not to get married. They were multilingual, well dressed, sophisticated. My female role models were women who were hyper-glamorous, hyper-intelligent, educated."

As she got older, the messages of privilege, entitlement and confidence began to sink in. Susan says she never fell for the stereotypes that "pretty girls were stupid," or "women who pay attention to their appearance are not nurturing." How could she, when her mother cooked three-course meals in full makeup and packed her and her brother's school lunches in false eyelashes and furs? Susan remembers being at her 30th birthday party and introducing her mother to the guy she was dating. "Your mother seems like she would be a very self-centered woman," her beau tells her. "Why are you saying that?" asks Susan, who is shocked. "Well, she's so glamorous," the guy responds with a shrug. But Susan isn't buying it. "Let me tell you, this self-centered woman was a great mom," she says. "Let me tell you all that this woman did."

Like so many other 30 somethings who live in a big city, Susan is trying to balance marriage and dreams of a family with her own career ambitions and goals. "Balance," that buzzword of the '90s, continues to be a bee in the bonnet of the 21st-century woman. Susan wants to have it all and she thinks that things have changed enough since her mother's day that she just might be able to pull it off. But she also looks to her mother's generation for important lessons about achievement and family and what you get in the end. "There are always trade-offs," she says. "What I want in a successful life is yes, a degree of intellectual achievement and professional achievement, but I also think there's emotional and spiritual achievement and I think that comes through relationships. I'm not saying that if you don't have a husband, you're not a success. But I think there's a growth that happens through being with other people and being in long-standing relationships with other people. Regardless of whether it's a parent or it's a child, whether it's a friend or a spouse. Balance is key."

Since her mother's death, she's what psychologists now call "a motherless daughter." She has seen the full arc of a woman's life and that has a profound effect on how seriously she plans her own. "The main message I got from my mother and her friends wasn't about having it all, it was about being it all," she says. "You could be a phenomenal artist and a great mom and a loving person and politically active. You could be all these incredible things. It was less about having it all because certainly, none of them got it all in the end. They all sacrificed something. My mother sacrificed a tremendous amount of her career and creative drive to raise us."

One of the gifts that Josephine Premice's Haitian-born parents gave her was the gift of entitlement; it was no small feat for a black woman in the 1950s to expect the very best that life had to offer and then to take the goodies, without guilt, when the metaphorical dessert tray went by. "My grandmother had a vision for her daughters," says Susan. "She would say, 'I will not teach you how to cook because you will only enter into a kitchen to give orders.' Which is kind of a loony thing to say to anybody that's not a member of the royal family."

At this point, Susan Fales-Hill throws back her head and laughs. It is an identical image of the picture in *Harper's Bazaar.* But her laugh is a revelation. It seems to come from two places at once—the back of her throat and the bottom of her belly. It is a soprano's trill of a laugh, so melodic, so huge, that she seems to need to throw back her head to release it. She giggles a little more, then continues talking about her grandmother and the pride she instilled in her mother. "There was a sense that you are to expect something of life and you are somebody."

Much has been written of the generations of the black elite, who made their fortunes in insurance and beauty products and publishing businesses. These are the sort of people who represent multigeneration alumni of schools like Howard and Spelman, who define themselves socially by attachment to social groups such as the Deltas, the AKAs and the Links. They are whom the author Lawrence Otis Graham called "our kind of people." But what's so intriguing to me about Josephine Premice and her circle is that they weren't those "kind of people." These black swans all married interracially, lived abroad, spoke foreign languages and traveled in racially diverse, sophisticated circles. "They were not part of the traditional black colleges, black sorority and fraternity, black middle-class world," says Susan. "My mother was certainly too dark to be completely accepted, though she had some very good friends who were part of that Delta and AKA axis who adored and respected her."

Not being part of the traditional black middle-class world liberated the swans. The pressure that black middle-class women felt to marry a certain kind of man and lead a sepia-toned Ozzie and Harriet life was never a concern. These women wrote their own stories and cast themselves as stars of films that Hollywood was way too limited to imagine. They stood out because of their personalities, clothes, adventures, travels and parties—and they knew it. "I met Warren Beatty a few years ago and he had known my mother," says Susan. "He said, 'Your mother was a complete original.' His whole attitude was that she wasn't representative of any race because she was so much her own person. She didn't fit in a box."

In the 1950s and early 1960s, interracial marriage was more than about bucking the trend for dark-skinned women like Josephine Premice. It was an important option. "She didn't tell me this, Aunt Diahann did, but black men were not paying attention to my mother," says Susan, who is herself very fair. "She was very dark. That's not what they considered pretty and even if they did, that's not what they wanted to marry. The color line of the 1950s was that they wanted someone light and bright. A lot of guys still want that. It's like Whoopi Goldberg said once in an interview. I guess Spike Lee was giving her a hard time about dating a white guy. She said, 'To Spike and any other black guys who are having a hard time, my only question is, where are my flowers from you?'"

On paper, it may have seemed that Josephine Premice and Timothy Fales had nothing in common. He was from a Boston Brahmin family that had relocated to New York without losing an iota of their WASP sting. She was the daughter of Haitian immigrants. But as Susan describes it, they had enormous amounts in common. "In terms of their mind-sets and their outlooks and their experiences and travels, they saw the world the same way," says Susan. "I saw my father a few weeks ago and he kept saying, 'Your mother and I, your mother and I.'" They may not have fit on paper, but Susan says, "They spoke the same set of languages and always considered themselves citizens of the world. They believed there's one race, the human race."

Her mother's life fills in an important gap in the question that I keep asking both myself and the women I interview. How did we get here? How have we moved so quickly; what's behind this generation of unprecedented success? Certainly, we all benefit by the audacity, curiosity and ingenuity of the black swans who came before us. Susan's life, more than most of the women in this book, was aided by the dual blessings of financial privilege and family connections. But if she were only the well-off daughter of a famous black actress, her story would be far less intriguing. As Susan tells it, her parents always made it clear that in America, she would be considered a black woman. She built a career writing and producing for two landmark black television shows. In the process, not only did she set about the difficult work of composing a life (to borrow a phrase from Mary Catherine Bateson), she also created characters that shaped America's perception of who we are as black women and the lives we are capable of leading.

Her first job was as a writer's apprentice on a new sitcom called *The Cosby Show*. Through a family friend, Susan submitted a writing sample to Bill Cosby. But she also sent along something else that she believes helped cinch the deal: a tape of her doing different voices and impersonations. "He loved the tape," she says. "Because I was there, in part through nepotism, I felt an added duty to give 200 percent, which I did." With the exception of one person and Susan, the writing staff was all white, all male and not necessarily receptive to the new kid on the block. "They hadn't picked me, they were wondering who the hell was this?" Susan remembers. "I was a woman and I wasn't 300 pounds and I'm attractive—there's a real prejudice in the comedy writing community that if you're not ugly, you're not funny." At this point, she laughs out loud. "Yes, that's a reality," she says. "Women, in general, are not that well accepted. Women who are not unattractive and Roseanne Barr-ish are viewed with suspicion and dismissed as, 'Oh come on. You couldn't possibly have a funny bone in your body.'"

For two months, the writers wouldn't even let her in the room. She showed up every morning at the same time and asked the same question, "Can I do anything?" Finally, she was tossed a bone. A very small bone. She was asked to research insurance laws in Brooklyn, where the show was set. "It was so stupid," she recalls, guffawing at the memory. But she was grateful for the chance to do something, anything. "So I gave them a dossier!" she says. "I knew every in and out about car insurance in Brooklyn. I typed it all up, quite innocently. Then they stopped and said, 'Wait a minute. She could actually be useful.'" She was invited into the room.

Susan was assigned the task of what's called keeping the book. "When you're writing for a television show," she explains, "it's a group of people, everybody's pitching outlines and ideas. Somebody's got to be what they call the scribe, you take it all down so it can be typed." Writer's apprentices that followed Susan balked at the task, considering it secretarial and beneath them. "That's really shortsighted and stupid," she points out. "Because the fact of the matter is, you should be shutting up and listening, 'cause that's the finest way to learn in that environment." Her life as the writer's scribe wasn't exactly a walk in the park. Every time she pitched an idea, the response was "Well, maybe that's funny at Harvard." Susan wasn't only the young black woman in the room. She was the only one with an Ivy League degree.

She stuck it out and was promoted to staff writer. In the meantime, at the request of Bill Cosby, she began doing warm-up—talking to the audience during the tapings. It was a spine-strengthening task. As Susan says with a laugh, "The audience definitely did not come to see you. They're thinking, 'Why doesn't she shut up?' and 'Why is this thing taking two and a half hours?' " But it taught her how to think on her feet; to learn to gauge an audience and play with them.

When *A Different World* was created, the one-time writer's apprentice got her big shot. "They said, you're young, you just got out of college, so you go do it." She was 24 years old. She had also just moved in with the love of her life and was heartbroken by the idea of leaving New York with all of its comfort and familiarity. She says it is one of the few times that her mother actually gave her career advice. "My mother said, 'You have to do it. You're much, much, much too young to make a decision against your career and for your relationship.' That was a really important point in my life. Even though it was breaking my heart, I knew, absolutely, that she was right. I was much too young and opportunities like this do not come every single day, you really do have to grab them."

In California, Susan learned how important it can be to leave behind the people who have trained you. Although she had been promoted to staff writer in New York, she still played the role of the eager apprentice. Los Angeles was tabula rasa and Susan began to flourish. For the first time, she began to pitch ideas with abandon. Three weeks after her arrival, Fales-Hill says her boss called her in for a meeting and said, "You know we were told that you were really hard-working, you were very good, quite talented, you turn in good scripts, but not to expect you to say much in the room." "From the moment I would arrive, I couldn't stop talking," she says, laughing and doing a fine impersonation of a duck's cry. "It was just squawk, squawk, squawk." Making a professional move after getting your first training is advice she now believes deeply in. "For any woman, you've really got to look at seizing those opportunities to be in a new environment with people who haven't trained you and not in a secondary, subservient, 'Oh, great ones teach me' position."

Her bosses in New York stayed mentors; both the head writer, John Marcus, and Matt Williams, who went on to create *Roseanne* and *Home Improvement*. "Matt Williams, in particular, took me under his wing and really trained me," Susan remembers. "So that's another thing I would say to people, Don't give up, even if initially people aren't being very friendly. If you just really keep saying, 'I'm here to work, I'm here to work,' somebody is going to say, 'Come here, let me give you some pointers.'"

By her fourth year at *Different World*, Susan had been promoted to executive producer. She was 28 years old, young even by Hollywood whiz kid standards, with a staff of sometimes much older people reporting to her. She was at the top of her game professionally, but far from personally content. "What was happening on the personal side? Zilch, zippo, nothing," she says with a grin. The long-distance relationship she had been carrying on with her boyfriend in New York eventually floundered. In Los Angeles, she had a lot of what she calls "non-starter relationships."

She says, "I think I had a real problem because I was so attached to my beau in New York that I wasn't necessarily open to anything. My heart was still really with him. I was also working 14 hours a day and often on weekends as well. There was not a lot of balance, time or opportunities to meet people. Clearly, you don't want to date people at work. That is not the move. It was really, really challenging." Susan began to feel the marriage crunch acutely, describing her late 20s as a period when she despaired of meeting a man of any color—white, black or other—who wouldn't be intimidated by a woman with a certain level of success and independence.

She could throw herself into work as long as the ratings continued to hold, but finally, after seven seasons, *Different World* was cancelled. She was 30 years old with a string of successes under her belt, but the deep desire to have a fuller, richer life. Seeing herself at a crossroads, she began to consider business school in Europe. She loved her friends on the West Coast, but in her words, "I hated Los Angeles with every fiber of my being. Which is another reason I was tempted to go to Europe.

It was everything that LA wasn't—cultivated, international, intellectual. Everything LA didn't have to offer." She also admits that she had begun to think, once again about marriage. "Business schools can be a good place to meet a potential mate."

She gave her plan considerable thought, even traveling abroad to visit the school. But she was seriously torn. When the producers at Carsey-Werner, creators of *The Cosby Show,* heard that she could be persuaded to stay in Los Angeles they offered her a deal to develop her own shows. "So I chose the familiar," she says. "Which looking back, I wonder what would have happened if I'd gone the other way. In some ways, that's a regret." She pauses for a second and I imagine her, as she sometimes must, married to an Italian manufacturing executive or to a French restaurateur that she met in business school. Then she smiles. "It's over now, so too bad."

At Carsey-Werner and tired of seeing just homeboys on the air, Susan developed a pilot for CBS about a black-owned family business. "I thought it's really time," she says. "We've never seen the really successful, the bourgeoisie in the black community—the John Johnsons. And a family business takes all the issues of family and writes them large. This was a publishing empire, a very upscale business, very multigenerational." Susan's project provoked strong responses at CBS—they either loved it or hated it. Such dissent meant only one thing: the project wasn't going to go forward. She was shattered. "That was a big, big, big disappointment," she says. "At that point, I was 31, I was really tired, I was very disappointed that the show didn't make it. I thought I needed to take a step back and I chose to come to New York." New York meant being near her mother and a chance to reconnect with her roots. It was also a chance to "meet some guys and have some fun."

New York was all that she hoped it would be. Then, over the holidays, her mother got very sick. She was diagnosed with emphysema; she ended up in a coma over Christmas and almost died. Before that, "I was very much in the 'bee in the garden of flowers' mode," she says. "New York had a lot of really cute guys of all colors. I was open to anything. I hadn't decided that I had to marry someone black. I was an equal opportunity dater, a Rainbow Coalition dater."

Equal opportunity dating is a tack she would advise for other black professional women. "You know what, it's just too hard," she says. "I think it's very dangerous to have that tunnel vision. You just need someone who understands you because there are black people who don't understand you and there are white people who don't understand you."

Her mother's illness brought the marriage crunch a little closer. At that point, she decided, "I needed to stop playing around, hone in and find my mate for life. Life is short and you don't know when your number is up. What do I want to say that I've done?" Again and again, Susan returned to a chilling question to which she knew the answer: "Do I want to be standing by myself at my mother's funeral? No, I don't."

She began to admit to herself that she had pushed away anyone who seemed seriously interested and was very into unavailable men. Then like a women's self-help guru, she begins to break it down, right there in the tearoom of the Mark Hotel. "I think women avoid commitment by choosing men who are commitment phobes," she says. "There you are, as a single woman…" Suddenly she slips into one of her famous impersonations, a breathless reverie. "I don't have a problem with commitment." She switches back to her own powerful alto, "Look at him! You've chosen this guy, on a motorcycle, with a tattoo. Honey, from date one he told you that he's dating five other women. Why are you blaming him?"

She says she's tired of hearing women, especially black women, say there are no men. "Yes, it's very challenging to find a guy for any woman, of any color, who has a brain and is strong and accomplished," she continues. "It's difficult, across the board, to find men who can contend with that and who aren't going to be insecure. However, we also push away men who are nice, men who are maybe not the flashiest guy in the room, who aren't the richest guy in the room."

Her own husband, Dr. Aaron Hill, is a nice guy that she blew off when she was in "my standoffish phase." When he began to call her again, after her mother's illness, she decided to give the relationship a chance. He's the consummate gentleman—rising when she enters a room, pulling out her chair when they enter a restaurant—and it seems hard to believe that she almost passed on him, dismissing him as having that fatal flaw of being too nice. "We've lost the attitude of gratitude and we want everything," she says. "Well guess what, the guy who is going to be the billionaire CEO is generally not interested in a woman who's also trying to have a career. The guy who's going to be the billionaire CEO is generally not all that warm and fuzzy. Know what the trade-off is and decide. There are alpha males who are successful, who have a lot to offer, who aren't going to be necessarily the richest guy, but who want a woman who is a real partner. If you're serious about your career and you're serious about your drive or just serious about being respected, that's what you need to be looking for. As women, we go for the bad boys, the hot shot, the flashy guy and we're not looking at the right person."

Susan Fales became Susan Fales-Hill and her new husband, a man she describes as "extremely strong," stood by her through her mother's illness and eventual death. Her marriage has been a joy, but she began to worry about her career. Could she have it all? Or was it true that nobody got to have it all? Suddenly, her agent at the time was not returning her calls. "I was somewhat concerned because I thought now that my personal life is in order, I have this wonderful man that I'm crazy about and love, and he loves me —now my career is going to go into the toilet and I'm going to be baking Rice Krispies treats and people are going to be snickering behind my back. They're going to say, 'She used to be Susan Fales. She used to have a career and she used to be impressive. Now look at her. What a loser.'"

She switched agents and got the call she had been waiting for. Actor Tim Reid approached Susan about writing the pilot for a show that would be called *Linc's*. Susan and Aaron's new Park Avenue apartment under renovation, they moved into a hotel and Susan began to write. Showtime picked up *Linc's* and Susan finally got the "Created by" credit she had hoped for all those years before at Carsey-Werner. It took five years and four failed pilots to get it. "That was a tremendous feeling of achievement and that ran for two seasons," she says. "Then *Linc's* was canceled and in the meantime, my mother was getting very, very ill." Being in New York was a major priority and yet, all the television work that she was being offered was in Los Angeles. For Susan, there was no choice. She didn't want to leave her husband. She couldn't leave her dying mother. "So I wrote one pilot for Showtime, which didn't get picked up," she says. "Then I wrote an article for *Vogue*."

During the course of her mother's illness, Susan began to think deeply about Josephine Premice and the black swans who had been her fairy godmothers growing up. She decided to write a book proposal about her mother's life that was quickly snapped up by a major publisher. "It's a big, big career shift," she says of her life now. "It's not working with other people. It's a lot less money. In some ways, it's really challenging. But it's also been really wonderful because for the first time, I'm writing from my soul and gut. And not worrying about will the audience get this? Will the network like this? I'm really writing from my own truth."

As a television writer, she had tried to pay homage to her mother and to the great black divas that she had grown up around but she had not managed to do it. Every time she wrote a character, people would say, "Who is this woman? We don't quite get it." Television executives knew Diahann Carroll because of *Dynasty* and *Julia* and they knew Eartha Kitt as Catwoman. They didn't know how multifaceted these women were. "I realized the only way I'm really going to be able to write about them is to write about them in the Great Dames way," she says, referencing Marie Brenner's book of profiles that ranged from Jackie Kennedy to her own mother, Thelma Brenner. "Now, I'm telling their stories from the perspective of someone who knew them well and grew up around them and had them as…" She pauses for a second, searching for the word that describes the black swans and the impact they had on her life. When she finds it, she bows her head and smiles serenely, "as someone who had them as kind of fairy godmothers."

CHAPTER 9

*Invisible Women: Professional
Women and the Media*

SOMETIMES IT SEEMS like a revolution. A Häagen Dazs ad with a beautiful woman in a fluffy white robe eating straight out of the pint, extolling the perks of an evening spent in a hotel on a business trip. A sister with natural hair in a snazzy Armani-style suit explains the virtues of Saturn cars. A Marriott ad features a black couple lounging under the sheets, happy with the hotel's promise that "We've been thinking about your love life all week." A dew-covered black woman reclines on an azure riverbed. "The world's in fast forward," the copy reads. "Hit pause." Calgon's promise to "take you away" is an old one, but the sister in the ad represents a new acknowledgment of our busy professional lives.

For all the change it symbolizes, it's still a drop in the media bucket. Black women are slowly creeping into starring roles in the mainstream blockbuster action flicks and romantic comedies. Twenty years after Mary Tyler Moore, no black career girl has ever gotten her own television show on one of the major networks. "When you think about black upper-class women, who see the world and have options, you don't see us," says Tracie Howard, who spent 15 years as an executive at companies such as Xerox and American Express before setting out as a novelist. "Even companies that want to target black women of means do so through Mary J. Blige and Foxy Brown. LVMH, which produces Louis Vuitton, has a deal with Lil' Kim. They think the way to get to our pocket is through this flamboyant, rap culture lifestyle. They think women like us, who have means, don't exist, and they don't realize we don't relate to the hip-hop world."

Corporate America is full of powerful, wealthy black women. But you wouldn't know it from the newspapers, magazines or television. Successful black women are still largely invisible to the media; and when we are covered, it's at junctures spaced so far apart that the message gets lost. There's not one of us doing well, there are hundreds of us. There are not 100 black women making six-figure salaries, there are thousands. It's nothing short of a revolution, and the media is missing it. Even smart, upscale publications like *Vanity Fair* are more interested in the curve of Eve's thighs than in the brainpower and economic power of women like BET President and Chief Operating Officer Debra Lee. "It's an image thing," says Tracie Howard. "Every time someone meets one of us, there's an exception. No matter that we represent hundreds of thousands of middle-class black women, we're always regarded as the exception. There aren't many icons that depict a black woman with means, who can roll with her own flow."

Jacqueline Bazan runs her own entertainment publicity firm and says, "With the exception of Roz Abrams or Sue Simmons, anchors on nightly news programs in New York, I rarely find black women in the media whom I feel represent me. And I happen to be in a profession where I represent them. Ironic, I think. I represent movies, and primarily movies about African Americans, and I stand in constant amazement of how I do not know or recognize any of those people who are represented on screen." There are exceptions. She points to Kasi Lemmons, director of the modern classic, *Eve's Bayou*, as someone who is "uncompromising when it comes to her belief and her representation of the black community." Angela Bassett, *The Practice*'s Lisa Gay Hamilton and Lorraine Touissant, star of Lifetime's *Any Day Now*, are other favorites.

Tamala Edwards, a political correspondent for ABC News, is grateful for the women who have broken through the media blackout. "I don't think folks of all colors are lying when they say they think Halle Berry —a brown-skinned, short-haired, clearly African-American woman— is beautiful," she says. "Back in the day, Pam Grier, Beverly Johnson and Iman were exotic. But today, I think folks honestly look at Halle and say what they'd say if she were Gwyneth Paltrow—she's beautiful."

How We See

IN 1975, LAURA MULVEY constructed a theory of the male gaze in cinema. She drew on the psychoanalytic works of Sigmund Freud and Jacques Lacan to argue that the male point of view was so standard in the images of film that women interpreted what they saw through a "gendered gaze." As scholar S. Craig Watkins explains, "The masculine gaze so thoroughly shapes the film-viewing experience that it socializes women into identification and compliance with the very patriarchal values and ideologies that reproduce their marginalized status." Mulvey's essay was so revolutionary feminists scholars argued that the same theory could be applied to any element of the mass media, particularly television and advertising. [32]

I would argue that black women experience the media through a double lens; we view the mainstream media through a racialized and gendered gaze, one largely constructed through whiteness and maleness, that renders us practically invisible in the process. "Not seeing our images reproduced—in particular in ads that constitute such a visible medium in our society—suggests to our children that we have no power, that having power is inconceivable," says Michele Wallace of her findings in *Invisibility Blues: From Pop to Theory*.

This is not to suggest that we are solely victims. The process of absorbing a point of view in which one's experience does not factor widens a black woman's perspective, giving her more information about the world and how it works. "I would have been delighted to see Lena Horne or Dorothy Dandridge photographed beyond the racial cloister of *Ebony* magazine," Margo Jefferson writes in a *New York Times* essay titled "Looking at What Black Looks Like." "Draped, say, on a divan in *Vogue* or exuding hauteur on the boulevard of some major European capital for *Harper's Bazaar* in the 1950s. And I despised the reasons they were excluded, if prejudice, ignorance and timidity can be called reasons." She goes on to say, "Thank goodness I could still love great non-Negro models like Suzy Parker and Lisa Fonssagrives. It is fine visual and imaginative training, this learning to be at ease with something that on the surface seems quite removed from you."

One might argue that a fashion spread in *Harper's Bazaar* is hardly a battlefield for black women's rights in the face of growing poverty and powerlessness among black women in the underclass. But as Patricia Hill Collins explains in *Black Feminist Thought,* in an age where black women are still relatively absent from the corridors of powers, too often, media images become the basis for political discourse. "The images of black women reflect the interlocking processes of race, class and gender oppression. Images like the mammy, the jezebel and the welfare mother have become staple icons in the popular mediascape, finding routine expression not only in popular media discourse but also in the arena of social policy discourse."

More and more, we are moving past this unholy trinity of stereotype. More black women anchor the news than ever before and this shapes both how we are presented and how we are perceived. We are still conspicuously absent from the big networks, but there are pockets of encouragement: ground-breaking shows like Yvette Lee Bowser's career-girl sisterfest, *Living Single,* Lisa Nicole Carson on *Ally McBeal,* Michael Michelle's role on *ER,* and her predecessor Gloria Reuben. Cable fares better, most notably Lifetime Television's *Any Day Now.* It's the top-rated show on the network and the only drama on television that explores cross-racial friendships on a weekly basis. It may be no surprise then, that while television viewing for African-American women in the all-important 18-34 demographic is down 22 percent, we make up a hefty 13 percent of Lifetime's audience, making it the most highly watched cable network on TV. [33]

The double lens (male gaze/white gaze) that black women view the media through has meant that we don't need to be represented in order to be extraordinarily loyal to what we see. We make up only 12 percent of the population, but we represent 37.7 percent of the daytime viewing audience.[34] The numbers are even higher when you look specifically at soap operas, which have had a long and consistent history of white-washing black story lines (if they carry them at all). There are 12 running soap operas on network TV, and they feature fewer than a dozen African-American actors at any given time.

Daytime talk shows and commentary programs fare better. You could argue that Oprah Winfrey is such a phenomenon, she doesn't belong in an analysis of blacks on TV. I say excluding her would be to adopt an apartheid-era perspective, by which celebrities are whitened by their fame and fortune. On the contrary, the presence of Oprah—and the way that she has broadened her "sister next door" appeal to encompass a universal audience—opens the way for other black women to enter daytime. The most notable of these is Star Jones on ABC's top-rated morning show, *The View.* I would also include in this group restaurateur and Food Network host, Barbara Smith, and rapper and talk show host, Queen Latifah.

The Dictionary That Defines Me

STAR JONES MAY HAVE a law degree, but it's her gift of gab that has brought her fame and fortune. As one of the five stars of *The View,* ABC's top-rated daytime talk show, she discusses everything from hair weaves and hunks to abortion rights and capital punishment. Star remembers that when she was first exploring a career in television, every station was looking for a new Oprah. It was an opportunity she passed on. She wanted to do social commentary, not a straight talk show, and she waited for years for the right opportunity to arise. "I said no. I want Oprah to do her thing and because she's so encouraging to other African Americans, I can do my thing," she told me when I was at *Newsweek.*

As the only African-American woman in a circle that includes three white women and an Asian, she has become America's sister-girlfriend next door. She may be the first woman in television to shush Barbara Walters with a "honey, please." As much as she enjoys representing a generation of high-achieving black women, she detests the stereotypes that go along with it—and the way the media is always trying to pin an "up from poverty" story on her. "You know, there's got to be a crackhead prostitute in the background or your story has no depth," she says, reclining into a leather sofa at her favorite New York cigar bar. "When I started doing television, everyone presumed that I was some black girl from some downtrodden family."

Star Jones, her given name, was born into what she likes to call a family of "have-somes." Her mother is a director of social services in Trenton, New Jersey. Her father is a security officer in the city. The man she calls her father is actually her stepfather who raised her from childhood. Her mother got pregnant with Star as a college student and decided to keep the baby. As a vocal supporter of abortion rights, Star says it's not the choice she would have made in the same situation. "If I'm really honest with you, I think I would've been too selfish to put my dreams on hold for someone else," Star says. "Thank God she did. She then went back to school, got a degree and married my stepfather, who is the love of my life."

Home, as a child, was split between her grandparents in North Carolina and a housing project in Trenton. "Housing projects in the late '60s and early '70s aren't what people think housing projects are now," Star says. "They were a wonderful place to grow up. You had the lady next door who would always look out for you when you came back from school if your mama was working and auntie next door made sure you had a snack and did your homework before you played outside. And if you didn't, they'd make sure your mama found out when she got home." Both Star and her sister attended charm school. "I had a debutante ball. My sister had a debutante ball. These were all things that were part of my life. The people I grew up with are part of the fabric of black society, but it's like they're not there. We don't talk about them."

She attributes the popularity of *The View* to the fact that America was ready to see a group of multi-cultural women interact as peers, and sometimes adversaries. According to Star, the gender bond is much stronger than the racial bond. "A black woman has more in common with an Asian woman who has more in common with a Hispanic woman who has more in common with a Caucasian woman than any of these women have in common with men," says Star. "Which is to say that we shouldn't allow anyone to divide us as women."

If professional black women are invisible in the media, perhaps it's only partly because the people who run the news organizations don't know—apart from the women in their lives that they might deem as "exceptions"—that we exist. According to Star, it always takes the news industry a while to catch up to what's going on in real life. "You know what it is? You don't see the evidence of black women who're getting their groove on as much because we're working, honey," says Star. "Obviously I have a public job. Oprah has a public job. Iyanla Vanzant, Lauryn Hill are public figures and you will see us. Then you hear about the have-nots: the ones who are on welfare, the ones who are having too many children, the ones whose husbands beat them, left them, got them on crack, threw them out, strung them out. You hear about those women because those are the ones that *Newsweek* and *60 Minutes* are doing stories on. But the ones in the middle, those 'have somes' who are just working every day, making love to their husbands, picking up the children from school, motivating their kids to do more; you rarely hear about them and what I'm here to tell you is that's the group I come from."

At the same time that she feels comfortable with her affluent status and her lower-middle-class background, Star says that there are moments that make her realize how much work still needs to be done in race relations. "When that man [James Byrd] was dragged on the streets of Texas, I came to *The View* that day and Barbara looked at me—on air—and said, 'I have never seen you so upset,'" Star remembers. "I told her, I woke up that morning depressed. I said, I cannot tell you the last day that I woke up depressed because I'm a happy person. I'm blessed with a good family, great friends and a great job. But I woke up depressed that day. For everything that I've accomplished: this law degree, my job is to sit at a table with Barbara Walters! If I meet the wrong white person on the wrong street, I too could be dragged in chains because all they would see is a nigger! I got to say that on air. Do you know how powerful that was? To be able to say that live on national television?" For all the pain she felt that day, she was ultimately cheered by the power of her position, the ability to speak, every day, to millions of white women about her experiences as a black woman.

One of the things I most enjoyed about my conversation with Star was that she seemed to have spent a lot of time thinking about the fact that while she feels a sisterhood with other black women, each woman's choices are her own. She says it's been a learning process to realize that while she loves the Knicks, not all black women love basketball. She's come to learn that there are some black women who prefer Laura Ashley to Gucci, Yanni to Motown and so forth. She remembers, for example, being vehemently opposed to Clarence Thomas, but having serious doubts about the allegations raised by Anita Hill. As an outspoken, let's-take-it-to-the-curb black woman, Star wondered what kind of sister would have put up with Thomas's antics. "I was raised by a very strong black woman," she says. "So if a man said something to me that I found uncomfortable, regardless of the fact that he's my boss, I would've told him to take a flying leap off a short pier. I know that about myself. I had trouble as a black woman, as a black lawyer who found myself saying to Professor Hill 'I don't understand why you did not cuss him out.'" Time and maturity have given her a different point of view. "Several years later I met Anita Hill and she hipped me to something that plays into this book that you're doing," Star says. "She said the kind of black woman I am is not the kind of black woman she is…and I got it! We don't all fit into a box. We're not all the ones who would tell you off. We're vulnerable just like other people. I got a great lesson in just meeting her and getting a chance to talk to her."

Throughout my conversations with successful black women, the topic that came up again and again was whether or not our education and our success made it harder for us to find a mate. As a 40-year-old single woman who has a lucrative career in television, it's a situation that Star is well acquainted with. "Financially, I can deal with my own life. I'm set," she says. "Intellectually, I have my friends. I'm challenged socially. I have a great time in my life but what I want is someone who can hold my hand on those days when I want to get into bed and put the covers over my head. And I want it to be a brother."

Star admitted that one of the things she finds so bizarre is that even white women express sympathy to her that she is so successful, but still single. "They say, 'It must be very difficult for you,'" she says with a tight smile. When I express surprise that anyone would be that blunt, her laugh is deep and from the gut. "People say anything they think of to me!" she chuckles. "They think because I'm in their living room every day they can just go for it. I've had several white women say to me, 'it must be very difficult for you to meet a mate. I can see how intimidating you would be.' What is that? Is that code for 'brothers aren't strong enough to handle you.' They don't know the brothers I know. I haven't found my mate, but I think there are a lot of brothers out there who I plainly admire. I don't think people get that as strong as I am in my professional life, how vulnerable I'd like to be in my personal life."

While Star will discuss her dating life on *The View*, her weight is a topic that is strictly off limits. Like many black women, she is overweight. "Let me tell you something, Veronica," she says. "Straight up. I don't allow the world to weigh in, if you will, on my weight. Your opinion is irrelevant. The only person whose business it is is mine and my doctor's. When my doctor says, 'you've got to lose 20 pounds Missy Missy, you're putting some stress here.' That's when I have to worry about it."

I'm certain, however, that she knows that she is an icon for plus-sized women. She tells me that she's aware of it, but for her, the issue of weight is much closer to home. "I'd like women to believe it and not be put into the box of you've got to be a size two to be considered beautiful," she says. "But you know, my mom is full-figured and my daddy loves her and my father is the sexiest man I have ever met in my life. He is fine, he is smart, he is funny, he's got it going on and he loves her. Why would I ever think that I need to please any other kind of man? I had that approval growing up and I never thought of my size as an issue so I never allowed the people around me where I worked to make it part of the dialogue."

One of Star's favorite sayings is "I am the author of the only dictionary that defines me." The words speak for every woman who was brown-skinned in an environment that preferred light-skinned, who was overweight in a society that worships thinness, who was black and female and refused to take her place at the bottom of the totem pole. It's also a saying for every sister who didn't fit into the black woman box, especially for those who had the courage to step out of boxes created by other black women. It's for Anita Hill having the courage not to react to situations in the same way that Star would. It's for Condoleezza Rice choosing to be Republican when blacks are the most loyal Democratic group in the country. It's for the women in this book, the have-somes and the haves, who have crafted successful lives without role models or media coverage.

The Color, and Pricetag, of Beauty

THE YEAR WAS 1992 and a dozen of America's most famous black models had assembled at Club USA in New York City. Iman was there; as
was her best friend, former model and management company owner,
Beth-Ann Hardison. Azzedine Alaia muse, Veronica Webb, had shown
up, along with *Sports Illustrated* cover girl Tyra Banks. Britain's most
famous bad girl, Naomi Campbell, had squeezed the meeting in. Cynthia
Bailey, Kersti Bowser, Karen Alexander, Beverly Peele, Peggy Dillard—
there were 20 models in all, a veritable who's who of black fashion for
the past 20 years. Seated on a dais, they were a feast for the eyes. But
they were here to speak their minds, not sashay the catwalk. One hun-
dred journalists gathered in the audience to hear what the models had
to say.

They called themselves the Black Girls Coalition and had formed
quietly as a non-profit group to aid the homeless. But they had come
together that winter afternoon for an altogether different purpose—to
talk about the business of being black and beautiful in an industry that
holds whiteness as the ideal. Iman spoke about the indignity of being
called a "white woman dipped in chocolate," and how the speaker
meant it as a compliment. Tyra Banks pointed out that while she had
graced 17 magazine covers in Europe, she had appeared on only 2 in
the United States. Hair was hotly debated—all the models were forced
to wear wigs and weaves to emulate the long, straight hair of their counterparts. Even Roshumba, the model who is most often photographed
with her short Afro, said, "I'm constantly arriving at a photographer's
studio and being told that I have to wear a wig."

It might have seemed like a glamorous pity party among the richest
and most well-known sisters in the city. But it was 1991 and the City of
New York Department of Consumer Affairs had just released a study
called "Invisible People: the Depiction of Minorities in Magazine Ads
and Catalogs."[35] Researchers found that in an analysis of over 11,000
magazine ads and 22,000 catalogue pictures, blacks made up only 3
percent of the models pictured. This was at the same time that we made
up 12 percent of the population and 11 percent of newsstand sales. Furthermore, the study found that the number of blacks in publications

such as *Vogue* and *Esquire* had either remained the same, or declined, since 1973. It probably goes without saying that we were most often portrayed in stereotypical roles, but as an example, 57 percent of the blacks pictured in *Business Week* were either athletes, musicians or service workers. The Black Girls Coalition might have been a glamorous group of privileged women, but their complaints struck a much deeper chord.

In 1956, when his evening variety show was cancelled after only one season, Nat King Cole famously remarked that "Madison Avenue is afraid of the dark." That might be the case, but they've come around. The Department of Consumer Affairs report pointed out that minorities made up a $400 billion business that advertisers were plain stupid to ignore. A decade later, the advertising industry has figured out that blacks, in particular black women, have serious clout. Retail sales of ethnic cosmetics cashed in at a hefty $291 million in 1991, a 22 percent increase from 1995. The figures are expected to jump another 28 percent by 2004, making ethnic cosmetics a $372 million business. The ads in the industry bible, *Advertising Age,* are hard to ignore: "At $446 billion, African-American buying power is more than the GNP of Switzerland." Middle-class black women regularly appear in ads for Visa, JCPenney and IBM. "Ten years ago, Americans' beauty icons were blondes with perfect figures and Cindy Crawford," said Janice Specter, VP of advertising at Avon. "In the last couple of years, the whole idea of what beauty is has been expanded extraordinarily."

Evidence suggests that the advertising campaigns are making a difference: especially when advertisers make an effort to tune in to what matters to black women. When Tampax sought to convert black women from "special occasion" tampon users to monthly users, they did more than run ads with black models. The company sponsored a health and fitness tour (including lectures, a wellness center and a "beauty escape" mini spa), which traveled to 22 markets in 2000, reaching a total of 64,000 African-American women. Sure, they promoted their products, but many women also got vital health information that might not have come into their community otherwise. As one woman wrote on the post-event comment card, "I love the sisterhood. It was a great opportunity to talk about issues that affect all of us."

ESPN won kudos in the summer of 2001 for its *Basketball Is Beau-*

tiful campaign, which featured lush black-and-white images of WNBA stars, including Dawn Staley of the Charlotte Sting, Teresa Weatherspoon of the Liberty and Sheryl Swoopes of the Houston Comets. A young African-American director, Nzingha Stewart, directed the five 30-second spots. As for the women in the Black Girls Coalition, they are doing just fine. Roshumba models, with her short natural hair, for Avon. Phina models for Oil of Olay. Tyra Banks enjoys a lucrative contract with Victoria's Secret. Iman started her own cosmetics line for women of color, I-Iman, and it's the top-selling new brand at Sephora.

It's not that Madison Avenue decided to do right by black women, it was simply that we became too big a market to ignore. In apparel spending, for example, we make up 14.5 percent of the American market. The question begs to be asked: ultimately, is being so heavily marketed to a good thing for the black community? When we have so little real wealth, why are we spending so much on the latest makeup, aromatherapy hair products and designer jeans? Robin Ghivan, the fashion editor for the *Washington Post* offers this perspective, "We all know that appearances matter a great deal and we also know that people of color tend to be judged even more harshly. When we still have executive vice presidents being mistaken for the janitor because of the color of their skin, it's not hard to see why someone might move from deciding to buy a good suit to buy an Armani suit. There's a sense that we need to take special care to make sure that we're regarded as professional and in charge and capable in a very material way."

When the 1991 Department of Consumer Affairs report came out, writer Lisa Jones explored the issue of black spending power and catalogue images in an article titled "1-800-WASP." Catalogues, she argued, serve as powerful tools of fantasy for all Americans, but even more so for middle-class blacks who'd like to imagine themselves among J. Crew photos that depict young couples "placing bids at Christie's" and "huddled in the stands at the Army-Navy Game." She writes, "For those of us who don't 'belong' in stores, the idea of shopping in the privacy of our own homes has a double meaning. Mail-order catalogues—24-hour hotlines—are a racially stress-free shopping encounter, no more hassles, no more watchful eyes. All you need is a major credit card and you're guaranteed unconditional acceptance. No one has to know your race, just buy. Or as some might say, buy in." It was a tremendously keen observation about professional blacks and the anonymity enjoyed by shopping in catalogues. It's a trend that's continued into the Internet arena. A 1999 study by the Yankelovich PR firm found that 39 percent of blacks with Internet access have household incomes above $50,000, and 14 percent shop online at least once a month, as compared to 5 percent of white Internet users.[36]

Beyond the politics of economics and spending power and professional perception, there is Michele Wallace's point: the powerlessness people feel when they aren't reflected in the media that surrounds them. In that sense, to use the Virginia Slims line, we've come a long way, baby. The current campaign for Evian pictures a chocolate-brown woman, perched upon a cloud (which discreetly covers her nudity), pouring Evian from the heavens. It isn't marketed specifically to blacks; it's the company's image on billboards, buses and in magazines from *People* to *In Style*. The model is a 21-year-old woman named Eva Cain, whose father told her she couldn't be a model because "models don't look like us." For Cain, the ad is a point of pride. She's too young to remember the "Black Is Beautiful" posters of the 1970s. But that's okay, she's living it. "The ad industry has figured out that beauty isn't always white," Cain told Bruce Horowitz of *USA Today*. "And that I, as an African-American woman, can be pictured as angelic tells you how far we've come."

Thinking out of the Box: A Television Actress's Perspective

AS BLACK PEOPLE we're privy to the white world—we've had to be in order to survive," says the actress Lorraine Touissant. "I think the world is structured in such a way that oftentimes white people can go through the world and not really invest in another culture or another race intimately, and be very fine and be happy, not really having it affect their lives. But that is changing." On *Any Day Now*, Lifetime's award-winning drama, Lorraine Touissant plays Rene Jackson, a black lawyer not unlike other women I've interviewed for this book. The show features two women—one black, one white—who grew up in the '60s in Birmingham who are now rekindling their friendship as adults.

It's the kind of front-and-center role that 30, 40, 50 years ago, actresses like Dorothy Dandridge and Lena Horne would have killed for. In 1964, acclaimed African-American actress Diana Sands broke the color barrier by taking over the female lead, opposite Alan Alda, in *The Owl and the Pussycat*. Of her Broadway turn, Sands told the *New York Herald Tribune* that she wished audiences could just "Look at me. Never mind my color. Please just look at me!" She won a Tony nomination for her role and enjoyed a successful run in the London production as well. It would be the kind of opportunity that comes only once in a black actress's career. "The Negro female has been categorized as the neuter, a mammy, an exotic," Sands sharply criticized. "Why isn't she a mother, wife, a woman desired? Someone who embodies all the characteristics of American womanhood?" On Lifetime's *Any Day Now* Lorraine Toussaint is all of these. And with each season, her character grows more complex.

It's a bright, sunny afternoon when Lorraine Toussaint welcomes me into her home, nestled high in the canyons above Los Angeles. It could be the set house of her character: replete with African art and Queen Anne vintage furniture. She waves me into the kitchen where she's preparing a formal tea; fruit and pastries dazzle on a silver tray like a picture in a woman's magazine. She is as famous, among her friends, for her teas as she is for the lush, tropical garden she designed herself.

She's agreed to be interviewed for a book about middle-class black women because her character is an icon to professional sisters (the Lifetime TV online message boards contain thousands of messages from the fans, black and white, who identify with her). "I run into black women who love this show because suddenly there's somebody who looks like them—working hard, looking good, all the things that I've talked about why I kept this role, which is who and what we are," she says. " Oftentimes the media has said that black women are strong, black women are powerful, black women are no-nonsense; we have this image on TV that is hard and tough and non-needy and all that stuff. I'm a lot of other things."

She's also living the life, fully enmeshed in the sweetness and the struggle of being an upper-class black woman in a world that has not quite caught up. "Most of the women that I grew up with were robust, working black women that had their act together," says Lorraine. "They may not have been as wealthy as my character, Rene Jackson, but they had their acts together, and I sometimes think that television is really behind the times because people see that and think that's an oddity, but I've known that all my life as I'm sure you have."

Touissant is well aware that, in many ways, her character is picking up where Clair Huxtable of *The Cosby Show* left off. It's a mantle she accepts gratefully. "This character allows me the opportunity to be somebody's mother, somebody's daughter, somebody's friend, to be somebody's lover," says Lorraine. "To be a professional woman who is extremely successful and good at what she does, but who's also questioning herself and questioning the choices she's made to this point. That really resonated with me personally because we're similar ages and obviously I'm playing her, you know what I mean?" Her character, Rene, has never been married. Lorraine, who was divorced in her 30s, recently became engaged. Neither woman has children, though it is definitely an issue that the show raises and that Lorraine still hopes is a possibility.

Her character's moved from Washington, D.C., back home to Birmingham, Alabama, to run her deceased father's practice. It's a scenario rooted in reality. Between 1990 and 2000, almost 600,000 young black professionals, blue-collar workers and black retirees moved or returned to the South. While the Great Migration of the early 1900s saw millions of blacks move North to escape racial persecution and limited job prospects, the reverse migration of the 1990s had a more joyous tone. Blacks came back to the South to middle-class communities, most notably in cities like Atlanta, where they thrived professionally and felt at home socially.[37]

My friend Joe Wood used to say that when it comes to race relations, he would pick the South over the North any day. The South is more open, he insisted, more blatant in their love and their hate. Kali Grovesnor, a 41-year-old business manager from Washington, D.C., agrees. "I feel at home in South Carolina although I am from New York City. My mother's family is from South Carolina and I visited her family every summer. When I'm down south, I feel I am with people who I understood and whose ways I am familiar with."

Certainly in the fictional Birmingham of *Any Day Now*, there's no topic too delicate or trivial to discuss: from homophobia in the black community to the word *nigger* to interracial dating to why black people have kinky hair. "Annie is so much the voice of white America, some aspects of white America," says Lorraine of her co-star Annie Potts. "She gets to ask all the stupid questions which aren't stupid at all."

In the previous season, Rene broke off an engagement after deciding that she couldn't commit to a man who makes less money than she did. It's a struggle that Lorraine can identify with: her fiancé, Curtis, is a working actor, but she's the star in the family. "The issue of successful black women meeting men is a myth that is based on some reality, you know," she says. " You get to a certain level of 'success' (and this is not just with black women) you want to marry someone to whom you are well suited spiritually, intellectually, emotionally, financially. And so what do you do? The pool starts to get smaller and smaller as your criteria grow as to what you're comfortable being with and whom you want to invest in. And then you add to that, if you do go outside your race that's a big kettle of fish, you know?"

She knows the struggles of the women in this book, not because she plays them on TV but because she's living it, too. She is practically sheepish when she admits that she met her fiancé at a Kinko's and struck up a conversation with him in line. "You've got to approach the brothers where you see them," she says with a smile. Love has made her optimistic about what some call the crisis between black men and women. Like a big sister, she hopes that her television character will find love as well. She says, positive relationships between black men and women are so rare on television.

The loving portrayal of Clair and Cliff Huxtable is just another one of the reasons we miss *The Cosby Show*. Not since then have we seen a major network feature a middle-class black couple with the same sweet, funny dynamic that you see on classic shows like *Mad About You*. (The WB's *For Your Love* being one of the very few exceptions.) In 1999, Eriq LaSalle publicly threatened to quit his job on the Emmy award–winning series, *ER*, if the producers didn't end his on-air relationship with a white woman. His character's previous relationships with black women had been tumultuous to say the least: "an adulterous affair with HIV-positive Jeannie Boulet (Gloria Reuben), then he fathered a son out of wedlock with Carla (Lisa Nicole Carson)." LaSalle's concern was that this story line, which showed a dynamic loving relationship, implied that a black man could only find happiness with a white woman.

If television finds it so difficult to script a convincing love story, perhaps it's because black women are just beginning to figure it out in real life. "Relationships are hard anyway," Touissant says with a sigh. LaSalle is a friend of hers and it's a discussion the actors have had more than once. "Black women have a history of being self-sufficient and in-dependent; sometimes that's a double-edged sword with our men. So I understand the theory from the sisters that the more education I get and the higher up I go, the less my chances are of having what my mother had and my grandmother had—home and hearth. But we're not our mothers or our grandmothers. The rules have changed and we're mak-ing them up as we go along."

CHAPTER 10

Guess Who's Coming to
Dinner Now? Black Women
and Relationships

IT IS PERHAPS THE MOST disturbing truth of our generation: that we are better educated, better paid, more fulfilled and more likely to be alone than any other group of black women before us. In *Kidding Ourselves: Breadwinning, Babies and Bargaining Power*, Rhona Mahony reports that the last time the sex ratio was equal for black men and black women was in 1840. The figures have been dropping ever since. There are 600,000 black men in the American prison system and another 200,000 married to non-black women. Add to that these grim figures: "tragically high homicide rates (51.4 black men among 100,000 as opposed to 11.3 for black women), higher rates of suicide (9.9 per 100,000 as opposed to 2.0 for black women) and their higher rates of death from disease and accidents."[38] In *Backlash*, Susan Faludi was able to tell her audience of women readers that the so-called "marriage crunch" so widely heralded by the media was a myth, a backlash against the ways in which single women are thriving today. When I write about black women, I can't send a similar message to my sisters. There is a backlash against successful black women, but the marriage crunch is very real.

Yet the statistics only underline what most sisters already know: too many black men are languishing in prison or unemployment. Our men die younger and more senselessly than any other group in America. The better educated we are, the less likely we are to meet brothers who can match our credentials. The more successful we are, the less likely we are to meet brothers who can match our pocketbooks. What neither the statistics nor the tunnel vision of our own experiences can tell us is that while there may be a hole in the black Love Boat, the ship has not sunk. Every day, black men and women fall in love, get married and have children. Increasingly, we are learning how to negotiate the very real economic differences. Black men are learning in relationships, what we learned in the work place a century ago—it pays to be stronger than one's pride. "All that most brothers want is for sisters to wish the same good fortune for us," writes Kevin Chappell in *Ebony*. "Be patient with us, encourage us and stop writing us off like the anchors do on the nightly news. We want sisters to share their life experiences with us. Tell us what it's like to be the top in your field. Tell us what it's like to have a 401K, an IRA, an MBA. Build up our confidence and we will do the same for you."

There are reports, though some call them urban legends, about partnerships that thrive despite the economic differences. "One of the more successful relationships I know is a woman who married someone who was in her mail room," says Melissa, a Miami office manager. "He seems very centered, very self-assured, very confident. He doesn't have an inferiority complex. At least not an obvious one. She was a fairly senior executive, a VP in a corporation. I know another woman who is a lawyer, very successful. She married someone who was a FedEx delivery guy, that was less successful." Melissa's first marriage broke up over money. "I just think it's too much of an ego issue, no matter what the guys say."

That said, what truly erodes the self-esteem of many professional black women is the widespread lack of commitment among many black men. I won't even call it a fear of commitment because at least on the surface, it's a blatant "Why should I?" A front page *New York Observer* article about a black investment banker who seemed, to his colleagues, awfully popular with the ladies, quotes him as saying "Well, 80 percent of my competition is in jail." It's the sort of flip comment I've heard from a lot of successful black men. Since professional sisters are in a marriage crunch, many educated, highly paid black men feel no rush to settle down. And when crank black psychologists and relationship experts advise us that "man-sharing was common in Africa and had its benefits for the community" then who can blame them?

At 40, Harriette Cole comes pretty close to having it all. She is the president of Profundities, a life coaching and style production company. Her nationally syndicated column, "Sense and Sensitivity," is replacing Ann Landers in many markets. She is happily married to photographer George Chinsee. The couple's work takes them on trips around the world. Back home, Harriette and George share a tony Harlem residence.

Yet Harriette is disheartened by the attitude many black men—and women—have toward relationships. Recently, Harriette spoke with a film executive who is in her early 30s. "She says that she and her friends have decided they're not going to get married," Harriette tells me. The men that are her counterparts are mostly interested in white and Asian women. If they're interested in black women at all, they want them young—in their 20s." Harriette pauses for a moment and adds, "These young women feel discarded, It's really sad."

While in the mainstream middle-class community, the question is often, "When and how can I fit in children?," for many black women, that assumes a big maybe in our lives—a man who is committed to partnership and family. While Harriette wanted to tell her young friend that she would definitely meet someone, she couldn't. "My friends who are over 35, successful and single are wondering if they are really going to live their lives alone," Harriette says. "That's a much bigger question than will I have a child."

For Debra Jackson, a 34-year-old single woman, black men's commitment issues are deeper than the statistics. It also has to do with how they are raised to view their role in society and how much they are taught to value black women. To paraphrase Freud, it's their mamas. "There's a saying that black women raise their daughters and love their sons," she says. "They need to switch that stuff around. It carries over from what we dealt with in slavery. It affects us to this day, it's ingrained in our personalities. As women, we have to be cognizant that we love our sons, that we're sending them into a world that is really harsh and that's not going to be supportive. But you have to hold him accountable. Not make everything a cushy experience for him. When my brother married outside of the race, my mother felt it was as if he didn't have respect for her. There's something to that. Black men need the discipline and the regimentation."

The challenge comes when you're holding a man accountable and there are so many other women who will coddle him in the name of being a good race woman. "Black women are very brand loyal," says Erika Kirkland, the 28-year-old owner of Polish, a Brooklyn nail salon and day spa. "When it comes to black men, they stick with them. Not that I'm opposed to the brothers, I still love them. I just laugh when I hear Angie Stone singing, "Black brothers, I love ya ... I'm here for you, for whatever." And Jay-Z follows with "Girls, girls, girls, girls, girls, to do and adore...girls all over the world."

Popular wisdom holds that the reason the number of interracial marriages between black women and white men are on the rise is because sisters are looking for other options. That may be true, but such explanations don't probe deep enough. What I've learned in my years of talking to professional black women is that in the work place, familiarity does not always breed contempt; it can breed attraction, flirtation and respect as well. We live in different neighborhoods and move in different social circles than women did 20, even 10 years ago. For today's sisters, marrying the boy next door may indeed mean marrying a white boy. One woman I spoke to is a 43-year-old former FBI agent. She has been married to her husband for 14 years. "My husband is a white Irish Catholic from Boston," she says. "I didn't go out with him 15 years ago because there was a shortage of black men. He was a wonderful, kind person with a great sense of humor who just happened to be white. I wasn't going to let race be a factor in determining whether or not I should get to know this wonderful human being or not."

Aisha Brooks-Lytle, a seminary student, says "Until I married Carl, 'Aisha will end up with a white man' was the mantra of my friends and family since elementary school. Growing up I had crushes on pop stars like Sting, Ralph Macchio—don't front and pretend like the Karate Kid wasn't cute! I loved Pierce Brosnan and John Stamos. At the same time, all of my boyfriends were black. Today, I'm married to a black man. If the man I am married to, right now, had come to me from a different ethnic background, I would have taken him with open arms."

Watching her friends' hesitation at dating interracially, Aisha says, "Life is too short for people to talk about who they absolutely will not date based on race. I wish more women would say, I will never date a man who didn't treat me as his equal. I will never date a man who is verbally abusive. I will never date a man who was emotionally detached from me during conversations and intimate encounters."

Not Every Sister Is Waiting to Exhale

THE MAN SHORTAGE and the marriage crunch are such popular topics of discussion among black women that we pay little attention to the fact that not all sisters are waiting to exhale. In my interviews I met black women who were absolutely not looking for marriage, who were having too much fun to settle down. Our newfound affluence has bought us newfound freedoms; far from crowding the singles bar, you can find affluent sisters jetting to Paris for the summer sales or chilling on the beach in Jamaica with her homegirls. She may be making deals on the slopes at the Sundance Film Festival or learning how to ride a horse on Sunday afternoons. And while you could gather any group of black women and get a lengthy list of what black men need to work on, black women are acknowledging that they have some work to do, too. One woman I interviewed was model beautiful, 38 and purposefully single. "Men have always chosen me, I never choose them," she said. "I have to turn that around. It's a whole soul-searching endeavor at this point."

It's part of our heritage that our sexuality has been quantified in extremes: either the asexual mammy or the oversexed Jezebel. I still re-member the day, at my first job, when one of my co-workers found out that I wasn't having sex with the man I was dating. A white colleague, a '60s era baby boomer who prided himself on his equal allegiances to Martin Luther King and Miles Davis, he reacted with shock. "I'm really disappointed to hear this," he said. "I thought black people were sup-posed to be more laid back about sex than white people." It's this kind of attitude, both within and outside of our communities, that has prompted many black women to take a sabbatical from sexual relations. You can't count these women among the mythical throngs of sisters looking for a man because right now they're avoiding men like the plague. Do you doubt me? In the year 2000, a black woman minister named Juanita Bynum sold more than a million videos of a sermon she gave entitled "No More Sheets: The Truth About Sex." Across the country, women gave viewing parties of the sermon not unlike the ones that heralded the video release of *Waiting to Exhale.* As Michelle Burford writes in *Essence,* "It's now widely known among black women as, simply, the video."[39] It is one that's prompting thousands of women to hold themselves and their relationships to a higher standard.

The usual recital of unavailable black men usually eliminates men who are in prison, men who have married outside of the race and gay men, in one fell swoop. Yet little or no attention is paid to the fact that for all the black men who are in gay relationships, there is an equal number of black women in gay relationships, too. "Our community is extremely homophobic," says Yvonne Durant, a writer. "That is why black women have a high risk of contracting AIDS. It is also why black men and women are less apt to come galloping out of the closet like whites do every day."

The black gay women's invisibility factor is even greater, filtered as it is through the lens of race, gender and sexuality. But just because the mainstream black community doesn't acknowledge them doesn't take away from the fact that large numbers of black lesbians are in loving, satisfying relationships. The homophobia of the black community makes it difficult for many of these women to come out. "I think what happens when you're black is you feel your community is an oasis against some of the white racist people you know," says writer Linda Villarosa. "And you become really afraid you're going to lose that."[40] In a community that's notoriously homophobic, it's entirely possible that the single woman who "can't find a good man" isn't looking for a man at all. When we state that black women are having a hard time finding partners that match their earnings and education, do we know that this is the experience of black lesbians?

As professional black women we have changed so much in a single generation: our education levels, our incomes, public perception of who we are and how we perceive ourselves. The ways in which our relationships have changed, are changing, is an important, dynamic piece of the puzzle. You can pass anti-discrimination laws and you can pressure corporations to enforce fair hiring practices, but love and marriage can't be legislated. Each woman makes her own way and, if she's lucky, finds what she's looking for. In that way we're no different from our nonblack sisters, even if within their own racial groups, the odds of their meeting a compatible mate seem to favor them more than our own. What's important is that we don't get so caught up in the numbers that we send the wrong message to our daughters; we don't want them to grow up believing that their strength, intelligence or economic success will become a romantic liability. In our own lives, as well as in the presence of the next generation, we have to watch our words, as well as our actions. This, not some statistical rendering of numbers, is what will keep black love and relationships alive.

A Love Supreme: Carla Harris

DURING HER 15-YEAR career at Morgan Stanley, Carla Harris learned to wheel and deal with the best of them. Rising to the rank of managing director, she was responsible for some of the most public IPOs (Initial Public Offerings) of the 1990s: Martha Stewart, Donna Karan and UPS. Over breakfast at a favorite midtown diner, she says, "UPS was probably the highlight. At the time, it was the largest IPO in U.S. history, it was $5.5 billion. Everyone knows United Parcel and it was a company that was very dear to my heart, being away from home for such a long time."

Home is Jacksonville, Florida. While Carla, 39, may boast two Harvard degrees and all the trappings of success, Jacksonville is never far from her heart. It's in the slight Southern twang in her voice, that nearly 20 years of living in the Northeast hasn't erased. It's in her connection to the church and the gospel music that she sings on the outgoing message on her answering machine. It's even, some say, in the gigantic gold and diamond earrings she wears—that look more like something the wife of a Texas oil baron would wear than a conservative New York stockbroker. That too, is not too far off from Carla Harris's roots. She was born in Port Arthur, Texas, though she grew up in Florida.

Her father managed a commercial fishing boat and was gone six months of the year. Her mother taught physical education and retired, at the end of her career, as the assistant principal of a middle school. She grew up watching her mother run the household—doing it all, and Carla believes, having it all. "My mother really managed everything, and so seamlessly," she says. "I never thought twice about working, having a family, having a social life. There was never a conflict for me because I just saw her do it. When I got to business school, and later after being on the Street (Wall Street), people would always say, 'How do you manage it all?' It was an interesting question to me because I thought you just do it. You just do it."

Carla and her mother remain close and what she remembers, as a child, is that her mother was always there for her. And not just Carla, but many of the young people in her neighborhood who came to her for advice and guidance. "She was always around for the things that I needed and she had a thriving career," Carla says. "The other kids used to come to talk to her about their life and what they wanted to do in the future, so I always saw her as a sort of counselor. There never seemed to be a sense of sacrifice, nor did she seem like she was tired, or that she didn't have the time."

Yet, the message was very clear that success—in life or work—would not come easy. Carla's paternal grandmother founded and ran the neighborhood tavern for 40 years. It's a business that her father now manages, since Carla's grandmother is retired. "My grandmother used to always say to me, 'Whatever you do, whatever you want to be, be good at it. Make sure you're at the top,'" Carla recalls. "My mother used to always have the same concept. Don't ever be on the margin. We live in a world that as a black woman, if you're on the margin, you will never benefit. Always be so outstanding that there's never a question." As a Harvard undergrad and later at Harvard Business School, Carla always focused on being in the top of her class. The Harvard name on her degree was never enough. She remembers that in graduate school, one of her professors asked her why is it so important to get to the top? She told him, "It's so that I have credibility. So I can tell somebody else, who dreams of doing the same thing. 'You can do this.'"

At the same time, she never neglected her social life. She always dated. She always attended church. She always indulged her passion for singing. In college, she sang in a band called the Rhythm Company. At business school, even with a hardcore curriculum and a laserlike focus on achieving top grades, she sang in a band called the Late Night band. "We did a little Madonna, a little Steely Dan, a little Aretha," she says with a grin. While she was quickly becoming a star at Morgan Stanley, she spent her down time performing at weddings, open-mike nights, she even recorded an album. The record sold 5,000 copies and all proceeds went to fund scholarships at parochial schools in Jacksonville and in Harlem. "My personal life has always been important because I found that there was one year in my life where all I did was work," she says. "It was my first year out of college and that was the year I realized I could never just be one-dimensional because then you become the function of somebody's day. If the only thing in your life is work, then if things go terribly at work, or you know, a client yells at you, or a manager yells at you, then your whole world comes tumbling down. But if you have a number of different things define you, and you still have a bad day at work, then it's not like the curtain is coming down because you have other aspects of your life that give you that positive feedback."

Love proved more elusive than professional success, but she refused to be discouraged. "I don't think the more successful you are, the harder it is," she says, firmly. "I would not buy into that because the corollary theory is, 'Don't become successful or you won't find a man.' And I absolute can't stand that. I would negate that, deny that, refute that all day long." She insists that dating can be hard not just for black women, but for working women of all races. Successful women, she says, may have less tolerance and time for some of the back-and-forth of dating games. But that is something that is individual to each woman and the choices she makes.

"On the other hand, there is an increasing number of guys who respect and want to have a woman that is ambitious, can think for herself and is not entirely dependent on him," she says. "I'll tell you, I was shocked when I went back to my business school reunions. The number of men in my section, my harddriving section, had decided that they were going to get off track and take a job that would allow them to spend more time with their families. They want their kids to know them in ways that they never knew their fathers because that generation of men was never home." As more men make that decision, the value of a woman who can substantially contribute to the family income rises. As I listen to Carla speak, I wonder if this changing focus of men is more specific to white men because black men don't have the same long history of confidence and achievement in the work place. I imagine that for many black men, taking a back seat to a woman financially still feels much more like emasculation than emotional liberation.

Although she did not marry until her late 30s, Carla says she never doubted that she would find her love supreme. What did surprise her is that she'd have to go all the way back to Jacksonville, Florida, to find the man she would spend the rest of her life with. "The guy that I married is the guy who took me to my senior prom in high school," she says, still a newlywed. Her face flushes slightly when she speaks of her husband, Victor Franklin. "If you had asked me on May 6, 1980, if this was the guy that I would be married to 21 years later, I would have said, 'No way!' " Breaking up after high school, the couple hadn't seen each other for years when they ran into each other in 1994. Victor was living in Georgia at the time. Despite a 13-hour date where they "talked and talked and talked," it would take another two years for the couple to live in the same city and another five years before they walked down the aisle.

Carla says it was worth the wait. Victor is an assistant manager at a New Jersey hotel and, by comparison, Carla's career is light years ahead. But the fact that they have known each other since they were children helps to bridge the economic gap. They are both church-going, family-oriented people who like long Sunday dinners and visits home to Jacksonville. Despite the differences in their income, they are, as the Bible says, evenly yoked. "When Victor saw Carla Harris again, after all those years," she explains, "he saw the girl that he met at age 12, that he took to the prom at age 17, that he's meeting again at 30 something. So he was able to then add on Harvard undergrad, Harvard MBA, Wall Street investment banker. He added all that onto the core. Whereas other guys that I would meet would just see the resumé first, then get to know the woman or sometimes *not* get to know the woman. But Victor knew the woman and so he just perused the resumé. That makes all the difference."

Black Men, Black Women and How the
Green Gets In Between

WE NEVER WANT to say it's about the money. Women don't want to be perceived as gold diggers. Men are hard-pressed to admit that they feel threatened when their partners outearn them. But the greenback dilemma is the number one issue when it comes down to relationships between black men and women; especially when you're talking about successful black women. We're often blamed for wanting partners who can be our financial and professional equals. "Black women have this American dream image in their head about their ideal man," says Audrey Chapman, a Washington, D.C., marriage therapist. "It's not Afrocentric or collective. It's a very Westernized and very capitalistic view of a relationship." My question is what is wrong with black women buying into the American dream? It sure beats lying prone in a thatched hut waiting for the master of the compound to swing by for a quickie.

For some men, our success is nothing short of a betrayal. If we're alone, they assert, it's because we shouldn't have been so darn uppity— putting ourselves through school and pursuing lucrative jobs. In *Do Black Women Hate Black Men?*, psychologist A. L. Reynolds III lays the blame for the fissure in our relationships squarely at black women's feet. "After World War II, progress for black women outpaced that for black men," he writes. "As black men were in uniform, black women were rising in the workplace. More opportunities opened up for them. Then many black women embraced a women's liberation movement which further separated them from black men as they sought, at long last, equality in the home as in the work place. Thus, black men felt not only the sting of discrimination and lack of opportunity in white society's job market. They also were being looked down on by the now better-educated, better-paid black women as well as the vocal women's libbers."[41] He overlooks the fact that black women, and white women, too, lost their jobs to men when the war concluded.

Black women are urged to marry men who are less educated and make less money than they do. "It's about what's in his heart," is the common refrain. And the truth is we do marry out of our economic class; a black woman is ten times as likely to marry a man who makes less than she does than her white counterpart. How does money affect the happily ever after in these relationships? The women I've talked to over the last three years say that when a woman earns more, she not only bears the brunt of the resentment but shoulders the responsibility of making sure that her partner doesn't feel outclassed in their shared conversations and activities. It's a heavy burden to bear. "It's really tricky," says Walteen Grady-Truely, who is divorced. "I see articles in magazines like *Essence* that talk about how highly educated black women need not be such snobs about our mate selections and that we should look at brothers who are technical workers or blue-collar workers. My husband was a technical worker and, while he was very supportive of all my aspirations and stayed home with our son while I traveled, some element of our differences ultimately came down to class."

Actress Lorraine Touissant thinks that middle-class women who don't date blue-collar men aren't being elitist. She says that it's too simplistic to assume that those men are any easier to meet. "Especially when you are moving up the ranks of corporate America," she says. "More than likely there's going to be one brother, maybe two if you're lucky, that's on a similar kind of track. And if you're moving up the track that means that you're putting in ridiculous hours to do what you're doing to get where you want to go. You really don't have time to go to the church socials to meet guys outside of the work place or outside of your own circle. We fall in love when we get thrown into certain situations, so it takes a lot of energy to go find the construction worker."

Money woes are the number one cause of divorces, but black women often ignore a mate's earning capacity in the name of racial unity. "I never thought about success from a purely materialistic standpoint until this was a downfall in my marriage," Walteen says. "I kept ignoring how my husband wasn't making money and was leaving jobs and having trouble getting stabilized and then I found myself shouldering more and more responsibility for those things to a point where it was detrimental to me."

As successful black women, we've worked hard to get where we are. There's a real question about whether we can fully enjoy our success, and more important, continue to grow, when we've made a life-long commitment to a man who inhabits a different socioeconomic sphere. "Let's put it on the table," said former HBO producer Tracey Kemble, in an interview with *Newsweek.* "Sometimes because we have achieved a certain degree of success there will be those people who will say, 'Well, have you looked at the mailman or the construction worker?' These are wonderful jobs. But why should we have to? I mean, how will we meet him? If we're in a certain demographic then shouldn't we be meeting men who are in that demographic?"

At 36, Robin Nelson-Rice has the kind of life—and husband—that many people dream of. Her husband is general manager of a major pharmaceutical company. After giving birth to twins last year, and having an older son, Solomon, Robin decided to try life as a stay-at-home mom. Before that, though, she was her husband's colleague, a product manager in the same company. She says that she never doubted that she would meet a black man who was her financial and professional equal. "I didn't think it would be harder, I actually thought that going to business school, and bringing more to the table, would make it easier," she says. "My personal situation was that I was running from marriage. I didn't want that and wanted to prolong it for much longer. I ended up marrying a very successful man, but I wasn't as ready as he was to be married at the time."

For our interview, I met Robin at a posh restaurant in the Kensington section of London. She isn't hard to spot, the only other black woman in the joint. She's wearing a pantsuit and has relaxed hair that's cut into a short, professional style that frames her face. The restaurant was her suggestion and, after four years of living abroad, London is very much home. "I can remember being in business school with several women who felt that if they weren't hooked up before they left school, that was their last chance," Robin says. "My girlfriend Sheila and I shared the same views in that regard. We always said that was other women's problems. Neither of us ever felt like 'Oh my goodness, what are we going to do? We must have a man!'"

It's easy to say that Robin was simply lucky, but I can't help but feel that would be throwing away the lesson of her experience. Certainly part of what made her attractive was her confidence. She also seemed to be keenly aware that despite the statistics, the hundreds of thousands of black men that aren't marriage material for one reason or another, she didn't need the entire scale to tilt in her direction. She only needed to meet one man. "My question was always, 'Am I compatible with this person? Can we grow together?'" she says, "As opposed to 'How much money does he make?' There was a saying in my business school called HIP: High Income Potential and it was used by women of all backgrounds."

What would Robin have done if she hadn't met her husband in business school? She says she was running from marriage then, but what if she was 36 and single? She's aware of the growing number of black women choosing interracial relationships, but it wouldn't have been her choice. "I've never been attracted to white men," she says. "I'm not against it. I have lots of white friends, I'm just not interested." It's a choice, however, that more and more black women are making.

Prince Charming Changes His Color

IN THE LAST 20 years, black women have begun to date and marry interracially in record numbers. In 1980, there were 27,000 new marriages between black women and white men. By 1990, that number had doubled to 54,000. By 2000, the number had exploded to 122,000 new marriages. Black men still marry outside the race in greater numbers, but the message is clear. "It's a way of taking charge," says Rita Dove, the Pulitzer Prize–winning poet, who is married to a white German man. "They're saying 'I'm waiting for Prince Charming, but the important thing is that he's charming, not that he's black.'" Feminist writer bell hooks puts an even finer point on it. "Keep this in mind, girlfriend," she has said. "This generation of black women is growing up in a truly integrated pop culture. Most black women under the age of 30 would rather have a rich white man than a poor black man."

Black men who marry white women have long encountered criticism from the black community. The arguments are old, vicious and familiar. Take for example, the joke that asks what's the first thing a black man gets when he has some money? The answer: a new car and a white woman. It's long been perceived that a white, especially blonde, woman is a status symbol and those who insist the myth is based in reality point to any number of black male celebrities and athletes.

Interestingly enough, black women who marry white men are

spared some of the same vitriol. Yes, there are those who argue that black women who choose white partners are siding with "the man" and are inherently powerless in the relationship. They say white men who choose black women look at them as exotics and sexual playthings, rarely anything more. But the critics of black women marrying interracially are in the minority.

At one NAACP Image Awards ceremony, the host, comedian Steve Harvey, asked film critic Roger Ebert to guess the name of an Isley Brothers song. When he guessed correctly, the camera panned to the black woman sitting next to him. "Is that your wife?" Harvey asked. When Ebert nodded, Harvey broke into a smile. "Two thumbs up," he quipped. And this is the telling thing, the entire auditorium gave Ebert a standing ovation. "If that had been a black man with a white wife at the NAACP Awards, the reaction would not have been that way," notes San Francisco psychologist, Julia Hare.[42]

"This is a gross generalization, but I've noticed that black men that date outside of their race will date whomever," says novelist Tracie Howard. "The standards for a sister are high, but for other women it lowers. Black women are different. I dated one white man and he was a multi-millionaire, he was one of the richest men in Atlanta. That's not why I dated him, he was a great person. But if I'm going to date outside of the race, the bar is going to be higher. For black men, it's lower. I don't get that."

Camille, a 34-year-old college professor, points to Octavia Butler's novel, *Kindred,* as a metaphor for the brutal honesty that must take place in black-white interracial relationships in the United States. In the novel, the protagonist is an African-American woman married to a white man. Throughout the story, the woman is inexplicably yanked back into the time of slavery, to its pain, to its cruelty, and then she's thrown back into the present, into the 20th-century legacy. The fluidity of past and present and how it rocks the couples' relationship speaks to Camille's sense that the past is *always* present. It sets a tone of openness in her own interracial marriage. "My husband is a white European man," she says. "I like the fact that he's not American. We learn a lot from each other. We're profoundly different from one another and also very much alike. We're very honest with each other and I feel no apprehensions about coming home from work and railing about racism and sexism in the work place, at the mall, in the grocery store. I have no reservations about pointing out the privileges he has as a white European man in the United States."

Yvonne Durant, who has lived in Italy, found that there was a difference between dating white American men and white European men, though she is quick to point out that she doesn't put either on a pedestal. "I've dated several white men and I'm here to tell you they can be just as creepy and trifling and hurtful as any other man." That said, she says, European men have a different history that puts less pressure on the relationship. "Race is always somewhere on the table with a white American man," she says. "When you go out with a European, he's not bringing 300 years of repressed guilt or the issues of the day."

Some critics suggest that there has always been a double standard. Black women celebrities have been marrying white men, without a backlash, since the 1950s. The long list includes Josephine Baker, Pearl Bailey, Lena Horne, Dorothy Dandridge, Eartha Kitt, Diana Ross, Diahann Carroll and Tina Turner. Black women who aren't celebrities are marrying interracially for a number of reasons. Our social circles are broadening. As the country's beauty standards broaden and gorgeous black women appear in ads, magazines, on television and in films, white men are taking a second look. "[The proliferation of beautiful black women in the media] would have to have a psychological impact on white men," says Harvard psychologist Dr. Alvin Pouissant. "White men are now seeing black women as desirable mates. We must remember that black women themselves in the early '70s were really opposed to dating white men. Now they are more comfortable with it and so are white men." [43]

The process of getting comfortable with it is one I am intimately aware of. Just months before completing this book, I became engaged to a white man. From the beginning, he's been far more comfortable with the notion of being in an interracial relationship than I was. When we first started dating I asked him dozens of questions, too embarrassing and personal to repeat, all designed to draw out any hidden racism he might possess. I worried that he had a fascination with black women. Then I worried that he wasn't familiar enough with black culture to understand me and where I was coming from. I cringed when black guys gave us the evil eye on the street. He was positively oblivious. "Too bad," he said, when I asked him if he didn't notice the looks we received. "They had their chance." When I met his family, I examined every interaction with a fine-toothed comb. At the first ugly comment, I would have broken up with him. He says that wouldn't have been fair. Too bad, I told him, I wasn't trying to star in the sequel to *Guess Who's Coming to Dinner?* I spent too much of my professional life doing ad hoc consciousness-raising among ignorant white people. I didn't want to spend my Christmases and Thanksgivings doing the same thing.

Although I'd dated white guys before, I never took them seriously. As Tracie Howard said, when I dated a white guy, my standards were excruciatingly high. That I am getting married is still very much a surprise to me. In 2000, I had met Jason, but I was also dating other guys. On some unspoken level, I always thought I would marry a black man. All of my serious boyfriends have been black and there's so much I love about black men. I love the way they trash talk on the basketball court and how a brother will call you "shortie" when he is holding you close. I love the tones of black skin and watching brothers style and profile: the way Ed Bradley wears an earring on *60 Minutes* and watching Wynton Marsalis jazz up a custom-made suit. I love their voices and the way educated brothers code-switch from the King's English to ghetto slang in the blink of an eye.

When I made the decision to marry Jason, I left behind the comfort zone of being with someone of the same race. As our relationship grew more serious, I had to admit that if Jason were black, I would have thought he was perfect. I began to pay close attention to the type of person he is—his generosity, his sense of humor, the way he was emotionally strong whenever I fell to pieces, which happened a little more often than I care to admit. When I ran my first ten-mile race, Jason rented a car, drove me to the start at 5:00 A.M. and was waiting at the finish line with Gatorade and cheers. He may not be a brother, but he is the very definition of what sisters call "a good man." By the time he proposed, I was convinced that he was perfect. He asked me to marry him, I said yes and, in the middle of writing this book, I became what I am writing about. I'm in love, but I'm also part of an upward slope in the statistics. I'm another sister marrying a white guy.

From Integration to Assimilation

FOR MARTHA SOUTHGATE, her marriage sometimes feels like the almost inevitable conclusion to a lifetime of being an Only. She grew up in the Glenville section of Cleveland, a predominantly black neighborhood that erupted into riots in 1968. Martha was only eight at the time and her street was untouched, so she had little memory of the violence that surrounded her. Her parents were born strivers, in the best definition of the word. Her mother was a social worker who specialized in adoption placement, then later worked at an abortion clinic—a very radical move for a middle-class black woman in the early 1970s. Martha's father was a music teacher in the Cleveland public schools and later became a librarian. Both of her parents continued their schooling into Martha's childhood, each earning a Master's degree, which Martha remembers made them very different from the other parents she knew.

The only whites on Martha's block were the local minister and his family. They moved out not long after the riots. "Partly because they felt too uncomfortable living there after all that had happened," Martha says. While it was strange to see a white person walking down her street, she says her mother always moved comfortably in the white world. Her mother's best friend was a white woman from New York. The two had been roommates in the city, after college. "My mother had a more integrated sensibility," Martha says. "She was always the sort of local hipster in my neighborhood. My dad was less so, more conventional."

Martha is the oldest of four children and was always academically advanced. She was bussed into a gifted public school program and from the age of eight, attended school in a neighborhood miles away from her own. But the real life change came when a group of boys from a prep school called Hawken came to the gifted program to recruit girls. The year was 1974 and the school was going co-ed. Her parents encouraged her to apply, though the school's high price tag was intimidating. She got a scholarship and entered the school the next year. "I really didn't know how different it was going to be," she says. "Some of the wealthiest people in Cleveland sent their kids there." None of her siblings followed in her footsteps to prep school and this set Martha on a permanent path away from her family. "We've had very different educations," she says of her two sisters and brother. "Which has led us to different lives."

Hawken was more than an hour away from Glenville, a big distance for a 14-year-old kid. It housed a working farm and a bucolic campus that was bigger, acre for acre, than some college campuses. Martha loved sewing and for her first day at school, she made a jacket. "It had huge prints, huge doll faces," she remembers. "And I was really proud of it. I got to school and no one had anything like that on. It was all puffy down coats and skinny corduroys. I remember thinking 'This is not right,' and feeling really uncomfortable on my first day."

There were other black students at Hawken but Martha didn't seek them out. She had been the nerd among other black kids: short, with glasses and slow to develop physically. It was the whole "you talk white" scene, and in her neighborhood, Martha remembers that "if someone hit you on the street and you tried to blow them off, they would call you a white bitch." Afraid of being rejected by other black students, who shared her skin color but maybe not her mind-set, she challenged herself to make white friends instead. By the time she enrolled at Smith College, she says, "I carried over this fear from Hawken, so my response was largely to avoid black people." Her closest black female friend was a Caribbean woman who had grown up in Puerto Rico. "She didn't have the American experience as a black person," Martha says. "Which is what I think allowed us to come together."

Martha says she didn't reach out to other black women at Smith, partly because "what I saw some of the black women going through at Smith, I had already gone through at Hawken. I'd had my shock of the white people experience." At the time, she never imagined that her experience of attending a white prep school could have been helpful to other women struggling in a similar environment. "I loved Smith," she says. "I would go there again, but I would change a lot of how I conducted myself there. I would get more involved in black associations. I had just made my decision that the black students were going to be mean to me. I just thought I can't join the Black Student Association because I'll be teased."

It was a decision that set up the social pattern of her adult life. She made few black friends in college and consequently she also didn't get to know any black men. "There's a black community that I feel completely cut off from," she says. "It's just the nature of my experience and I could find my way back if I wanted to, but I just haven't." Having dated mostly white men in college and in her 20s, she wasn't surprised that the person she fell in love with and married was also white. What she can't shake is a feeling that if she had been "blacker," if she'd made more of an effort to be a part of a black community, she might have another life. "In my experience, the black women who are married to white men feel like we were passed up by black men," she says. "We didn't feel like waiting around for them to ask us out. White guys were the ones who asked us out." What feels like a rejection from black men has become, on some level, a symbol of a rejection from the black community at large. "I don't think my friends who are married to white men did it because they prefer white men," Martha says. "Or because of any self-hating kind of thing. There has been a struggle with where they fit into the black community. Among the three or four I know, they have all gone through some version of it. There's this 'you talk white' or you 'do this' and there has been, in all our history, a sense of not quite cutting it." Martha remembers distinctly that when she got a job at *Essence* magazine, the publishing nexus of the black women experience, she still felt left out. "I remember thinking, I don't go around calling everybody 'sister,'" she says. "I don't have the memories they talk about of my grandmother braiding my hair. I would feel like 'this is not me,' so I must not be authentic. This has been my big struggle. What is black? And where do I fit in?"

Martha has been married to her husband, Jeff, for ten years. They have two children, Nate and Ruby, and they live in the Park Slope section of Brooklyn. There are a number of interracial couples in the neighborhood and this helps to make her feel at home. "Every now and then I feel a twinge that perhaps I should live in a predominantly black neighborhood," she says. "I mean the lack of infrastructure presents both political and practical problems. You have to be really committed to stick it out."

Having children has added another level to Martha's experience of living her life entirely in a white world. "I think there have been a couple of times when people have thought I was Nate's sitter and not his mom," she says. "Because there are very few black women in the neighborhood who are at home with their children." Martha has a friend who has had more blatant experiences of the same phenomenon. The woman's daughter is lighter than she is and Martha says, "On more than one occasion, when she was nursing her daughter, she was asked, 'Do you get paid extra to do that?'"

She doesn't want her children to grow up being as uncomfortable around other blacks as she has been. She's started a play group with other black and bi-racial parents. "Jeff and I both feel like we're not bumping into enough black people," she says. "So we have to make a deliberate effort, especially since we've decided to send our children to private school." Oddly enough, she notices that her sister, who lives in a predominantly black neighborhood, is facing the opposite issue. "If anything, my niece Helena is going to have to meet white people," Martha says. "She's going to have to be taken somewhere to meet people, it will require an effort."

That same sister, Martha notes, dated one white guy, then made a decision she would not date white men at all. Now she is married to a black man, lives in a black neighborhood, and lives a life that is the photo-negative opposite of the life that Martha has chosen. Now that she is 40, it seems a wonder to her that one decision could have led her so far from where she began. The riot-torn streets of Glenville, Cleveland, are a million miles, in emotional and psychological distance, from the biracial parents' group she's now a part of in Park Slope.

When the phone rings and a guy asks you to a movie, it hardly seems like a momentous decision. But it continues to be a decision of weight for black women. Especially if the person on the other end of the phone line isn't black. Interracial marriage is a permanent commitment to living life, at least partially, in another world. It's a passport to the most personal kind of integration, one that is guaranteed to change your relationship to both black and white people. "It's like which came first, the chicken or the egg," Martha says. "I ended up hanging around a lot of white people because of where I went to school, the jobs I got, the things I was interested in. I ended up not being in predominantly black situations so that cut down the number of black men that I might meet and who might ask me out. At certain points, I was not so committed to the idea that I would have the marriage I have now. But I really love Jeff and this is where I am."

What Love Teaches Us About Race

BEEN AROUND THE WORLD AND I CAN'T FIND MY BAAAABBBY
27-year-old journalist/filmmaker looking for a man of any color,
who likes himself and loves his mother

BACK IN 1994, when documentary filmmaker Luchina Fisher placed the above ad in a Chicago newspaper, she had no idea that it would lead to meeting her future husband. She did know that as an African-American woman, her male peers seemed not to be overwhelmingly interested in commitment. Dressed in a simple cream scallop-necked blouse and mini skirt, Luchina has wavy shoulder-length hair and big, round eyes that seem to shine with energy and curiosity. "They're always shopping!" she says, unabashedly, about the commitment-phobic black men she has observed. "The supermarket is always open. Their attitude is, "I can always run back and get something else. Or if I go back next week, there'll be something new.'" One gentleman she had a long distance relationship with was 40 and successful. He was wealthy and never hesitated to fly into town, just to take Luchina to dinner. "I was shocked to learn how much of a player he was," she says. "What I took as a romantic gesture that said something about our relationship was essentially a booty call. An expensive booty call, but a booty call all the same."

Growing up as an Army brat, Luchina and her siblings lived in Germany, before settling in Fayetteville, North Carolina. Over the years, she says with a wicked grin, "All of my siblings, including my brother, have been involved with white men." It's something she once thought might worry her father, as a smart, ambitious black man of another generation. It didn't. "He told me, 'I raised you kids to be exposed to all different kinds of cultures,'" she recalls. "That's what he and my mother wanted."

Her "Been around the world" personal ad netted 55 responses the week that it ran. Luchina went out on dates with six guys, the fifth guy was the man who would become her fiancé, David. An Irish Catholic guy who grew up in western Pennsylvania, David appealed to Luchina from the start. "He had lived in France and spoke fluent French," she says. "He was getting his Ph.D. in psychology. My father earned a Master's in psychology and I always loved talking to my father. I wanted to be with someone whom I could talk to on this deeper level. It was the kind of conversation I hadn't had in previous relationships."

On a personal level, Luchina says that being involved with David has taught her to put down the black superwoman mantle she once carried so proudly. "It's so hard for us, as black women, to be vulnerable," she says. "Some of my black girlfriends who aren't in relationship *say* that they want a man who will be there for them and rub their feet. But we can be *so* hard. David showed me this because he doesn't carry the same baggage. He says, 'You're tough. You're a survivor. Your strength is what you needed to get to this point, but you don't have to continue that into our relationship. There has to be room for me to feel needed, that there's a role I play in your life.'"

THE RELATIONSHIP got off to a rocky start. The couple dated for over a year, then broke up. They got together again and once again broke up. Almost three years had passed when they began to consider giving it one more try. "I thought, well, we'll just be good friends," Luchina remembers. "But there were always sparks when we got together or spoke on the phone. We started talking, by e-mail and over the phone, about what it would take to build a lasting relationship. It had to go to another level. We couldn't just date each other casually." When David was offered a job in New York, the couple decided to go for it. Two years later, they are now engaged.

One of the things that interests me about Luchina and David's relationship is how seriously they take the responsibility of being in an interracial relationship. The very first year they began dating, they took a six-week course called "Healing Racism." Luchina says this course gave them a common language with which to discuss race that has shaped and supported their entire relationship. "It's not just talking about my pain, oh, my pain," she says. "It's about empathizing with each other. I learned how to empathize with whites and realize that their privilege makes them *so* blind. Sometimes they are so lonely, they want to reach out to a person of color, but they're scared."

In the course, Luchina and David were surprised to learn how often human problems masquerade as racial problems. This, they say, makes it easier for them not to racialize their own issues. "For example, a white person looks at a group of black people and says, 'Black people are so loud,'" she says. "It's not necessarily that black people are loud, it's that you feel small in your voice because you grew up so repressed. There are actually very few black-and-white issues in our world."

While some may blanch at the notion that interracial relationships promote racial harmony, Luchina says, "We *are* making a difference with our relationship. We go to Riverside Church. One day, we were having a difficult time and our reverend came up to us and said, 'The world needs you.'" Certainly, their relationship has made a difference in how their families view race. David's mother, in particular, has been challenged to think differently. She had always been open to Luchina, but when the couple became engaged, the mother of the groom had what Luchina calls "a moment." It was a difficult period for David, but Luchina says, "I understood that she just needed some time. Two weeks later, she was right behind us. We went to our house and she surprised us with champagne and toasted our relationship. My engagement ring is made of diamonds that belonged to her mother."

As the wedding gets closer, the couple is prepared that more of their relatives may have "a moment," before they accept the relationship, but Luchina and David are ready. "The whole family has to think about race now," Luchina says, a game-face smile planted squarely on her face. "It may be uncomfortable at times, but it's an opportunity."

CHAPTER 11

The Price of the Ticket:
New Challenges and Old Demons

FAMILY RESPONSIBILITY RELATIONSHIPS SUCCESS MOTHERHOOD BALANCE

MAYBE THEY WERE always there—these warnings that money can't buy happiness and that no matter how successful you get, you're still going to carry some of that historic black baggage. It could be that I pay more attention now that I'm in my 30s and planning, for the near future, a wedding and beginning to shape my ideas about family. It is entirely possible that the next generation seems entirely more real, now that I know who the father of my children will be. I think this is why my mouth is on the floor when my friend's teenage daughter tells me that bulimia is such a problem at her school that the pipes in the girl's bathroom were rotted through with stomach acid and were closed for three months because they needed to be replaced.

Mocha Moms founder Cheli Figaro says that she's heard a 100 stories just like it. "Because we are black in America, we are going to be challenged on every level with respect to raising children," she says. "I know a woman whose daughter is concerned about her weight because all the little white girls weigh 62 pounds and she weighs 82 pounds. Our girls end up hating themselves, hating their hair, their faces, their features. I don't want that for my baby. And what they do to black boys, that's a whole 'nother other. That's even worse. They destroy them."

Another day, visiting a new mommy friend, I sat in horror listening to a story about an affluent black couple that sent their kids to the most elite school in New York City. The girl came home and said the other kids told her that her butt was too big. The girl was eight. Countless studies have shown that black women have higher "body esteem" than white women. One recent study, published in the *Journal of Social Psychology*, found that "general positive or negative social feedback influenced the body esteem of white women, but did not influence the body esteem of black women—a difference that occurred despite the fact that both groups reported similar reactions of pleasure or displeasure to the feedback." [44]

In layman's terms, black women don't like being called names any more than white women; however, we do seem more able to not take insults about our weight personally. What we haven't begun to study is how class and environment affect these attitudes. Does a black girl growing up in Palo Alto have the same thick skin as a girl growing up in southside Chicago? Does a girl from the suburbs care that her look would be more accepted, even revered, in the 'hood? Or are the children of black middle-class families more conditioned by friends and fashion magazines than by their family and people who look like them? "We're seeing a homogenization and globalization of beauty ideals," Toronto psychologist Niva Piran told *Maclean's* magazine. "It's white. It's thin. And the result is that people come to identify less with their own cultures and more with an image in the media." [45]

Even in the field of psychology, where scientists work so hard to be specific, we are still speaking—and studying—in broad strokes. More often than not, it's black or white, not rural white versus urban white versus middle-class black versus poverty-level black. It was easy, when I was growing up in predominantly black neighborhoods, to dismiss certain societal bugaboos, such as bulimia and body image, as a "white girl thing." But now I know that by pure dint of being brought up in integrated middle-class neighborhoods my children won't have the luxury of dismissing certain challenges as being purely out of their cultural milieu.

The next generation of young black women—the daughters of lawyers, doctors and swans—will live in a more integrated world than most of their mothers could imagine. Yet, they will still be charged with negotiating the politics of difference—how are they different from their peers in upbringing and how are they the same? How important are physical differences (the shape of a young girl's behind, a young boy's darker skin) when they live in the same up-scale neighborhood as their white peers and their parents drive the same kind of car? The answer is, of course, that it varies. The problem is that there is so little precedent that each teen must negotiate a changing set of boundaries on her own.

When I went away to college in 1987, there were still large numbers of white kids who had little or no introduction to either black people or black culture. Other students routinely asked to touch my hair. One girl paraded around a letter from her family's black maid as if it was as exotic and impossible as a telephone call from the family dog. The next wave of the integration generation will benefit from greater familiarity. Turn on MTV and it's easy to see that just as Motown was the "Sound of Young America" in the early 1960s, hip-hop has become the sound of young America today. Rap music supplies the unifying fashion, lingo and aesthetic for black kids and white kids, adolescent Latinos and Asian-American teens.

Recently, on a train in New Jersey, I saw two girls riding home from a Michael Jackson concert at Madison Square Garden. They wore their hair in the same elaborately braided style. The girl with red hair was either white or a very fair-skinned black young woman. Sitting a few rows behind them, it was impossible to get any clues from their language. They spoke in the same lilting accent, used the same slang, had the same body language. When they turned to leave the train at the New Brunswick stop, I could see that the girl with red hair was white and it was hard not to stare.

For a short while, when I was much younger, Bo Derek braids had been the trend, but the white girls who wore them seemed pitifully affected. Even now, when I travel to the Caribbean, the airport is full of them—young white girls (and sometimes mom) who got their hair braided on a Jamaican or Trinidadian beach. Everything about this girl, from the natural way she spoke about going with her friend to "get her weave tightened up" to the way she described Michael Jackson's performance as "banging," bespoke an intimacy with black culture that is hard to fake.

While it may be true that many young people, of all colors, speak a universal hip-hop language, parents of black children are still concerned that when push comes to shove, their kids will be the ones that will suffer for not speaking the King's English. "I don't care if the white kids speak the same slang," one older white man said, talking to me about his bi-racial, college student son. "When it comes to getting a job after he graduates, they are going to think the white kid is hip and that Eric is ignorant."

If the challenge for those of us who came of age in the '70s and '80s was to bridge the predominantly black world of our neighborhood or our families with the predominantly white worlds of universities and workplaces, then the challenge of the next generation has only become transmuted, it hasn't disappeared. For Eric's generation, there is still the pressure of never being able to entirely let down their guard. "I have a very close group of white girlfriends, but I put limits on the interactions I have with them because their perspective is different," I was told by Sheila, a 20-something lawyer with a prominent Seattle firm. "I know that I can rely on them if I ever needed anything, but I'm not always as open with them, because they won't be able to relate to all the things I come into contact with." I wonder if she is ever guarded around other blacks. "I'm most guarded in all-white rooms," she says. "But I can be equally guarded in all-black rooms, especially among the more elitist black organizations: Links, Jack and Jill, most of the sororities."

I found it intriguing that this woman also felt uncomfortable in some black organizations, especially ones like Jack and Jill, an organization that was started in 1938 by 20 middle-class black women, looking to form a strong social foundation for their children—exactly the sort of organization that fosters high achievers like Sheila. At the same time, I wasn't surprised. Several of the women that I interviewed spoke with real pain in their voices about being excluded from black sororities and of having their children, and by extension, themselves, rejected from Jack and Jill. No matter how much black middle-class parents do to prepare their children, to fill them with a sense of confidence and entitlement, there is nothing they can do about the ways race and racism will surface in their child's life except to warn them not to get too comfortable—that inevitably, the ground beneath their children's well-soled feet is bound to shift. As we are learning in this post–civil rights era, there is no immunization against prejudice, and, in contrast to the days when to be suspicious of white folks was a good rule of thumb, now we know that some of the people who are going to make us feel most uncomfortable are actually going to share our color. For a people raised with a healthy sense of "us versus them," these shifting dynamics of community, loyalty and trust can be unsettling and disturbing.

Not More Than We Can Bear, More Than We Should Have To

AS BLACK WOMEN, the single biggest health challenge we face is our weight. If bulimia and anorexia are still more prevalent among white women, then let's be clear. I'm not talking about schoolyard mean fat, but life-threatening, heart-stopping fat. We're not alone. According to the National Center for Health Statistics, one in two Americans is obese. The problem is that sisters are the most overweight group in the country. (Latinas are second.) In 1998, the average black woman wore a size 18. Today, she wears a size 20. "The mistake that is happening is this 'full-figured title,'" said obesity specialist Dr. Soundrea Hickman in the March 2000 issue of *Ebony*. "She's no longer considered obese. She's just full-figured. It's a death sentence for the black woman. I'd like to choke the person who came up with that title because it's killing us and I'm sick and tired of going to funerals of black women in their fifties."

"I speak from experience and the extra weight I put on due to health issues," says Kencle Satchell-McKoy, who is married to her college sweetheart. "My weight gain has affected my entire life. I don't feel as confident, cute, or sexy. I'm also very self-conscious of how others view me as well. I think time is a huge dynamic in black women and weight gain. We are wearing a lot of hats as mothers, wives and professionals and time is limited. Self is put on the back burner and is often neglected, which will affect one's health. Exercise is not a necessity but a luxury."

Many experts say that our weight issues are the outward expression of inner turmoil. We've overcome so many of society's limitations on us: stereotypical and punishing beliefs about our abilities, our sexuality, our beauty and our intelligence. We no longer cling to the myth of the black superwoman and, if we sometimes get a little greedy and want it all, we're becoming increasingly comfortable with the idea that having our dreams and desires, the plums of marriage, family and career success, one at a time. Yet the stress of combating issues of race, class, gender—not to mention all the universal stresses of modern life— takes its toll. Increasingly, black women suffer from clinical levels of depression.

Having little historical experience with the concept of therapy and the idea of depression, we are likely to dismiss our problem as a simple case of one rough day too many. When we're down, we try to rally by recalling Bessie Smith and the notion that "wild women don't wear no blues." We turn our anger inward by exhibiting self-sabotaging behavior such as over-eating or we criticize ourselves by calling ourselves lazy when we can't accomplish 20 things in a single day. (The last of these being a phenomenon I'm way too familiar with.) In 1998, writer Meri Danquah broke an all-too-common silence with the publication of *Willow Weep for Me: A Black Woman's Journey Through Depression.* The thorns of Danquah's pain are ones that were familiar to many black women: sexual abuse, domestic violence, single motherhood and a pervading sense of fatalism—darkness and exhaustion that she could not shake.

While sisterhood is powerful, seeking professional help is still anathema for many black women. Therapy is another one of those things that is too easily dismissed as a "white girl" thing, even when the cost of therapy is not an issue. "Culturally, African Americans tend not to go to counseling, period, for anything, let alone depression," psychologist Paula Mickens-English told the *Cleveland Plain Dealer.* "Mostly because we have tended to deal with things within the family and have also used what could be considered nontraditional counseling approaches, like going to a minister." In her doctoral dissertation, Mickens-English studied the stress levels of 90 black women in support groups. While therapy helped, she found that even after 12 weeks of mental health support, the black women's stress levels were still skyrocketing and were equal to white women patients in a psychiatric ward. In an effort to combat what she sees as dangerously high stress levels, she has led a black women's support group for over a decade, through her Cleveland Heights private practice, Northcoast Afrocentric Counseling Services.

In the 1990s, suicide among successful, high-profile black women began to make the news. In 1995, black women were shocked by the suicide deaths of singer Phyllis Hyman, famous for her rendition of "Betcha By Golly Wow," and author Terri Jewell, *The Black Woman's Gumbo Ya-Ya*. For the most part, suicide is not our métier. White women are three times as likely to end their own lives, black men are eight times as likely to commit suicide and white men are fourteen times as likely to kill themselves.[46] Still, as Esther Iverem pointed out in an *Essence* article titled "Over the Edge": "For every sister who makes that fatal leap, there's another who has thought about it or tried it or is taking the long, slow route. Mental health experts point out that many black women are also killing themselves softly in ways not measured by suicide statistics, with drugs, alcohol or compulsive overeating."[47]

Ain't Nothing Going on but the Rent

THERE HAVE ALWAYS BEEN black women who were material girls. Long before Lil' Kim and Eve rapped about being laced in platinum and ice (diamonds), there have been black women who made it clear that the best things in their world were far from free. In the 1960s, Eartha Kitt created a classic hit when she purred, "Santa baby/forgot to mention one little thing/A ring/I don't mean on the phone." In the 1970s, Jessica Folker topped the charts with "Ain't Nothing Going on but the Rent," urging her sisters to take up her "no romance without finance" battle cry and warning potential suitors that they had to have a "J-O-B, if you want to be with me." In the 1980s, hip-hop artists began to name-check for every designer under the sun: Bally, Calvin Klein, Gucci, Chanel, you name it.

Increasingly, young black women and men began to define success in startlingly materialistic terms. Because they weren't buying their designer clothes with stock earnings, the drug culture was glorified more than ever before. This, in itself, is a tragedy that our community continues to reel from. But the real tragedy is how the more gangsta-oriented elements of hip-hop culture are married to the notion that drug dealing is the only realistic road to riches and set up women as nothing but gold-digging skeezers. As Lisa Jones writes in her collection of essays, *Bulletproof Diva:*

> The woman-as-gold-digger image is as old as the hills. The *Oxford English Dictionary*'s first reference is this from 1920: women who "dig for the gold of their gentlemen friends and spend it on being good to their mothers and pet dogs." By way of rap etymology, skeezer comes from the verb to skeeze (to fornicate, particularly a rap entourage with groupies on the road). When you dig behind the skeezer/gold-digger character you find a storehouse of male fear and insecurity. Music videos that feature skeezers are more successful as portraits of male ineptitude than paeans to machismo. EPMD's "Gold Digger" begins with the rappers in a group therapy session with a white shrink. Later, the guys twiddle their thumbs while axe-toting women, spray painted in gold, work the EPMD gold mine.

In the 1990s, the material girls took their gloves off, making straightforward connections between the size of a man's wallet and the likelihood to get into a sister's pants. TLC made it clear that they had no interest in penniless chumps in "No Scrubs": "Want to get with me with no money? Oh no, I don't want no scrubs."

In 1999, Destiny's Child shot to fame with "Bills, Bills, Bills," a song that proclaimed that the singer could "chill" with someone who paid the bills, but a suitor who was low on cash shouldn't waste her time.

In 2001, Blu Cantrell charged her way to pop stardom with her advice to women on how to make a cheating man pay with "Hit 'Em, Up Style," a song that suggested the best way to get back at a boyfriend is to swipe his credit cards and charge them to the limit.

What does the consistent emphasis on materialism in relationships and marriage say to our young daughters? What does it say to our sons?

Just as important, what message are we sending to ourselves? For one, we've become a community of consumers who wear our wealth. We've also allowed our search for love to be tinged by a desire for material wealth. So many young black women seem to be looking for a man with money, and so many young men seem to be looking for a woman who looks like money. Not to say this phenomenon doesn't exist in the mainstream culture. But in black culture, this rampant materialism pervades not only the dating scene and the stories we tell anecdotally, but every aspect of our media: music, magazines, television, movies and the ever-popular nouveau chitlin circuit of black comedians. We complain about the bills, bills, bills, but seem unwilling to acknowledge that culturally we are writing checks our relationships and our self-esteem must cash.

Some might say that by powerfully co-opting the skeezer moniker (As in, "Yeah, I'm a skeezer and you're not enough of a big money baller to get with me"), black women entertainers are de-fanging the term in the same way that some rappers appropriated "nigger" and some feminists appropriated "bitch." But were the young women who danced along to these songs and appropriated these anthems really that savvy?

The songs I've quoted here are not just emblematic of hip-hop kids. In the October 2000 *Journal of Family Issues,* psychologist Faustina E. Haynes wrote about her study of black middle-class Americans. In her study, a man's ability to provide was "a strong expectation among male and female respondents." In turn, black men tended to suffer from what is known as "provider role strain" while black women created "gender strategies and family myths to maintain a balance between their autonomy and their husband's presumed need to maintain his masculinity through the auspices of the provider role." As one study respondent, a 42-year-old divorcée, put it, "Employed? Yes sir, he better. He better have a job or [he is] out of here! I ain't taking care of no grown man." Compare that comment, published in a sociological journal, with lyrics from TLC and Destiny's Child and it becomes clear that there's more truth than fiction in black women's R&B.

It's interesting to note how the pure numbers game among black professionals and the ways in which black educated men are believed to have their pick among women intersects with the hip-hop notion of the gold-digging skeezer. The skeezer is set up, again and again, as the romantic rival to the professional woman. Both desire an affluent man as their partner, though perhaps not for entirely the same reasons. In turn, the men are looking for a woman who embodies some, if not all, of the traits of the "trophy" girls of the hip-hop videos. Regardless of her educational background, a woman who hopes to land a high-status man must be as well groomed as a French mistress—perfect manicures and pedicures, a stylish haircut, the best designer clothes she can afford to buy.

In a 2002 article in the popular young black women's magazine *Honey* there is a sidebar entitled, "How to Snag a Baller"—basically a ghetto version of *How to Marry a Millionaire*. In some ways, the advice is enough to make anyone with vaguely feminist leanings cringe, everything from tips on "hair, makeup, nails, figure" to advice that urges women to "Close your mouth" and "Never let him see you sweat." But that's too simplistic. There is a lot of America in African Americans. Doesn't it make sense that now that we've begun to achieve the level of prosperity that white folks enjoyed after World War II, that we are also, however covertly, harking toward those ideals? After a turbulent 20th century that saw the political, economic and emotional breakdown of the black family, is it really so surprising that black middle-class families lean toward tradition? "I found that although these [black] men and women say that they want egalitarian marriages, their ideologies and expectations about marital life reflect neo-patriarchal gender ideals," writes Bryn Mawr sociologist Faustina Haynes. "This finding speaks directly against the popular theory in family scholarship that proposes that black families are typically matriarchal."

The yearning is understandable, but the manifestation—the consistent emphasis on luxury goods, money for sex or money for punishment for sexual betrayal—and the confusing ways that it manifest in our marriages ("provider strain" and "gender games") are all indications that what held our families together through hundreds of years of slavery is not holding us together now. Our ancestors deserve better. We deserve better. Our children want better.

Cruising black websites, I read this post from a young black woman: "Understand that there is more to life than a model-type woman, wearing ice and driving an expensive car. That was someone else's dream, that belongs to the spirit of consumption and greed—the heart of capitalist America." The message was followed by this response from a young black man: "Hey, this is dynamite stuff," he writes. "I've long felt that materialism is a profound curse in the black community. It's very difficult to get a handle on, too, because we are inundated from birth. We will never be rid of it, but our people should learn to temper it, and control it, so it doesn't eat us alive. It's tough, I know!"

I read the back-and-forth of their message board post, quietly whispering Amen, and then I got to the young man's final message: "As soon as we quit trying to hustle up the cash to front a gold-plated Lexus or a sparkling new BMW... then we can focus on more important things like taking time out to talk to one another; helping our kids with their homework; owning the roof over our heads and so on." The challenges I've discussed in this chapter—body image, social integration for black middle-class teens, weight issues, depression, materialism—are all powerful reminders that if we want to have it all, we need to begin with, to borrow a phrase from Gloria Steinem, revolution from within.

CHAPTER 12

Black Cinderellas: Finally,
Sisters Are Going to the Ball

FAMILY RESPONSIBILITY RELATIONSHIPS SUCCESS MOTHERHOOD BALANCE

ANNA PEREZ HAS A MOVIE STAR smile: each tooth an ivory door in a doll's house, with a distinctive gap between the front two. Her laugh is more Tinseltown than Washington Beltway, it's mischievous, slightly bodacious and never, ever buttoned up. She made her reputation (and some news) as someone who says what she thinks during George Bush's presidency, when she acted as the First Lady's press secretary—the first black woman to do so. There wasn't any of the usual smoke-and-mirror publicity stuff that's routine among those who are gatekeepers to celebrities and public figures. A reporter who asked her about Barbara Bush's hair, wardrobe or decorating preferences would be rebuked with a cheerful, "No way!" When one reporter asked to trail along on a designer fitting with the First Lady, Anna let her know, "In a pig's eye!"

She was as straightforward and no-nonsense as her boss. While reporters grew to love her during her four-year tenure at the White House, she never stopped letting them know when she believed they were way out of line. When Bush lost the 1992 election, Anna scoffed at reporters who theorized that Barbara Bush was secretly relieved. "What rot!" Perez told *Seattle Post-Intelligencer* Christopher Hanson, drawing on one of her favorite phrases. "What rot! Absolutely not! She hated losing. She feels George Bush is by any measure...best for the country."[48] When it became known that the Bushes were building their retirement home on a modest lot in Houston, the *Los Angeles Times* commissioned an architect to design a home that would remedy the obvious space problems of the large Bush extended family. The proposed solution was a home with multiple levels beneath ground—three to be exact—a kind of luxe bomb shelter/retirement home. Perez promptly shot back that the *Times* deserved the "Dumb Story of the Year" award. "For goodness sake, it sounded like something out of a James Bond movie," she said. "Three levels underground. Subterranean life. I know they're going to be more private than they have been before, but three stories underground is ridiculous!"

The friendly fire wasn't aimed simply at the media. Anna and Barbara Bush enjoyed taking their shots at each other. Bush publicly and repeatedly urged the no-frills Anna to do something about her short, curly Afro—she never cared for it. In return, Anna made good-hearted cracks about the first dog. One year, Perez was photographed at a White House correspondents' dinner, donning sunglasses and smiling mischievously with Donald Trump's ex, Marla Maples. Not long afterward, she showed up at an event only to be greeted by Barbara Bush, the First Lady's staff and Secret Service agents all wearing dark glasses and plastic ID tags with the Perez/Maples photo laminated for posterity. "Utter humiliation," she says with a giggle. The two women began their work together as strangers and left the White House as friends. Every year, Anna, her husband, Ted and their two children visit the Bushes at their summer home in Maine.

But her time in the White House wasn't all about newsbreaks and quick comebacks. After eight years in Washington, four as a press aide in Congress and four in the Senate, she had furiously campaigned for the job on the First Lady's staff. Fans on Capitol Hill noted that although she didn't have a college degree, she was extraordinarily well suited for the job because of her "sense of humor, fearlessness and ability to work very hard." During the course of her interviews, she was relentlessly covered by the media: a sister on the White House staff is always news. She met the President on Martin Luther King day and he introduced himself by saying "I'm George Bush and you're Anna Perez. I've been reading about you in the papers." The timing of the event moved Anna. "What a way to celebrate Martin Luther King's birthday," she says. "Dare I hope, he would really be proud of his country."

The most fairy-tale moment of all came when she accompanied the President and First Lady to China. She arrived at the first evening's dinner via presidential motorcade and, in an evening dress, made her way up the stairs to the Great Hall of the People in Beijing. She paused at the door and considered the significance of the moment. She was a black girl from Queens, raised by a single mother. She could have become so easily another statistic, another casualty of the underclass. At best, she might have hoped for a white-collar job, something that paid the rent, fed the children and allowed for a few, treasured indulgences. Unlike so many other successful black women, she didn't have an Ivy League pedigree to help overcome racial and gender obstacles. But she had made it, vaulting farther and higher than she had ever imagined. "The whole thing was so wonderful," she says. "I felt like, 'Is this me?'" It was like something out of a fairy tale. She was a black Cinderella, taking her place at the ball.

In the years after her historic position at the White House, success followed success. She moved to Hollywood and landed a position as director of communications at CAA, then the most powerful agency in the city. She became an intimate of the legendary agent Michael Ovitz and learned the movie business inside out. She followed Ovitz to his short and ill-fated stint as head of Disney studios, where she bridged her Washington experience with her movie experience as Vice President of Government Relations. When she was offered a job as director of corporate communication for Chevron, she jumped at it. It was, above all, a chance to move back to Marin County where she and her husband first met. It's there that I visit the couple, in their hilltop house with views of both bridges and Alcatraz Island. We spend the evening talking and eating and drinking wine. Her husband is a retired engineer. He and Anna tell jokes about how on one of their first dates, Ted took her for a ride in his plane—a well-oiled gambit he used to impress the ladies. Anna took to flying small planes like Amelia Earheart. "She never flinched," he says, his voice rich with respect after more than 20 years of marriage.

Poverty wreaked a particularly awful kind of turbulence on her youth. "I never had the experience of not being thrown out of an apartment until I signed my first lease," she says. One memory stands out in particular. "I was walking home with a very cute, popular girl from school. All of a sudden I looked up and saw the furniture from our house sitting on the pavement two blocks away and realized that my family had been evicted. The blood started draining from my face. I was in real pain. Somehow I steered my friend away from my house. Then I went to the library and stayed for hours." She's happily married now, but she knew that the key to her success wasn't in meeting Prince Charming. "Growing up, I loved fairy tales," Anna tells me. "But I never thought someone was going to come along and take care of us. It sure didn't happen for my mother who raised six kids by herself."

What intrigues me about Anna is that growing up poor has not affected her belief that she has the right to be in circles of tremendous influence. "I was your Fresh Air Fund child once," she says saucily. "But I'm not now." The fact that black women have declared ourselves worthy is a big part of why we are now succeeding in so many areas. "These women have a sense of entitlement that is not affected by laws, affirmative action, public approval or affection," she says. Because we aren't looking to the mainstream to validate us, they can't take our new-found self-esteem away. Anna, for one, stays out of the gossip circles. "If someone has a problem with me, I'm the last person to know," she says.

Now she is in Washington again, serving as deputy assistant to President George W. Bush and counselor to the National Security Advisor for Communications. She has no foreign policy experience, but she has used Chevron's global presence to learn about international issues of commerce and policy. Ted will stay in Marin County, tending to home in much the same way that women have for years. They will log plenty of frequent-flyer miles, but it's nothing they're not used to. Her relationship, like her career, has long defied gravity.

A New Twist on the Old Tale

FOR GENERATIONS, black women have been the societal embodiment of Cinderella. Like Cinderella, black women have often been relegated to the cooking and the cleaning, watching enviously as the women they worked for lived a more privileged life. Think about *Gone With the Wind*. Wouldn't Scarlett O'Hara have laughed like an evil stepsister if Butterfly McQueen said she wanted to go to the ball, that she wanted to dance with Rhett Butler? For years, the idea of a black girl playing the role of Cinderella was unthinkable. But in the late 1990s, the actress and singer Whitney Houston decided to produce a multiracial version of Rodger's and Hammerstein's *Cinderella*. She chose the young pop superstar Brandy, then 18, to be the star of the Disney/ABC production. The ratings soared, as did the hopes of black women. Finally, black women intoned with hand-on-the-hip attitude, a sister is going to the ball.

The casting of Brandy as Disney's latest Cinderella is especially significant because for many black women, the 1940 animated Disney *Cinderella*—all blonde hair and blue eyes—sent the painful message that only white women could be princesses. "It's hard when you don't fit the traditional view of beauty," said Whoopi Goldberg, who played the prince's mother in the new version. "I've gotten letters from people that say if I'd just gotten my nose done or if I wasn't so dark, I'd be OK-looking. That's why I love this *Cinderella*, because Brandy is a beautiful, everyday-looking black girl."

The new twist on *Cinderella* took multiracial casting to a never never land extreme: Whoopi was the queen, while the king (Victor Garber) was white. Bernadette Peters was the stepmother with one white daughter and one black. Whitney Houston played the fairy godmother, in a soulful performance reminiscent of Lena Horne's in *The Wiz*. Jason Alexander was the prince's much-maligned valet. And the prince was played by a Filipino actor Paolo Montalban.

The version sparked some controversy in the community. "I'm genuinely bothered by the subliminal message that's sent when you don't have a black Prince Charming," said Denene Millner, author of *The Sistahs' Rules*. "When my stepson who's five looks at that production,

I want him to know that he can be somebody's Prince Charming." But the casting mirrored, albeit unwittingly, what some might call a growing loss of faith in black men by many black women. Just as Brandy's Cinderella falls in love with a prince of another color, so have black women begun to date interracially in record numbers.

There's an irony here. For white women, the *Cinderella* myth is one of passivity. For black women it's about actively seeking a partner who's their equal. For many successful black women, the issue is hardly about becoming dependent. One woman I spoke to put it this way, "The man I'm looking for has to have a salary close to what I make or more. I've gone down the road with someone who didn't and it's not a good road."

For all the talk about a marriage crunch in the black community and the paucity of available men, black girls still believe in fairy tales and still dream about Prince Charming. Young black women learn, from example, that having it all requires an extraordinary amount of work. They learn, from example, that their legacy as black women is one of strength and independence. Far from undermining their self-esteem or recycling antiquated notions of gender, Whitney's Cinderella gave young black women a powerful image to hold onto: a princess who looked like them. "Racism is so universal in this country, so widespread and deep-seated," Shirley Chisholm once wrote. "It is invisible because it is so normal." It means something that Brandy didn't see her role in *Cinderella* as particularly ground-breaking. "I grew up listening to the *Cinderella* stories," she said. "Just because she was white didn't mean that I couldn't live the same dream." [49]

What gives *Cinderella* such staying power is the myth's malleability, the many ways in which it continues to be transformed. Author Virginia Hamilton, a MacArthur "genius" award winner, was partial to a plantation myth called "Catskinella," which appears in her book, *Her-Stories*. In this version, Cinderella is strong and wily. The prince wants to marry her, but she makes him wait until she is good and ready. Hamilton told me that she loved the story because it is evidence that "when black women were at their most oppressed, they had the extraordinary imagination to create stories for themselves, about themselves."

For bell hooks, Zora Neale Hurston's classic novel, *Their Eyes Were Watching God*, is the best Cinderella story going. "Janie rejects her rich husband for Tea Cake, the laborer," she told me when I was at *Newsweek.* "Janie talks about how there is a jewel inside of her. Tea Cake sees that jewel and brings it out. Which is very different from the traditional Cinderella myth of the prince holding the jewel and you trying to get it from him."

In the multicultural version of *Cinderella,* Disney made a subtle, some might say feeble, attempt to give the myth a more feminist slant. When they first meet, Cinderella tells the prince that she's not sure she wants to get to know him. She says, "I doubt if any stranger has any idea how a girl should be treated." He gives her a knowing look and says, "Like a princess, I suppose." And she looks at him, with her big brown eyes, and says, "No, like a person. With kindness and respect."

Both Princesses and Fairy Godmothers

I REMEMBER the precise moment I decided to write this book. I had picked up a copy of Elsa Walsh's *Divided Lives,* a book about how successful women balance family, work and relationships. I was single, without the prospect of a husband or the thought of a child in mind. I didn't have anything to balance but my checkbook. That didn't stop me from wanting to know how it could be done, how had different women approached this new territory of having it all. I read the book in two sittings, riveted—as if being told a fable or a fairy tale about these women's lives and the challenges they faced.

At the time I was a freelance writer, contributing to a range of publications that included the *New York Times Magazine* and *Glamour.* One of the women Walsh featured was Meredith Viera, who I had first seen on the television news show *West 57th Street.* She had gone on to capture a much-coveted post on *60 Minutes,* the granddaddy of all news feature shows. I read Viera's story the closest because she was a journalist and seemed a closer role model than the other women featured, a musical conductor and breast cancer surgeon.

It became apparent early on that these were women who were, in the ghetto vernacular, paid. Their incomes all topped $500,000 a year. Later, some reviewers would carp that the women in Walsh's book were so privileged that they offered no meaningful perspective on the work-family fulcrum that was at the center of modern women's lives. But I believed Walsh had a point when she said that these women were useful as examples. If with all the money and help they had at their disposal, these women were still having a hard time having it all—what did that say about the rest of us? In my mind, I took the question one step further than perhaps Walsh could have. If white women, with ample incomes, unfettered by racial obstacles, were still struggling, then what did that say about the rest of us? And by us, I meant black women. Sisters.

I can hardly remember a time when I didn't think of myself as a woman first—when I didn't define my achievements, my failures and my challenges from a female-centered point of view. When I was eight or nine years old, someone introduced the concept of reincarnation to me. I ran home, hid underneath the covers and fell into a deep panic. Could it be that in some previous life I might have been a boy? Worse, might there still be some boy left in me, sour and stale like milk left in the bottom of a dirty cup? I shivered at the thought. I wanted to be all girl, all the time. And because I was a girl growing up in America, I was keenly aware that being a black girl meant something different than being a white girl.

Like many children, I learned to read with a simple Dick and Jane primer. I loved to read, but it also filled me with a kind of helplessness about what this new skill—reading—could change. I learned quickly that reading was not wishing, because no matter how many times I read the story, Jane was always white.

Although I now hold blaxploitation heroines such as Pam Grier and Cleopatra Jones in my pantheon of kick-ass goddesses (right alongside Michelle Yeoh and Luc Besson's *La Femme Nikita*), as a black girl in the 1970s, my pop culture icons were seriously limited. I liked Thelma on the television sitcom *Good Times,* but I didn't want to live in the projects. I thought Florence on the sitcom *The Jeffersons* was hilarious, but I didn't want to be a maid. When a boy at my school brought in the Farrah Fawcett swimsuit poster and all the boys went crazy, I wondered why they didn't also have a poster of '70s sex symbol Jayne Kennedy. My father made us watch *Roots* on television, but his exaltations that

Cicely Tyson was a beautiful, talented woman that I should aspire to be like were lost on my nine-year-old self. After the miniseries was over, all I could think was that Cicely Tyson might be all those things my father said, but she was also a slave. I didn't want to be a slave. I wanted to be the first black Charlie's Angel. I wanted to have hair that bounced, wear really tight jeans and chase down bad guys while looking fabulous.

I never, ever wanted to be white, but there was a freedom white girls seemed to have and I wanted it, too. There is a picture of me at age seven or so. It's Christmas morning and I am holding two dolls—one black, one white. The white one is Barbie and the black one is Christie, Barbie's black friend. In the photo, I am grinning with toothless exuberance. I had asked for both dolls, sure I wouldn't get two dolls for Christmas. Money was always tight in our household and I had no illusions about a fat, white guy named Santa Claus. But it must have been a good year or my mother must have understood something about my need for both the doll that all my friends would have as well as a doll that looked like me.

I think back on that image—me with two dolls—because I think it's a telling illustration of the life I have constructed for myself. Long before I became a "successful black woman," before I went to college, landed my first big job, moved to a posh neighborhood or bought my first pair of Gucci boots—I longed for an experience of womanhood that reflected the best that both the black world and the white world had to offer.

I wanted to be a strong black woman: like my mother, like the women in my neighborhood. At basement parties and crammed apartment jams, I listened to funk classics that gave me powerful views of my impending black woman self. "She's a bad Mamajamma," went the words to one song. "Just as bad as she can be." In another favorite, the singer marveled that the object of his affection was a "Brick...House. She's mighty, mighty. Just letting it all hang out."

A bad Mamajamma? I could be that.

A Brick House? I'll take it.

Mighty Mighty? You bet.

HOWEVER, GROWING UP in the 1970s, in the heart of urban black America, I knew that being a strong black woman wasn't without its down sides. My neighborhood was full of fatherless children and when, at the age of ten, I joined their ranks, I saw how hard my mother's life truly was. I learned that even a brick house was susceptible to the huffing and puffing of the wicked wolf. I had cheered because my father wasn't around to use my mother like a punching bag anymore. But I was hardly prepared for the laundry list of things he took with him. Not just his violence and his money, but my mother's chosen soul mate, sexual partner and friend. He took a lot of what was feminine about my mother with him and left behind a stern shell of a woman whose primary concern was raising her children and paying the bills. She was strong, but until she started dating again, she was hard around the edges, too. And the thing was that most of my friends' mothers never started dating again and fell easily and regularly into choruses about how a good black man is hard to find.

It was around the time of my parents' divorce and my mother's most stoic period that I saw *Gone With the Wind* for the first time on TV. I abhorred the depictions of Hattie McDaniel and Butterfly McQueen, but I'd be marked for a liar and justly so, if I didn't admit that old Scarlett had her appeal—even to a black and proud girl like me. She was simply brimming with what my friends and I called that white girl thing—Cry at the drop of a hat? Check. Bat your eyes and expect it to mean something to a man? Check. Act the fool (in this case, dress up in curtains), be a drama queen and not be the least bit ashamed of how trifling you are? Check. Miss Scarlett had all the bases covered and deep inside there was a part of me that didn't want to be cool, didn't want to be strong, that wanted to settle in for a good cry or a good cotillion, too.

Over the past five years, I've watched the women in this book wrestle with the most primal issues of what Mary Catherine Bateson calls "composing a life." Walteen Grady-Truely moved from Brooklyn to the Poconos to give her son a more stable environment, at the cost of a major career change for herself. In the fallout of the Internet boom, Angela Kyle went from VP of a Web-related company to a surprising and soul-searching unemployment that prompted her to start a relationship and to begin considering family in a serious way. Within the course of a year, she had found her current job at Live Planet and was back on the career track. She wants to make a mark in the entertainment field, she says. At 31, love and family can wait. Lynette Hall has gone from being unsure of her value as a full-time mom to a quiet confidence that she made the right decision to leave her television career. During the course of this book, Robin Nelson Rice, whom her friends called the sister most likely to make CEO, made the same decision to stay home with children. A wealth of black at-home mom support groups have begun to crop up around the country, suggesting that this is a choice more and more well-educated, affluent black women are struggling with.

While most of the women in this book are quoted with their real names, I did respect the wishes of the women who wished to be quoted anonymously or wanted to use an alias.

In a 1999 *New York Times* profile of art consultant Kim Heirston, artist Greg Crewdson is quoted as saying, "I know being fabulous is a full-time occupation. But what exactly does she do?" Six foot tall and rail thin, Heirston, like Susan Fales-Hill, is a favorite of society photographers and glossy up-scale fashion magazines. One might call them black Cinderellas except for the fact that they are not ash sweepers transformed into princesses. They are modern-day princesses, transformed through no small amount of hard work, into media icons. "I guess the biggest surprise is that I've been able to make something so fabulous almost out of thin air," Kim told me, over lunch at the Four Seasons in 2002. "Sometimes I think, 'My God, I shape my day and I shape what it is that I want to do. I sculpt it.'" After attending Yale, studying in London and Florence and years of working in both blue-chip midtown galleries and cutting-edge Soho spaces, Heirston has created a career where she buys art for wealthy collectors. She visits galleries, auction houses and artists' studios and is considered an expert on not only what is most exciting creatively, but how to build a collection that will continue to grow in financial value. "I've created my job description," she says. "That's not to say there haven't been other art advisors, but I do it in a way that is particularly me and I work with the people I want to work with. It's a very powerful feeling not to have to answer to anyone."

My interviews with Thelma Golden taught me so much about what it means to be a strong black woman in a post-modern age. From her, I learned the importance of separating oneself, at least periodically, from the lens of race and gender. In the five years I've been interviewing her, Thelma has done an incredible amount of work on herself: becoming comfortable with failure and finding the strength to re-invent herself. Thelma is a firecracker, a small yet potent ball of power, enthusiasm, intelligence and excitement. I've watched her move with the utmost confidence in the elite Manhattan museum world, then be forced to reckon with a shattering loss of identity after her resignation from the Whitney. Every professional black woman goes through daily and weekly doubts about all the micro-inequities of her life. When we are rejected, passed over, critiqued, ignored, offended, we are always asking ourselves: Is it because I'm black? Is it because I'm a woman? Is it because I'm me? I watched Thelma wrestle with these questions in a very public way as the media covered the shakeup caused by a new director at the Whitney and focused on the diminutive black woman who some in the art world thought had gone too far, too fast.

I also watched Thelma in private, as she mourned the security of a post she felt fully entitled to. That year she came to my annual tree-trimming party, dressed to kill as always in a brightly colored designer suit. Her garments were flame red, but her eyes were dimmed. Within half an hour, she left. "I'm not ready to talk about it," she said quietly, as she pulled me aside. "Too much asking me what I do." A year later, she resurfaced as chief curator at the Studio Museum, a process that has brought her new challenges. She's learning, for the very first time really, what it's like to be in an all-black world. The early reports are good and her first show, *Freestyle*, which highlighted the works of 28 young artists, was a critical success.

Although she isn't a real person, Aunt Jemima became a vivid character for me in this book. I am deeply indebted to the work of M. M. Manring, author of *Slave in a Box*, and other writers who have mined the heavy batter of her legacy. The image of Aunt Jemima, along with such historical figures as Hattie McDaniel, Butterfly McQueen, Josephine Baker and others helped me to focus on the evolution of black women's self-image over the generations. My own grandmothers, both deceased, were not as much help. They were Panamanian immigrants, from Costa

Rica and Martinique respectively. They only lived in the United States at the end of their lives. Flora Jean Baptiste and Connie Chambers followed a different journey and their lives tell a different story—one I hope to tell in a future book.

In the current climate, any discussion of women's success will be met with a certain amount of defensiveness by black men. No matter which way you slice it, brothers are going to feel that they are getting a bad rap. I'd ask them to look again closely at the words and portrayal of men like Paul Hall and Anna Perez's husband, Ted Simms. It's not true, as some agitators insist, that black women hate black men. But we are, as Toni Cade Bambara once wrote, in love and in trouble. The women in this book—Erika Kirkland, Aisha Brooks-Lytle, Robin Nelson Rice, Tracie Howard, Debra Jackson among others—have a deep faith in the importance of black relationships and the ability of brothers to move forward from the crisis we are now in. "There is an incredible amount of magic and feistiness in black men that nobody has been able to wipe out," Toni Morrison once said. "But everybody has tried." [50]

My own life has changed immeasurably during the course of this book. I gave serious consideration to adopting a child, as a single person. I felt the first longing to keep him when he came to stay with me at my Brooklyn Heights neighborhood and said, at the age of four, "I like it here, there's no crack bottles on the street. I like it here, there's no gunshots at night." When his guardian failed to call or pick him up after a week, I began to get serious about adoption. I was also worried. One afternoon, he came up to me. I was sitting in the living room, my head bent into my lap. "Don't take anything," he said, patting my back. "It will be okay." I eventually decided that the challenges of the situation were too great, the most insurmountable of them being that his mother thought she was doing a fine job raising him. But I made a decision that someday I will adopt, a decision my future husband supports me in. I've discussed him in earlier chapters. By the time this book is published, reader, I will have married him.

I think of the women in this book as black Cinderellas because they have gone from being the lowest on the totem pole to being architects of their own dreams. For the most part, their stories don't entail glass slippers, horse and carriages or fairy godmothers. But our successes

have more permanence than fairy tales, and we feel a deeper entitlement to them because we know we have earned them. For all the ways
in which her White House post was a dream come true, Anna Perez
came to work every day at 1600 Pennsylvania Avenue with the deep
conviction that "I belong here."

This generation of sisters has overcome the stigma Zora Neale
Hurston so powerfully invoked when she described us as "being tragically colored." I know this because of people like the two sister execs
that I met at the Canyon Ranch Spa, earlier this year. They were there,
as were my friend and I, doing what professionals do when they're trying to relax. I know this because of the 50-something black woman I
saw, strolling with an impossibly handsome older black man, in Milan's
Piazza della Signora. She was tall and thin, wearing a white shirt, Capri
pants and big Audrey Hepburn sunglasses. The light seemed to make
her chocolate skin glow and her head was thrown back in laughter. And
I know she was American because a week later, I ran into her at the airport, shopping in duty free. I overheard her American accent, even stole
a peek at her Michigan driving license. These were just regular women,
living their lives and enjoying the world in a way their mothers and
grandmothers could never have imagined. We may not all be at the ball,
but middle-class black women are having a ball.

Even educated and affluent sisters have their struggles. Black
women are the most overweight group in the country. Studies are quick
to report that we have stronger body images than white women and
higher self-esteem, but our weight is an issue, a symptom of our mental
and emotional insecurities. For all the ways in which our lives are
steeped in conflict and obstacles, we are still reticent to seek out therapy and other crucial forms of support. It's little wonder that a recent
study found that out of black men, black women, white women and
white men, black women have the highest rates of depression.

Because this is America, we know that our paths to success are
made jagged by the vicissitudes of race, class and gender. We also know
that we are up to the task. There are so many of us, out there, working
it. And at the same time, there are too few of us. We need, as Star Jones
says, to reach out and pull some of the have-nots into the worlds of
have-somes. Through mentoring and other community outreach efforts,

professional black women have the opportunity to be fairy godmothers to girls who don't know that there are paths to glory more sure than the sexy shenanigans of Lil' Kim and other rappers of her ilk. We need to let young women know that *The Cosby Show* may be off the air, but the Clair Huxtables of the world are alive and well.

Notes

[1] Lynette Clemetson and Allison Samuels. "We Have the Power." *Newsweek,* September 18, 2000.

[2] Audrey Edwards and Dr. Craig K. Polite. *Children of the Dream: The Psychology of Black Success.* Doubleday, 1992.

[3] "Women of Color Executives: Their Voices, Their Journeys." Catalyst, 2001.

[4] Ronnie Crocker. "Homage to Aunt Jemima Remains a Tricky Business," *Houston Chronicle,* April 5, 1996.

[5] "The African-American Education Data Book: Volume I: Higher and Adult Education." Frederick D. Patterson Research Institute of the College Fund/UNCF, 1997.

[6] Stat Abstract 2001.

[7] Mary Catherine Bateson. *Composing a Life.* Atlantic Monthly Press, 1989.

[8] Liz Atwood. "Church Plan Meets Neighbors' Opposition." *Baltimore Sun*, August 26, 1999. Laura Sessions Stepp. "How to Make a Church Grow." *Baltimore Sun*, August 9, 1991.

[9] Beverly Hall Lawrence. *Reviving the Spirit: A Generation of African Americans Goes Home to Church.* Grove Press, 1996.

[10] "Women of Color in Corporate Management: Opportunities and Barriers." Catalyst, 1999.

[11] Michele Wallace. *Black Macho and the Myth of the Superwoman.* Warner Books, 1983.

[12] Lynette Clemetson and Allison Samuels. "We Have the Power." *Newsweek*, September 18, 2000.

[13] Bill Sheeline. "Hunting for the First House." *Money*, December 1993.

[14] Ellis Cose. *The Rage of a Privileged Class.* HarperCollins, 1994.

[15] Reeves, Tracey A. "Trading Suits for Sweats: Black Moms Unite Against Pressures to Return to Their Jobs." *Washington Post*, November 12, 2000.

[16] Patricia Hill Collins. "The Meaning of Motherhood in Black Culture and Black Mother-Daughter Relationships." *Double-Stitch: Black Women Write About Mothers and Daughters.* ed. Patricia Bell-Scott, et. al. HarperPerennial, 1991.

[17] Bart Landry. *Black Working Wives: Pioneers of the American Family Revolution.* University of California Press, 2000.

[18] Deborah Straszheim. "Black in a White-Collar World: Book Tells Tales of African-American Women Succeeding." *Daily Press*, October 26, 1998.

[19] Julianne Malveaux. "What's So New About Juggling Many Roles?" *USA Today*, February 11, 2000.

[20] bell hooks. *Ain't I a Woman: Black Women and Feminism.* South End Press, 1981.

[21] Suni Petersen. "Multi-Cultural Perspective on Middle-class Women's Identity Development." *Journal of Counseling and Development,* Winter 2000, Vol 78, Issue 1.

[22] Richard Morin. "Major Changes in Black Family Structure." *Washington Post,* March 25, 1997.

[23] Suni Petersen. "Multi-Cultural Perspective on Middle-class Women's Identity Development."

[24] Holland Cotter. "Shaking Up a Harlem Museum." *New York Times,* February 28, 2000.

[25] Gerda Lerner. *Black Women in White America: A Documentary History.* Vintage, 1996.

[26] Kimberle Crenshaw. "Whose Story Is It Anyway? Feminist and Antiracist Appropriations of Anita Hill." *Race-ing Justice, En-gendering Power: Essays on Anita Hill, Clarence Thomas, and the Construction of Social Reality.* ed. Toni Morrison. Pantheon, 1992.

[27] Gerda Lerner. *Black Women.*

[28] Gerda Lerner. Ibid.

[29] Gerda Lerner. Ibid.

[30] Veronica Chambers. "The Myth of Cinderella." *Newsweek,* November 3, 1997.

[31] Paula Giddings, *When and Where I Enter: The Impact of Black Women on Race and Sex in America.* William Morrow, 1984.

[32] S. Craig Watkins. "Feminist Media Criticism and Feminist Media Practices." *Annals of the American Academy of Political and Social Science,* September 2000.

[33] Chuck Ross. "O&M Says Black Women Tuning Out TV." *Advertising Age.* March 8, 1999; Gerry Khermouch. "Hard to Hold." *Mediaweek,* May 10, 1999.

[34] Alan Carter. "All My Sistuhs." *Essence,* August, 1992.

[35] Invisible People: the Depiction of Minorities in Magazine Ads and Catalogues: a study by the City of New York Department of Consumer Affairs; Mark Green, Commissioner, July, 1991.

[36] Kate Fitzgerald. "Connecting Confirmation." *Advertising Age*, November 29, 1999.

[37] William H. Frey. "Migration to the South Brings U.S. Blacks Full Circle." Population Reference Bureau, April–June 2001.

[38] Fahizah Alim. "Following Their Hearts." *Sacramento Bee*, May 2, 1998.

[39] Michelle Burford. "Carnal Knowledge." *Essence*, May 2001.

[40] Linda and Clara Villarosa. "Coming Out." *Essence*, May 1991.

[41] A. L. Reynolds III. *Do Black Women Hate Black Men?* Hastings House, 1994.

[42] Fahizah Alim. "Following Their Hearts." *Sacramento Bee*, May 2, 1998.

[43] Lynn Norment. "Guess Who's Coming to Dinner Now?" *Ebony*, September 1992.

[44] Jack Demarest, Rita Allen. "Body Image: Gender, Ethnic, and Age Differences." *The Journal of Social Psychology*, August 2000.

[45] Susan McClelland. "Distorted Images." *Maclean's*, August 14, 2000.

[46] Martin W. Jones, M.D., and Brenda Davis Jones. "What Are the Warning Signs?" *Essence*, July 1996.

[47] Esther Iverem. "Over the Edge." *Essence*, July 1996.

[48] Christopher Hanson. "First Lady's Aide Didn't Mind the Press—Usually." *Seattle Post-Intelligencer*, December 22, 1992.

[49] Gerda Lerner. *Black Women*.

[50] Toni Morrison, in Dexter Fisher. *The Third Woman: Minority Women Writers of the United States*. Houghton Mifflin, 1980.

Bibliography

FAMILY RESPONSIBILITY RELATIONSHIPS SUCCESS MOTHERHOOD BALANCE

I consulted a wealth of research material. But the following are the ones for which I am especially grateful.

Bateson, Mary Catherine. *Composing a Life: Life as a Work in Progress: the improvisations of five extraordinary women.* Plume, 1989.

Bell, Derrick. *And We Are Not Saved: The Elusive Quest for Racial Justice.* Basic Books, 1987.

Campbell, Bebe Moore. "Women Who Go for It!" *Essence,* August 1989.

Clark, Caroline V. *Take a Lesson: Today's Black Achievers on How They Made It and What They Learned Along the Way.* John Wiley and Sons, 2001.

Collins, Patricia Hill. *Black Feminist Thought: Knowledge, Consciousness and the Politics of Empowerment.* Routledge 2000.

Contemporary Black Biography. *Anna Perez.* Gale 1992.

Cose, Ellis. *The Rage of a Privileged Class.* HarperCollins, 1994.

Davis, Angela Y. *Women, Race and Class.* Random House, 1981.

DuBois, William E. B. *The Souls of Black Folks (Three Negro Classics).* Avon Books, 1965.

Edwards, Audrey, and Dr. Craig K. Polite. *Children of the Dream: The Psychology of Black Success.* Doubleday, 1992.

Ehrhart-Morrison, Dorothy. *No Mountain High Enough: Secrets of Successful African American Women.* Conari Press, 1997.

Faludi, Susan. *Backlash: The Undeclared War Against American Women.* Anchor, 1992.

Fortune Magazine. "The New Black Power: A New Generation of African Americans Is Seizing Real Power in the World of Business." August 4, 1997.

Foxworth, Marilyn Kern. *Aunt Jemima, Uncle Ben and Rastus: Blacks in Advertising Yesterday, Today, and Tomorrow.* Greenwood Publishing, 1994.

Giddings, Paula. *When and Where I Enter: The Impact of Black Women on Race and Sex in America.* William Morrow, 1984.

Greene, Marilyn. "Guardian of the First Lady's Image: For Anna Perez, It's Just Saying No." *USA Today,* July 17, 1989.

Hanson, Christopher. "First Lady's Aide Didn't Mind the Press— Usually." *Seattle Post-Intelligencer.* December 22, 1992.

hooks, bell. *Ain't I a Woman: Black Women and Feminism.* South End Press, 1981.

Hull, Gloria, Patricia Bell Scott and Barbara Smith, eds. *All the Women Are White, All the Blacks Are Men, But Some of Us Are Brave.* Black Women's Studies, Feminist Press, 1986.

Lawrence, Beverly Hall. *Reviving the Spirit: A Generation of African Americans Goes Home to Church.* Grove Press, 1996.

Lerner, Gerda. *Black Women in White America: A Documentary History.* Vintage, 1996.

Mahony, Rhona. *Kidding Ourselves: Breadwinning, Babies, and Bargaining Power.* Basic Books, June 1996.

Malveaux, Julianne M. "What's So New About Juggling Roles?" *USA Today.* February 11, 2000.

Manring, M. M. *Slave in a Box: The Strange Career of Aunt Jemima.* University of Virginia, 1998.

Nelson, Alondra, Thuy Lihn N. Tu and Alicia Headlam Hines, eds. *Technicolor: Race, Technology and Everyday Life.* New York University Press, May 2001.

Orenstein, Peggy. *Flux: Women on Sex, Work, Love, Kids, and Life in a Half-Changed World.* Doubleday, 2001.

Parker, Gwendolyn M. *Trespassing: My Sojourn in the Halls of Privilege,* Houghton Mifflin, 1997.

Peterson, Karen S., "Having it all—Except Children." *USA Today,* April 8, 2002.

Petersen, Suni, "Multi-Cultural Perspective on Middle-Class Women's Identity Development." *Journal of Counseling and Development,* Winter 2000, Vol 78, Issue 1, p. 63.

Reeves, Tracey A., "Trading Suits for Sweats: Black Moms Unite Against Pressures to Return to Their Jobs." *The Washington Post,* November 12, 2000.

Simms, Margaret C. and Julianne Malveaux, eds. *Slipping Through the Cracks: The Status of Black Women,* Transaction Books, 1986.

Wallace, Michele. *Black Macho and the Myth of the Superwoman.* Dial Press, 1978.

Walsh, Elsa. *Divided Lives: The Public and Private Struggles of Three American Women.* Anchor Books, 1995.

Wilson, William Julius. *The Truly Disadvantaged: The Inner City, the Underclass, and Public Policy.* University of Chicago, 1987.

Acknowledgments

I am very grateful to many people but, above all, to the women in this book—they gave generously of their time and rarely pulled their punches. They are swans. All of them.

I am grateful for the research assistance of Judy Ganeles and Matt Dulany. Without you, I'm just a bobble head with a library card. I really appreciate all of your time and effort. A special thank you to Adrienne Roberts for her unbelievably smart feedback. Andrea Polans is an encouraging and kind first reader. Thank you.

Over the years, I have been fortunate to have learned from a number of great editors. They include Chris Connelley, Adam Moss, Stephanie Stokes Oliver, Dawn Raffel, as well as a number of *Newsweek* staffers: Jeff Giles, Cathleen McGuigan, John Capouya and Mark Whitaker.

A posse of homegirls have always gone above and beyond for me and for my work. Thank you to Liba Daniels, Lynette Hall, Tracie

Howard, Debra Jackson, Shay Youngblood, Michelle Burford, Karen Moore-Greene, Lynette Clemetson and Cassandra Butcher.

The soul sisters at Princeton provided insight, support, good company and Tofutti Cuties. Thank you to Saje Mathieu, Daphne Brooks and Valerie Smith.

Thelma Golden is an inspiration in every way. Lynn Harris is as charming as he is clever. What a dream boy. A. J. Verdelle and Alexa Birdsong educate through their work, but also teach by living. Carla Harris gave me excellent wedding day advice. Thank you.

I have only one word to say to the unbelievably wise and supportive Peggy Orenstein: shoes.

Thank you to my webmaster, Dave Cooksey, at www.saturdave.com. You are Cary Grant cool.

Sandy Dijkstra and her associates: Margaret, Elisabeth, Julie, Jill and many others provided invaluable feedback and assistance. Thank you, Sandy, for keeping faith in me during truly difficult times. Many thanks, as well, to the indomitable Toisan Craigg. Shake what your Mama gave you, girl.

For a woman who makes her living with words, Janet Hill defies description. All I can say is thank you. Having you as my editor is, professionally, the very meaning of having it all.

Jason Clampet read more drafts and worked harder on this book than most melanin-challenged brothers ever could. He is wise. He is kind. And I really like the food.